ROUTLEDGE LIBRARY EDITIONS:
SUSTAINABILITY

Volume 3

THE WAY FORWARD

THE WAY FORWARD

Beyond Agenda 21

Edited by
FELIX DODDS

Routledge
Taylor & Francis Group

LONDON AND NEW YORK

First published in 1997 by Earthscan Publications Ltd

This edition first published in 2019
by Routledge
2 Park Square, Milton Park, Abingdon, Oxon OX14 4RN

and by Routledge
52 Vanderbilt Avenue, New York, NY 10017

Routledge is an imprint of the Taylor & Francis Group, an informa business

British Library Cataloguing in Publication Data
A catalogue record for this book is available from the British Library

ISBN: 978-0-367-18630-2 (Set)
ISBN: 978-0-429-26895-3 (Set) (ebk)
ISBN: 978-0-367-18644-9 (Volume 3) (hbk)
ISBN: 978-0-429-19738-3 (Volume 3) (ebk)

Publisher's Note
The publisher has gone to great lengths to ensure the quality of this reprint but
points out that some imperfections in the original copies may be apparent.

Disclaimer
The publisher has made every effort to trace copyright holders and would welcome
correspondence from those they have been unable to trace.

At its inception in 1993, United Nations Environment and Development UK Committee's (UNED-UK) mission was to promote global environmental protection and sustainable development. It did so by supporting the work of the United Nations Environment Programme, the United Nations Development Programme, and the former United Nations Commission on Sustainable Development, primarily in the United Kingdom of Great Britain and Northern Ireland.

During the early years following the 1992 Rio Earth Summit, UNED-UK's work focused on mobilizing the UK political process through effectively engaging the Westminster Government, local government, and the nine Agenda 21 stakeholder groups in the work of the United Nations and related intergovernmental institutions on sustainable development.

Today, some twenty-five years later, UNED-UK is Stakeholder Forum for a Sustainable Future, an international organization working to advance sustainable development at all levels. Stakeholder Forum continues to provide a bridge between those who have a stake in sustainable development, and the international forums where decisions are made in their name.

The Way Forward

Beyond Agenda 21

Edited by Felix Dodds

First published in the UK in 1997 by Earthscan Publications Ltd

Copyright © United Nations Environment and Development –
UK Committee (UNED–UK), 1997

A catalogue record for this book is available from the British Library

ISBN: 1 85383 437 8 (paperback)

Typesetting and page design by Saxon Graphics Ltd, Derby

Printed and bound by Clays Ltd. St Ives PLC

Cover design by Declan Buckley

For a full list of publications, please contact
Earthscan Publications Ltd
120 Pentonville Road
London N1 9JN
Tel: 0171 278 0433
Fax: 0171 278 1142
email: earthinfo@earthscan.co.uk
http://www.earthscan.co.uk

Earthscan is an editorially independent subsidiary of Kogan Page Ltd and publishes in
association with WWF-UK and the International Institute of Environment and
Development.

Contents

PART 2: MAJOR GROUPS

PART 3: MAJOR ISSUES FOR THE FUTURE

PART 4: PERSPECTIVES ON THE FUTURE

List of Contributors

Tom Bigg has worked for the UN Environment and Development UK committee since its creation in 1993. He has focused particularly on the work of the UN Commission on Sustainable Development. This has entailed contributing to sessions of the Commission, and also working for UNED–UK's national Round Tables addressing Agenda 21 implementation. Tom has written a number of reports on follow up to the Rio Summit and also on the World Summit for Social Development and issues of UN reform.

Barbara J Bramble is director and founder of the International Office of the National Wildlife Federation, the largest US conservation organization. The Office is dedicated to ensuring that environmental issues become core considerations in international economic decisions. Ms Bramble served on the Steering Committee of the International NGO Forum, the principal conference of NGOs that took place at the Earth Summit in Rio. Before joining NWF, she was legal adviser to the President's Council on Environmental Quality, and represented a variety of US national and local conservation groups.

Jeb Brugman has been Secretary-General of the International Council for Local Environmental Initiatives since 1990 and has represented ICLEI at the Rio and Istanbul Conferences. He is also a member of the Editorial Board of the Urban Age (World Bank), a member of the Earth Council Institute and the IUCN Commission on Environmental Strategy and planning. He has also served on the Global Forum 94 Advisory Board, and was Executive Director of the Cambridge Commission on Nuclear Disarmament and Peace Education.

Henrique Brandao Cavalcanti was chair of the UN Commission on Sustainable Development 1995–96. In 1972 he was a member of the Brazilian delegation to the United Nations Conference on the Human Environment in Stockholm, and was responsible for the setting up of the

Brazilian Federal Environmental Agency in 1973. In 1994 he was Minister of Environment and the Amazon. He has also held major executive positions in electricity and power utilities in Southern Brazil, as Chairman and CEO of SIDERBRAS, the recently privatized Brazilian steel-making group, and on the board of private pulp and mining companies of the CAEMI group.

Charles Arden Clarke is Senior Policy Analyst in the Sustainable Resource Use Programme of WWF International in Gland, Switzerland. He has worked for WWF International for six years, mostly on the GATT/WTO and international trade. Prior to joining the WWF he worked for nearly seven years in an environmental consultancy in the UK, on issues ranging from the environmental effects of nuclear power to conservation of the Antarctic.

Nitin Desai was the Deputy Secretary-General of the UN Conference on Environment and Development, and since 1993 has headed the Department of Policy Co-ordination and Sustainable Development at the UN headquarters in New York. Before his work in the UN, Nitin Desai was a senior official in the Planning Commission and the Ministry of Finance of the Government of India. He also worked on the staff of the Brundtland Commission and was deeply involved in the drafting of its report *Our Common Future*.

Felix Dodds is the Co-ordinator of UNED–UK and has attended the Rio and Habitat II summits and all the Commission on Sustainable Development meetings. He was a member of the Global Forum 94 Advisory Board and the Editorial Board for the Centre for Our Common Future's publications. He is co-author of *Three Years Since the Rio Summit* (UNED–UK, 1995), editor of *The Urban Agenda* (UNED–UK, 1995) and *Into the 21st Century: An Agenda for Political Re-alignment* (Greenprint, 1988). He co-founded Green Voice in 1988, which looked at building links between parties on a green agenda.

Elizabeth Dowdeswell joined UNEP as its third Executive Director in January 1993. Before joining UNEP she was Canada's principal delegate to the Intergovernmental Panel on Climate Change and Co-chair of the working group on mechanisms leading to the Framework Convention on Climate Change. She has been Canada's Permanent Representative to the World Meteorological Organization, twice being elected to its Executive Board. Prior to her service with Environmental Canada, Ms Dowdeswell worked as a management consultant to the federal government.

Winston Gereluk is education and communications representative with the Alberta Union of Provincial Employees, a component of the National Union of Public & General Employees in Canada which is affiliated to the Public Services International in Geneva. He was involved in documenting the ICFTU case studies presented to the UN CSD for the 1996 'Day of the Workplace'. He also instructs and develops distance education courses in industrial relations for Athabasca University in Alberta, Canada.

Gary Lawrence is Director of the Centre for Sustainable Communities at Washington University. Until 1994 he was Chief Planner of the City of Seattle and introduced some of the key sustainable development plans for the city. Gary is an adviser to the President's Council on Sustainable Development and recently was involved in the production of the Local Agenda 21 Plan for London. He attended the Istanbul Habitat II Conference as a member of the US Government delegation.

Caroline LeQuesne is Oxfam UK/I's policy adviser on trade and environment issues. She is the author of *Reforming World Trade: The Social and Environmental Priorities* (Oxfam, 1996) and co-authored a revised version of *The Trade Trap: Poverty and the Global Commodity Markets* (Oxfam, 1996).

Chip Lindner is currently Senior Adviser to the Chairman and Executive Secretary of the 12th World AIDS Conference to be held in Geneva in June 1998. He was Executive Director of the Centre for Our Common Future, and International Co-ordinator responsible for organizing the 1992 Global Forum in Rio de Janeiro during the Earth Summit. He was Secretary of the Brundtland Commission; Director of the Energy Department with Société Générale pour l'Energie et les Ressources, and Deputy Director of WWF International.

Angela Mawle Angela has a professional background in health and environmental management. Previously academic administrator of the Imperial College Centre for Environmental Technology. She was subsequently Director of the Women's Environmental Network and more recently Director of the International Coalition for Development Action (ICDA) – a Brussels based development NGO. Angela was very active in the preparatory processes for the World Women's conference and attended Beijing as the sole UK lobbyist on women and the environment.

Fiona McConnell headed the UK negotiation teams for both the Montreal Protocol and the Biodiversity Convention and was a member of the British delegation to the Earth Summit. She is author of *The Biodiversity Convention: a Negotiating History* (Kulwer Law International, 1996).

Peter Mucke was born in 1958 and has a degree in biology. He was a member of the German NGO delegation to the 1992 Earth Summit in Rio de Janeiro and headed the Forum for Environment & Development from 1993 to 1996. Today he is Managing Director of Terre des Hommes.

Peter Newell is a lecturer in International Studies in the Department of Politics and International Studies at Warwick University. He is completing a PhD project on *The International Politics of Climate Change: A Non-Governmental Account* which he studied for at the University of Keele. He has taught Environmental Politics and held a position as researcher at Climate Network Europe in Brussels.

Derek Osborn is Chair of the United Nations Environment and Development UK Committee. He is also Chair of the European Environmental Agency and a member of the board of the UK Environmental Agency. He co-chaired the 1997 CSD Intersessional Meeting preparing for Earth Summit II. Previously, he was the Director General of the UK Department of the Environment and attended the Rio Summit and all the meetings of the Commission on Sustainable Development.

Peter Padbury is a futurist by training, with an interest in the relationships between vision, strategy and action. From 1990 to 1996 he worked as Co-ordinator of the Sustainability Team and then worked with the Multilateral Policy Team at the Canadian Council for International Co-operation. During that period, he played leadership roles in the Canadian Participatory Committee for UNCED; the International NGO Forum (which hosted the NGO Alternative Treaty Process in Rio) and the Projet de société (a multi-stakeholder process which attempted to create a sustainability plan for Canada). He was a member of many Canadian Government delegations to the UNCED process and to the UN Commission of Sustainable Development.

Lucien Royer is the Health, Safety and Environment Officer for the International Confederation of Free Trade Unions (ICFTU). He co-ordinates programmes throughout the world and represents the ICFTU at the United Nations and other international agencies with respect to health, safety and environment. Originally from Western Canada, he was involved in environmental litigation and environmental law reform, and was a founding member of the Canadian Environmental Network. He formed part of the Canadian Government delegation at Bergen in 1990 and at Rio in 1992.

Carole Saint-Laurent is currently the Director of Forest Instruments for the World Wide Fund for Nature – International's Forest for Life Campaign, she is also the co-ordinator for UNCED follow-up for WWF–International. She attended the Rio UN Conference and all the meetings of the Commission on Sustainable Development. She has trained in Environmental Law and specialized in taxation law.

Philippe Sands is a lecturer in law at SOAS Law Department, London University, and is Legal Director of the Foundation for International Environmental Law and Development (FIELD). He attended the Earth Summit in 1992 and is a member of UNED–UK executive.

Björn Stigson has had extensive experience in international business. He began his career as financial analyst with the Kockums Group, then the world's biggest shipyard, and ESAB, the world's leading supplier of equipment for welding, before joining ABB Fläkt as President and Chief Executive Officer in 1982. From 1991 to 1993, he was Executive Vice-President and a member of ABB Asea Brown Boveri's Executive Management Group. From 1993 to 1994, he ran his own management consultancy, and served on the board of a variety of international companies. On 1 January 1995 he was appointed Executive Director of the World Business Council for Sustainable Development (WBCSD) in Geneva. From its formation in 1990, Mr Stigson was actively involved with the Business Council for Sustainable Development (BCSD), one of the two organizations which led to the creation of the WBCSD.

Professor Dr Klaus Töpfer was the second Chair of the UN Commission on Sustainable Development in 1994–95. He was the German Minister for Environment, Energy and Nuclear Safety until 1995 when he became the Minister for Urban Affairs. He attended the Rio and Istanbul UN Conferences and is a strong supporter of sustainable urban development.

Camilla Toulmin directs the Drylands Programme at the International Institute of Environment and Development (IIED). An economist by training, her work focuses mainly on issues of land management and agricultural development in the semi-arid areas of West Africa. She formed part of the UN Panel of Experts set up to advise the negotiations of the Convention to Combat Desertification. Currently she is engaged in a series of research programmes examining land tenure and resource access, traditional methods of soil conservation and how farmers manage soil fertility in a range of African farming systems.

Zonny Woods is currently a Gender and Development Consultant with experience and a focus in Latin America and Asia. Zonny worked as the International Youth Coordinator for the NGO Forum on Women, organizing youth participation and input to the UN World Conference on Women. As a youth activist, she was one of the organizers of Youth 92, the world youth preparatory for UNCED. Following UNCED, she worked for the IISD and edited the *Youth Sourcebook on International Development*. She is a member of the board of the IGLHRC (International Gay and Lesbian Human Rights Commission), and Canada World Youth.

Preface

James Gustave Speth
Administrator, United Nations Development Programme

Harold Wilson once said that a week is a long time in politics. But the same cannot be said for sustainable development – which requires a long-term perspective and commitment. Indeed, nearly 250 weeks have passed since the UN Conference on Environment and Development – the 'Earth Summit' – took place in Rio de Janeiro. What has been accomplished since 1992?

Although there has been progress since the Summit, it can hardly be said that we have reversed the major trends that threaten our common future. If we ask whether there are more poor people today than in 1992, the answer is yes. If we ask whether environmental deterioration persists, the answer is also yes. And if we ask whether governments have forgotten the financial commitments they made at the Summit, the answer is again, sadly, yes.

For any Summit participant interested in the fight against poverty around the world, it is hugely disappointing that official development assistance has dropped significantly since 1992. Support for sustainable development is not only essential to the eradication of poverty, but also for the protection of the environment.

To realize the goals of Agenda 21, the blueprint for environmental action into the 21st century, significantly more funds are needed – both development assistance and private investments. Development assistance is needed to help countries face their environmental challenges, move ahead with sustainable development programmes, and build the capacity for designing and carrying out measures to raise the living standards of the poor.

Fortunately, the international community still has a chance to come forward with these funds and to honour the commitments made in Rio de Janeiro. This June, governments will again come together for a special session of the UN General Assembly to take stock of progress since the Earth Summit. I am hopeful that at this event, already being referred to as 'Earth Summit II', officials from all countries will muster the political will and the financial means to create an environmentally sustainable world for future generations.

The availability of fresh water will be just one of the concerns for everyone in the near future. In only 25 years, water shortages could affect nearly one-third of the Earth's population. Deforestation continues nearly unabated in much of the world. The Earth Summit resulted in a number of agreements on forest preservation and management, but they were modest and did not change the deforestation trend. Much the same can be said for desertification and the buildup of climate-altering gases in the atmosphere. Rio showed the path but too few have taken it.

But the past five years have also resulted in a number of advancements. Significant among these is that governments now recognize they cannot achieve environmental and development goals alone. One of the main roles for governments in the 21st century will be to create legislative and other frameworks that will enable all countries to work together. Rio also buried the myth that environmental protection is a luxury of the rich, it is now widely seen as a necessity for the poor.

New thinking in development is yet another advance. Development that fails to benefit the poor has no soul, and development that fails to safeguard the environment has no vision. Sustainable development does not take place in a political or social vacuum but depends both on effective governance and on the empowerment of communities in civil society to participate in the decisions that affect their lives.

The Way Forward: Beyond Agenda 21 is an important contribution to the body of knowledge we have developed since the Earth Summit. Produced by the UNED-UK, which is UNDP's focal point in the United Kingdom, it provides yardsticks and benchmarks for progress – and failures – since Rio and guides us on our journey toward a more sustainable planet.

I hope the next five years of the journey will include large strides that take us beyond a world of words and promises, and a global awakening to the need for real and concerted action.

James Gustave Speth
Geneva
February 1997

The Adventure of Change

Felix Dodds

If we fail to dare, if we do not try, the next generation will harvest the fruits of our indifference; a world we did not want — a world we did not choose — but a world we could have made better, by caring more for the results of our labors.

Senator Robert Kennedy

The Way Forward – Beyond Agenda 21 is an attempt to try on the fifth Anniversary of the UN Conference on Environment and Development to explain a little about where we have come from, what has been accomplished and where we might be going.

The people who have contributed to this book have themselves helped frame where we are today, and continue to do so. I am indebted to all of them for agreeing to work with me on this project. We all hope it will not only help the debate in 1997, but also help people to understand the first five years since the Earth Summit.

This book is dedicated to all the people around the world who have embraced complexity and are experimenting in trying to make sustainable development a reality. To people who believe in social justice, equity and who have hope that by working together we might create a better world.

In particular to Maria Figueroa, Megan Howell, Matthew Layton, Lova Andre, David Denny, Zonny Woods, Mike Marcolongo, Stacy Gilbert, Ingi Isalm, Mario LaVoie, Giulietta Melessaccio, Alex Gozzi, Craig Boljkovac, Juliet Le Breton and Ozlem Verdar, who are showing the leadership for the next generation. My heartfelt thanks go also to Claire Nugent and Tom Bigg for all their help in putting this book together.

This book is also dedicated to the memory of Mike Harskin – without the Mike Harskins of this world or the next, oppression would be just a little more deep rooted and injustice more widespread.

Without the help of David Boyle and the encouragement of Peter Padbury and Earthscan this book would never have become a reality.

We are all engaged in the 'Adventure of Change' as President Clinton said in his inaugural address in 1993:

The urgent question of our time is whether we can make change our friend and not our enemy.

Felix Dodds
Asgard
February 1997

Introduction

Jonathon Porritt

It seems to have become standard practice for many media cynics and world-weary environmentalists to dismiss the 1992 Earth Summit as 'just another UN talk shop'. I am therefore very grateful to Felix Dodds (UNED-UK's indefatigable and inspirational coordinator) for reminding us just how idiotic this throwaway contempt sounds when set against the principal outcomes of those two frenetic weeks in Rio de Janeiro five years ago. He summarises these as follows:

- Agenda 21;
- The Rio Declaration;
- The Forestry Principles;
- The Climate Convention;
- The Biodiversity Convention;
- The Desertification Convention;
- The UN Commission on Sustainable Development (CSD);
- The CSD NGO/Major Groups Steering Committee to interface with the UN in the work of the CSD;
- The Conference on Small Island Developing States;
- The Conference on Straddling and Highly Migratory Fish Stocks;
- The Inter-Governmental Panel on Forests;
- Over 2000 Local Agenda 21s around the world;
- Over 120 National Sustainable Development Councils;
- Over 120 National Sustainable Development Strategies;
- The development of sustainable development indicators at the local and national level; and
- Enhanced involvement of stakeholders in the UN, national and local decision making process.

Not bad for just another UN talk shop. In fact, the last five years have seen a most impressive take-up of both the spirit and output of certain parts of the Rio agenda. This has been going on within *all* political parties, within local authorities, within the business community, within a host of the establishment institutions, such as architects, engineers, planners, etc, and of course within the NGO community – though it's true that a recurring theme of many of the chapters in *The Way Forward* is the frustration felt at the lack of progress in the intervening five years.

But there is another recurring theme that made an even more powerful impression on me in reading this stirring book: that sustainable development as a concept means very little if its two fundamental elements – environmental sustainability and social justice – are not being given *equal* attention. In mainstream political discourse in most OECD countries today one gets the disturbing impression that sustainable development has become all but synonymous with conventionally defined environmentalism.

So it's worth remembering (however many revisionist interpretations of it there may now be!) that there was undoubtedly a 'deal' on the table at the Earth Summit. G77 and emerging countries *implicitly* agreed to sign up to a variety of action plans for addressing some of the big environmental issues (global warming, deforestation, loss of biodiversity etc), whilst OECD countries *implicitly* signed up to the idea of increased aid flows and other forms of development assistance as the quid pro quo for their buy-in on the environment agenda. This deal was brokered quietly by a lot of diplomacy behind the scenes, despite the prevailing political climate engendered by the Reagan/Thatcher years.

But the deal couldn't quite be made to stick even at the time. At the behest of the United States and the UK, the crucial concept of over-consumption in northern industrialized countries was entirely excised from the conference documentation and discussed only on the fringes. This did not impress delegations from the South. 'Conventionitis' broke out in a bad way, masking the kind of political challenges which should really have been addressed.

From that point on, the deal began almost immediately to unravel. Within Europe, for instance, the European Union proved itself completely unable to agree on ways for coming up with the three billion-ecu aid pledge made as part of its Agenda 21 commitment at Rio. The usual fights broke out: what proportion of this should be determined by the EU itself and what proportion by member countries? Over what period should the money be spent? Under what budget titles should it be allocated? etc, etc. That pledge has *never* been turned into additional assistance.

This (and many similar decisions elsewhere in the developed world) has led to a profound sense of cynicism amongst most Southern countries. Some of the consequences of that retrenchment (with the total volume of aid declining from around $65 billion then to under $55 billion today) were starkly mapped out in last year's very powerful *Human Development Report* published by the UN Development Programme. Richard Jolly, the chief author of the report, pointed out that whereas the richest 20 per cent of the world's population was 30 times better off than the poorest 20 per cent in 1960, it is now *61* times wealthier. The one statistic that really does concentrate the mind in all these discussions is the fact that the wealth of the world's 358 billionaires is equal to the combined annual incomes of around 2.2 billion people. In a splendidly provocative article that sets the tone for the whole report, Nobel economics prize-winner Robert Solow goes to the heart of the environment and social justice issue: 'Those who are so urgent about not inflicting poverty on the future have to explain whey they do not attach even higher priority to reducing poverty today'.

Not a question that one hears asked very often here in the UK, let alone answered, by any of the major groups involved in Agenda 21. The business community, for instance, has retreated from what proved to be the uncomfortable and still unfamiliar zone of ethical and socio-economic engagement into the much more reassuring territory of *eco-efficiency*. Though this is a powerful enough agenda in its own right, it's *not* the same thing as genuinely sustainable development.

By the same token, the environmental NGOs in many developing countries went along with the 'Rio deal' in full knowledge of its significance, but the exigencies of moving the environment agenda forward since 1992 mean that they too have been largely sidelining the social justice aspect. The principal exception to this would appear to be in the United States where NGOs have consistently pursued an agenda driven by the concept of *environmental justice*, with an uncompromising emphasis on the disproportionate environmental impact on communities of colour and lower incomes. In this context, sustainable development can be explained to people as the next phase of the environmental justice movement, with the output of the Earth Summit providing a powerful confirmation of the centrality of this whole approach to environmental issues.

Whichever way you look at it, however, it is hard to deny a *cumulative* loss of momentum on the integration of environmental and social issues since 1992, as is confirmed by many of the authors in this comprehensive review of the post-Rio scene.

But if the Earth Summit (and the Brundtland Commission process that led up to it) really did mark a step change in the way nations both think about and practically address the twin crises of poverty and ecological degradation (as I would argue strongly they did), then it seems highly regrettable that we should be giving up that hard earned territory without much more than the occasional whimper.

Jonathon Porritt
Cheltenham
5 February 1997

Part I

AGREEMENTS FROM
THE RIO SUMMIT

Agenda 21

Chip Lindner

The real message of success will be what happens now, after Rio, when government leaders and citizens alike have returned to their countries, to their organizations, to their immediate preoccupations. It is up to all of us to build on the foundations laid by the Earth Summit to ensure that the decisions that have been taken at the global level be translated into national politics and practices at all levels. A new world order, as we move into the 21st century, must unite us all in a global partnership – which always recognizes and respects the transcending sovereignty of nature, of our only one Earth.

Maurice Strong, Secretary-General to the UN Conference on Environment and Development

On 22 December 1989, the General Assembly of the UN adopted a resolution[1] that called for the convening of the United Nations Conference on Environment and Development, later to be known as the Earth Summit.

The Earth Summit had been inspired by the publication of the Brundtland Report in 1987[2]. The Brundtland Report tried to balance the responsibilities of the North and the South and the need to integrate environment and development. As such, Agenda 21 was negotiated by government representatives with a strong input from a wide range of non-governmental organizations (NGOs).

Four preparatory meetings took place between the summer of 1990 and April 1992. The first Preparatory Committee (PrepCom) was held August 1990 in Nairobi. Two working groups were set up to start to put together the Platform of Action (Agenda 21). Working Group 1 dealt with atmosphere, land resources, biodiversity and biotechnology and Working Group 2 with oceans, seas and coastal areas, fresh water, and hazardous and toxic waste.

The second PrepCom in March 1991 in Geneva established a third working group which dealt with legal and institutional issues. It also opened the possibility for a forest convention, which eventually became the forest principles, and the Earth Charter, which became the Rio Declaration on Environment and Development.

Agenda 21 started to take shape at the third PrepCom in August 1991 in Geneva. As much as 90 per cent of it had been agreed by the final PrepCom in April 1992 in New York, leaving only the most controversial areas such as finance, technological transfer, climate, biodiversity, institutional issues, poverty, consumption, fisheries and biotechnology to be argued over at Rio. The draft Rio Declaration on Environment and Development was also agreed at the final PrepCom.

By the end, Agenda 21 consists of 40 chapters that cover almost everything about the planet and how humans interact with it. Many of the chapters overlap and a number of the issues are reinforced by repetition and are elaborated throughout the document. As such, it is a comprehensive strategy for global action on sustainable development, dealing with today's problems and trying to set the framework within which the problems of tomorrow can also be addressed.

Agenda 21 does not constitute a legally binding commitment for anyone – in many ways this is one of its strengths. It is designed to stand as a blueprint for sustainable development, providing some ideas on the problems that confront us all and on the ways in which these could be tackled. It is also the most comprehensive document negotiated between governments on the interaction between economic, social and environmental trends at every level of human activity.

As many as 178 government delegations attended the Rio Summit and endorsed Agenda 21. Many of the representatives were at the highest level – over 120 heads of government attended the conference, including leaders from all the G7 group of industrial countries. Although US President Bush was one of the last to announce that he was attending, when he arrived he also became intoxicated with the Rio spirit.

Addressing the other heads of state, he said:

The Chinese have a proverb: if a man cheats the earth, the earth will cheat the man. We must leave the earth in better condition than we found it. Some find the challenges ahead overwhelming. I believe that their pessimism is unfounded. It has been said that we don't inherit the earth from our ancestors, we borrow it from our children. When our children look back on this time and place, they will be grateful that we met in Rio, and they will certainly be pleased with the intentions stated and the commitments made. But they will judge us by the actions we take from this day forward. Let us not disappoint them.[3]

Rio was the largest gathering of heads of government that the world had ever seen. If you add to this 50,000 non-governmental representatives, over 5,000 press and thousands of civil servants, the Rio Summit helped to provide the means for vast numbers of people in positions of influence to find ways of implementing sustainable development through Agenda 21.

Possibly the biggest failure at Rio was that no new money to implement the programme was pledged. The secretariat was asked at PrepCom II to work out how much it would cost to implement Agenda 21. They estimated that it would take around $625 billion a year, of which $125 billion would come from developed countries transferring funds to the South through increased aid.

At Rio the overall aid contribution to the South was around $60 billion, and $55 billion in 1996. The 4 billion ECU that the EU promised did not materialize. Financial support for the Global Environmental Facility, which was supposed to be in addition to existing funding is today being seriously questioned by NGOs as it seems that funds paid to other sources have decreased as a result. Many feel that sleight-of-hand has taken from one budget and put into another when the original idea was to create a new instrument to augment existing institutions and processes.

INTERNATIONAL INSTITUTIONAL ISSUES

To make sure that Agenda 21 was implemented at local, national, regional and international level, the agreement called for the creation of a new commission of the UN Economic and Social Council. The Commission on Sustainable Development (CSD) was to meet annually.

The Commission is dealt with in greater depth in Chapter 2, but it is relevant to stress here that the CSD has become a political forum and its work in reviewing the implementation of Agenda 21 has benefited greatly from the presence and active participation of government ministers with a range of different portfolios, approximately 50 of whom have attended each annual session.

The involvement in the work of the CSD of politicians with knowledge and understanding of the national context, and also of many nongovernmental organizations with a focus on activities at national and local level, has been significant. Agenda 21 places great stress on the principle of subsidiarity – that is, implementation of the programmes at the appropriate level. The direct involvement of such government ministers and actors of civil society in the work of the CSD brings the world's concerns, problems and successes to UN efforts to realize sustainable development.

Setting up the Commission has also caused some blurring of the roles it shares with the United Nations Environment Programme (UNEP), which was set up out of the 1972 Stockholm UN Conference on Human Settlements. The UNEP and governments have endeavoured to be clearer about what the roles of the two bodies should be.

Agenda 21, however, is quite clear about this: the UNEP 'will continue to play its role with regard to policy guidance and co-ordination in the field of the environment, taking into consideration the development perspective'.[4]

The CSD's role is also identified quite clearly in Chapter 38 of Agenda 21: 'To monitor progress in the implementation of Agenda 21'.[5]

The two bodies cover some similar areas of work, however, and it is this that has caused the problem. The UK and Indian governments called a meeting of 13 environment ministers from key governments, North and South, and UN agencies to Brocket Hall in the UK to review the way forward before the third session of the CSD.

A relevant paragraph in the chairman's conclusions stated:

> *The high profile of the CSD, whilst welcome, has to some extent deflected political attention from UNEP. We agree that UNEP should be reaffirmed as the international focus for the environment. Its role should be to monitor and assess the state of the world environment; to provide a forum for global*

environment concerns and to catalyse necessary regional and global action; to provide advice and guidance on environmental capacity-building; and to be the voice of the environment within the UN system.[6]

This blurring of the roles between UNEP and the CSD was revisited at the 1996 G7 environment ministers meeting in Cabourg when they said that: 'The CSD should continue to be the high level forum for setting broad policy directions and long term goals.'[7]

The G7 heads of state meeting in Lyon in June 1996 carried on the discussion:

UNEP's role should be confirmed as the environmental voice of the UN responsible for environmental policy development, scientific analysis and monitoring assessment. The current restructuring of UNEP and its governing bodies should be supported.[8]

One of the hopes of the Special Session is that it will clarify the roles of these two very important bodies once and for all.

Agenda 21 allocates some responsibility for implementing aspects of the programmes outlined to nearly all UN agencies and programmes. The UN Inter Agency Committee on Sustainable Development, chaired by Under Secretary-General Nitin Desai, has the responsibility for seeing that there is co-ordination between different UN bodies.

Carrying out their duties as UN task managers overseeing aspects of Agenda 21 (*see* Agenda 21, Chapter 38) has also led parts of the UN system into a closer relationship with each other in the implementation of Agenda 21. Many have developed their own implementation programmes, such as the UN Development Programme's (UNDP) Capacity 21 initiative, which was designed to strengthen the institutional capacity of developing countries to implement Agenda 21 and other related activities at the national level.

The strength of giving nearly all UN agencies work in the implementation of Agenda 21 is that they have to meet and co-ordinate their activities and report to the CSD. This has brought with it some peer group review. The Food and Agricultural Organization's (FAO) work on forest issues was criticized at the CSD session in 1995 to the extent that when the Inter-Governmental Panel on Forests was set up that year, a new body was created as secretariat rather than locating it in FAO.

Criticism of UNESCO over their work on the implementation of

Chapter 36 was audible around the coffee bars and meeting-rooms of the UN at the 1996 CSD and may yet have a more tangible effect at the five-year review of Agenda 21.

REGIONAL CONTEXT

A variety of mechanisms look at the implementation of Agenda 21 at the regional level. These range from UN regional commissions, regional development banks, and regional economic and technical co-operation organizations, such as the European Union. In the EU's draft Common Platform for 1997, the Fifth Action Programme *Towards Sustainability* is identified as an approach to realize many of Agenda 21's priorities.

Towards Sustainability was prepared in parallel with Agenda 21 and is the EU's 'blueprint for achieving sustainable development in the EU by the year 2000'. The EU produced its Progress Report in 1995. It recognised that there had been a move to greater integration in the manufacturing sector, but less positive developments in the agriculture and tourism sectors. It went on to say:

> *Applying the analogy of a large ship which takes considerable time and space to manoeuvre, the 1992–95 phase should be viewed as a priming period, changing the sense of direction and commitment, and the 1996–2000 phase as getting the operation under full steam.*[9]

The Progress Report identified new elements for the work of the Community. It suggested that stronger measures and actions in addressing urban issues, climate change, agriculture and tourism were necessary.

NATIONAL ACTION

Agenda 21 states that 'national level efforts should be undertaken by all countries in an integrated manner so that both environment and development concerns can be dealt with in a coherent manner'.

CONSULTATION WITHIN GOVERNMENT

To make sure that there is an effective review system, countries were asked to report to the CSD on their implementation of Agenda 21.

Through the three full years of the Commission's life, 74 countries have produced national reports on their activities to meet the objectives in Agenda 21.

There has been much criticism of the reporting process. In many countries it has not entailed much more than a consultant being employed to produce the report. In other cases, one government department has produced a document with little or no input from other relevant departments, or from organizations outside central government. Just as there is a need to ensure that the UN agencies integrate their work to implement Agenda 21, so government departments should be exhorted to make stronger efforts to work more closely together.

CONSULTATION OUTSIDE GOVERNMENT

One of the criticisms which is often made is that there has been little input to the process of national reporting by non-governmental organizations. Agenda 21 goes so far as to suggest that 'states may wish to consider setting up national co-ordination structures responsible for the follow up of Agenda 21'. The national commissions, or round tables for sustainable development, which were set up in many countries could have been used for this, but in most cases they have not been.

There are now over 120 such bodies. Unfortunately they have tended not to use Agenda 21 as a 'blueprint', but to determine what they feel are the priorities for their country outside the Agenda 21 framework. The US and the UK are thought to be examples of this.

In a number of developing countries, such as China and the Philippines, Agenda 21 has been used as the starting point. If the national commissions or councils are not used as the mechanism for reviewing Agenda 21 implementation, then another organization or group of organizations has often taken on this interaction with government.

NATIONAL STRATEGIES

Many countries, including the UK, have also produced a national strategy for sustainable development. Work towards a strategy was initiated in early 1993: Prime Minister John Major had promised in Rio to have a strategy produced by the end of that year. The government decided to take the year 2012 – 20 years from Rio – as their time horizon.

An environment strategy had been produced under Margaret Thatcher in 1990 when a Cabinet Committee was brought together to agree policy proposals. With the sustainable development strategy, however, they had to integrate social and economic issues with environmental protection. It was also felt to be important to initiate a wider debate on what the UK strategy for sustainable development should look like. This included four key areas of consultation:

- A seminar with stakeholder groups in Oxford.
- Responses to a consultation paper – over 500 organizations from different sectors responded.
- The *Daily Telegraph* ran a series of articles culminating in a questionnaire about people's attitudes to the environment. It drew over 8,000 responses.
- Discussion with other countries.

The government tried to tie the structure of the strategy to Agenda 21. By doing so, it structured the report into four areas:

- Principles of sustainable development.
- The state of the environment.
- Economic activity in the different sectors.
- Types of policy response.[10]

This also led to specific strategies being adopted for particular areas, including climate change, biodiversity, forests, air quality, and a town and country quality initiative. The strategy document then helped the government to prepare its reports to the CSD.

INDICATORS FOR REPORTING

Indicators have been proposed for the chapters of Agenda 21 as a way to make the reports more useful. Organizations such as the Worldwide Fund For Nature (WWF) and the New Economics Foundation have made some suggestions of what this could entail.[11] The CSD indicators programme is intended to deliver a set of indicators on each chapter of Agenda 21 by 1999.

Some are already available and a number of countries are already testing them. As work on the indicators for sustainable development starts to deliver more concrete results, the reporting process will give us a clearer idea of what is happening. Part of the problem has been that we have not known whether we are moving towards or away from sustainable development. Indicators give us that information and then allow us to set targets to change their direction if necessary. Gary Lawrence discusses this in more depth in Chapter 14.

MAJOR GROUPS

One of the real successes of Agenda 21 was the recognition of the role of stakeholders – Agenda 21 calls them 'Major Groups' – in implementing Agenda 21. The nine major groups in Agenda 21 are: women, children and youth, indigenous people, non-governmental organizations, local authorities, trade unions, business and industry, the scientific and technical community, and farmers.

Each has a chapter (Agenda 21, Chapters 23–32). There are other chapters of this book that deal with the work of some of those major groups (Chapters 8–13). But the work of local authorities around the world to establish what Agenda 21 means at a local level is worth highlighting.

Many of the commitments in Agenda 21 need to be enacted at the local level. The Local Agenda 21 process, called for in Chapter 28 of Agenda 21, has been vital in translating the theory of sustainable development into practical local action. In many instances this has also furthered the debate about new forms of governance in which local stakeholder groups are drawn into local decision-making processes.

This is echoed at the international level with major groups gaining more and more access and rights to participate in relevant UN meetings. If such stakeholder groups are to be asked to implement agreements, it is right that they should have a say in agreeing them. Perhaps the most disappointing major group response has been from business and industry, although that is also starting to change. A number of leading companies that have local bases are finding that they are becoming involved in their local Agenda 21 process. National and international companies are also being asked about their corporate responsibilities.

THE WAY FORWARD

The Earth Summit focused the world on sustainable development, and by doing so created the possibility that we might take the right path in future. If the UN Special Session in June 1997 is a success, it will give a great boost to the work that is already under way. To do this it needs to focus on the main road blocks to implementing Agenda 21, while at the same time giving impetus to the driving forces which will make sure that those decisions are implemented.

Areas in which Agenda 21 is weak, where there will need to be work over the coming five years, include transport, energy and tourism. No UN bodies are dealing with these areas and no individual chapters of Agenda 21 cover them. Nevertheless, all three have a massive impact on sustainable development.

The following four areas will also receive special attention:

- **Forests**   The next five years of implementation will also have to deal with the problems associated with natural resources such as forests, oceans and fresh water. There are growing signs that these three will require new legal frameworks over the coming years. The Special Session may start the process for an internationally agreed convention on forests.
- **Fresh water**   Although water-related issues are principally regional in nature, there are examples of global framework conventions, such as that being considered for chemicals, which could set the global principles for sound management of scarce resources, pricing, capacity – building and a set of regional priorities.
- **Oceans and seas**   There are already four international agreements on fisheries and marine pollution, in addition to the Law of the Sea Convention. Even so, more legal instruments in the area of offshore installations, maritime transport and fisheries may well be part of the package coming out of the Special Session.
- **Finance**   Agenda 21 did not fully address the role of finance. A sharper focus on the role of transnational corporations is now seen as a major objective by many NGOs and some governments. The use of pension funds for supporting sustainable development, and the role of insurance and the banking industry are some of the areas that the UNEP has started to look into. Charters now exist for both – how they develop will be crucial.

Local authorities, trade unions and charities are now looking at where the money in their pension funds and other investments is going. The Local Agenda 21 process will start to look at this area over the next five years. Some of the key UK companies are already repositioning themselves to deal with this.

We are now better able to see how the implementation of Agenda 21 is progressing. The reporting process has allowed countries to start to prioritize their needs. The main stumbling-block to implementation in many countries, especially developing countries, is funding. This is a crucial issue to be addressed in the coming years; it was fudged in Rio when many developed countries cited the world recession as a reason for their failure to take decisive action then.

Success next year will depend on finding new resources to fund the implementation of Agenda 21. Barbara Bramble outlines what some of those might be in Chapter 15, but the most obvious is a tax on air fuel. This was supported for the first time by the UK Government in the speech by John Gummer, Secretary of State for the Environment, at the climate negotiations in Geneva in June 1996. It would generate \$2–\$4 billion – a long way short of the \$70 billion that is needed according to the figures presented at Rio, but it would be a start.

A new form of governance is emerging – that of 'stakeholders'. Local stakeholders in communities are linking together, whether they are local businesses or local authorities, non-governmental organizations or community-based organizations, women's groups or residents' associations. Groups that have an identifiable 'stake' in the future of the community are making these links to create a vision for the future which has a set of goals and measurable criteria or indicators.

This is an innovative approach that, if done well, enables a community to move forward together so that decisions taken are based on a shared set of values. This means moving to a more sustainable community, working at a level that most people relate to and feel they have some influence over. The Local Agenda 21 process is helping this all to take root.

We are seeing the growth of interest in stakeholder involvement. President Clinton and the UK Labour leader Tony Blair now use the rhetoric of stakeholder approaches to issues such as finance, education, health and social policy as the new organizing model for society. As Tony Blair said in a speech in Singapore in February 1996:

Successful companies invest, treat their employees fairly, value them as a resource not just of production but of creative innovation... We cannot by legislation guarantee that a company will behave in a way conducive to truth and long-term commitment. But it is surely time to assess how we shift the emphasis in corporate ethos — from the company being a mere vehicle for the capital market, to be traded, bought and sold as a commodity; towards a vision of the company as a community of partnership in which each employee has a stake, and where a company's responsibilities are more clearly delineated.[12]

Agenda 21 will become a household term in various ways over the next few years. It has given people the assurance that there is now a framework to work within that links the local to the national to the regional to the international. Individual action can now be seen in the context of a worldwide programme of activity. Those who said in 1992 that Rio was a failure may not have appreciated the impact it was going to have on the world. We are now starting to see what that might be.

NOTES

1. UN General Assembly Resolution 44/228, 22 December 1989.
2. The World Commission on Environment and Development (The Brundtland Commission), *Our Common Future*, Oxford University Press, 1987.
3. President Bush's address to the United Nations Conference on Environment and Development, June 1992.
4. Agenda 21, Chapter 38 (38.21–23), Regency Press 1992.
5. Agenda 21, Chapter 38 (38.11–38.14), Regency Press, 1992.
6. Informal meeting of environment ministers, Brocket Hall, UK, 10–11 February 1995.
7. G7 Environment Ministers Communiqué, Cabourg, May 1996.
8. G7 Heads of State Communiqué, Lyon, June 1996; Major Group Chapters are Chapters 24–32 of Agenda 21.
9. EU Progress Report on *Towards Sustainability*, 1995.
10. UNED-UK, *Three Years Since the Rio Summit*, September 1995.
11. WWF Recommendations to CSD94/95, April 1994 and April 1995.
12. Tony Blair, Singapore, February 1996.

2

The UN Commission on Sustainable Development

Tom Bigg and Felix Dodds

To most people, the United Nations is synonymous with international efforts to prevent organized violence in troubled parts of the world. Appreciation of the UN's role may extend to an awareness of the existence of some of the specialized agencies such as the United Nations Children's Fund (UNICEF), the World Health Organization (WHO) or even the UN Environment Programme (UNEP). But for the vast majority, the workings, activities and potential of the UN are seen to have very little relevance to everyday life.

This common perception is at odds with much that has happened in the UN over the past decade. A series of major international summits have attempted to focus on problems experienced by every inhabitant of the planet. These have placed a burden of responsibility not just on the international community and national governments, but on individuals, local government and local communities, trade unions and businesses – the whole range of organizations and perspectives which make up societies.

The implications of this change in priorities for the UN is reflected in the documents agreed by governments at the Rio Summit, the Copenhagen Social Summit, the Beijing Women's Conference and in preparation for the Cities Summit in Istanbul in June. The former UN Secretary-General Boutros Boutros-Ghali put it in these terms:

The battle for people-centred and sustainable development will be won or lost not in the corridors of governments, but in every hamlet and home, in every village and town, in the daily enterprise of every member of the global community and every institution of civil society. The charter of the United Nations begins with a pledge by 'We the Peoples....' It is the people, on whose behalf we all act, who are the true custodians of the emerging new vision of development. It is for them that we must work to achieve a new framework for development, co-operation and the revitalization of the United Nations system.

Boutros Boutros-Ghali, UN Secretary-General, Agenda for Development, 1995

One of the main outcomes of the Rio Summit was the establishment of the Commission on Sustainable Development (CSD) as the principal focus for monitoring and promoting the implementation of the agreements reached.

The CSD is the body within the UN system that is particularly responsible for the follow-up to the Rio Summit. Yet while Rio attracted tens of thousands of non-governmental participants and 116 heads of state, the CSD has received little attention. Nevertheless, over 40 government ministers attended the 1996 session, with a growing core of active representatives from different major groups, more than 300 of whom were present that year.

There is still a widespread lack of appreciation of the ways in which this body is developing. Government representatives at CSD sessions have predominantly been from environment ministries, and non-government representatives come mainly from environmental organizations. But this is steadily changing as ministers from housing and urban development, overseas development, transport, forestry and even finance departments have put in appearances. Indeed, Bulgarian finance minister Rumen Gechev chaired the fourth session of the Commission.

The CSD has been given a pivotal role at every level, from the activities of intergovernmental bodies to the implementation of Local Agenda 21s at community level. New instruments, such as legally binding conventions on the use of natural resources, are also likely to be initiated at the Commission.

Governments have been required to report annually to the CSD on the implementation of specific parts of Agenda 21. The concept of, and criteria for reporting have proved contentious. Even so, five countries made presentations on their national reports in 1995, and opened themselves to comment and criticism in ways which would not have been considered possible at the Earth Summit. A further six presented their experiences in 1996.

Strengthening the links between the intergovernmental process at UN level and the activities at national level has been crucial to the success of the CSD. This is a factor which we will explore in more detail later, but it is important to note that strong emphasis has been placed on the work of the Commission on the role of the other actors, apart from governments.

The identification of nine 'major groups' of civil society in Agenda 21 has led to active participation by a wide range of organizations in the CSD's work. The Commission itself has come to be seen as a testing ground for new ways of involving non-governmental organizations in UN processes, and the involvement of organizations which work principally or exclusively at national level has had a major impact. In future, it may not be just governments that hold up their records for scrutiny in the CSD: increasingly, there is pressure to allow equivalent opportunities to major groups.

With these opportunities for non-governmental organizations come additional responsibilities. The legitimacy of such organizations derives from the degree to which they represent civil society. If the role of the CSD after the five-year review is to push further forward with implementing the Rio agreements, and if the involvement of the major groups is to increase accordingly, it will be vital to ensure that NGOs working at the international level adequately consult with, inform and enhance the involvement of those on whose behalf they claim to speak.

THE BEGINNING

The CSD was established in 1993 as a functioning commission of the UN Economic and Social Council (ECOSOC). Agenda 21 provided for the creation of the CSD:

> *In order to ensure the effective follow up of the conference, as well as to enhance international co-operation and rationalise the inter-governmental decision-making capacity for the integration of environment and develop-*

*ment issues and to examine the progress of the implementation of Agenda
21 at the national, regional and international levels, a high-level
Commission on Sustainable Development should be established...*

(Agenda 21 38.11)

Agreement to the creation of the CSD was achieved against considerable initial opposition from many Northern governments, including the
UK and the USA, who opposed in principle the creation of any new
body in the UN system. This position was eventually overturned, in no
small part because of the persistence of NGOs and a number of
Southern governments.[1]

The 1992 General Assembly debated setting up the Commission
and resolved that:

- The Economic and Social Council has been requested to establish a
  high-level Commission as a functional council body.
- Representatives of 53 states have been elected by the council for up to
  three-year terms.
- The Commission will meet once a year for two or three weeks. It is a
  functional ECOSOC commission with a full-time secretariat based in
  New York. Care has been taken to ensure that the secretariat has a
  clear identity within the UN system.
- Relevant intergovernmental organizations and specialized agencies,
  including financial institutions, are invited to designate representatives
  to advise and assist the Commission, and also to serve as focal points for
  the members and secretariat of the Commission between sessions.

SECRETARIAT

The CSD secretariat is located within the Department for Policy
Co-ordination and Sustainable Development (DPCSD). The Head of
the DPCSD is UN Under Secretary-General Nitin Desai, who was
number two to Maurice Strong during the Earth Summit process. In
addition to its role in the follow-up to the Rio Summit, the DPCSD
includes secretariats that deal with outcomes from the Copenhagen
World Summit for Social Development and the Beijing Women's
Conference, both held in 1995.

The organization of the CSD, its place within the UN system, its staffing and funding levels and consequent credibility were painstakingly established over the first two years. At its inception, the Economic and Social Council stated that the CSD Secretariat should:

- Be an identifiable entity, highly qualified and competent.
- Aim for geographical and gender balance.
- Draw upon the expertise, method and structure of the preparatory process leading to UNCED.
- Be supplemented by secondment from other relevant bodies, notably UNEP, UNDP and the World Bank, while not 'negatively affecting the work programmes of these organizations'.
- Call upon members of national governments and appropriate specialists on limited term contracts.
- Be funded from the regular UN budget and depend to the maximum extent possible upon existing budgetary resources.

COMMISSION ON SUSTAINABLE DEVELOPMENT (CSD)

A third of the CSD's 53 members are up for election each year on a regional basis. The allocation of seats are: 13 seats from Africa, 11 seats from Asia, 6 seats from Eastern Europe, 10 seats from Latin America and the Caribbean, and 13 seats from Western Europe and North America. Each country has a three-year term of office on the Commission.

It is one of the few ECOSOC commissions for which countries actively 'run for office' to be members. In 1993 the UK Secretary of State wrote to all member states of the UN asking for their support in the UK's re-election to the Commission.

THE CSD BUREAU

The CSD Bureau is made up of the chair and the four vice-chairs of the Commission. The chair and the co-chairs are elected at the beginning of each session and then preside over work done in the inter-sessional period by the previous chair. The problems this causes were highlighted during the first two CSD sessions and are likely to resurface at the 1997 General Assembly Special Session.

HIGH-LEVEL ADVISORY BOARD

The High-level Advisory Board was called for in Agenda 21 as an additional tool to strengthen the follow-up to Rio. Agenda 21 defined the board's mandate:

> *Intergovernmental bodies, the Secretary General and the United Nations system as a whole may also benefit from the expertise of a high level advisory body consisting of eminent persons with knowledge about the environment and development, including relevant sciences, appointed by the Secretary General in their personal capacity. In this regard, the Secretary General should make appropriate recommendations to the 47th session of the General Assembly.*
>
> Agenda 21, Chapter 38

The board has helped the Commission to identify areas of concern and by giving the necessary gravitas to its operations. Its main task has been to advise the Secretary-General on matters of sustainable development.

Disquiet has been expressed both from members of the board and others that it has not lived up to its potential. It has been criticized for not taking a sufficiently active role in the Commission's work and in endeavouring to involve other actors between sessions of the CSD.

The future of the board and its relevance to the programme of work that has been established, may be called into question at the Special Session.

THE CSD's MANDATE

The CSD's mandate was agreed at a Special Session of ECOSOC in February 1993 (Resolution 1993/207) to:

- Monitor progress on the implementation of Agenda 21 and activities related to the integration of environmental and developmental goals by governments, NGOs and other UN bodies.
- Monitor progress towards the target of 0.7 per cent GNP from developed countries for overseas development aid.
- Review the adequacy of financing and the transfer of technologies as outlined in Agenda 21.

- Receive and analyse relevant information from competent NGOs in the context of Agenda 21 implementation.
- Enhance dialogue with NGOs, the independent sector, and other entities outside the UN system, within the UN framework.
- Provide recommendations to the General Assembly through ECOSOC.

The CSD's programme of work for the following four years was agreed at its first session in 1993.

RELATIONSHIP WITH OTHER PARTS OF THE UN SYSTEM

The CSD is linked both vertically and horizontally to other parts of the UN system. In the first direction, its secretariat, the Division on Sustainable Development, reports to one of the Under-Secretaries-General, who in turn assists the Secretary-General. Secondly, it relates to UN agencies and bodies and takes part in an Inter-Agency Committee on Sustainable Development with over 20 members.

This co-ordinating instrument allows for good co-operation and valuable inputs to the analysis of specific topics, for which members are designated as task managers or collaborators in the preparation of the basic documents and in actively participating in the discussions. Agenda 21 recognizes the important role that many agencies and programmes of the UN System have in implementing Agenda 21. It has therefore made sure that, where agencies have relevant programmes, they are brought into some relationship with the CSD.

THE ADMINISTRATIVE COMMITTEE ON CO-ORDINATION (ACC)

The ACC was set up under ECOSOC Resolution 13 (III) of 1946. Meetings are attended by the Secretary-General and the executive heads of specialized agencies and programmes. It has been suggested that this could become the 'cabinet' of the UN.[2]

How can we transform the ACC into a real cabinet wherein I do not pretend to be the Prime Minister, but at least play a role of chief of orchestra in order to have a minimum of co—ordination among the different agencies?

Secretary-General Boutros Boutros-Ghali, April 1993

If this enhanced role for the ACC were to be combined with an affirmation by governments of the UN General Assembly's authority to co-ordinate across the system, many of the difficulties currently experienced could be avoided.

The ACC has the task of co-ordinating the policies of the different parts of the UN and is chaired by the Secretary-General. In the past, ACC activities have been primarily administrative and rather low-key, but since UNCED in 1992, the ACC has regularly placed sustainability issues on the agenda which might be implemented throughout the United Nations system.

To follow up the series of summits has been placed high on its agenda. The streamlining and reorganization of its subsidiary machinery have been designed to enhance its efficency and synergy to give shape to the programme areas of Agenda 21. The Inter Agency Committee on Sustainable Development has been created as a subsidiary to the ACC specifically to provide fresh impetus and a new focus for the integration of poliies and programmes.

INTER AGENCY COMMITTEE ON SUSTAINABLE DEVELOPMENT (IACSD)

The IACSD is a subsidiary body to the ACC, focusing specifically on sustainable development issues in the UN system. It is made up of senior level officials from nine core members of the ACC – FAO, UNESCO, WHO, WMO, World Bank, UNDP, UNEP, ILO and IAEA (International Atomic Energy Agency). Officials from other UN bodies and intergovernmental institutions are able to attend meetings. The IACSD was asked by the ACC in 1993 to focus on four issues:

- Streamlining the existing interagency co-ordination machinery.
- Allocating and sharing responsibilities for Agenda 21 implementation by the UN system.
- Monitoring the new financial requirements of UN system organizations that relate to Agenda 21.
- Assessing reporting requirements that are related to the implementation of Agenda 21 and making recommendations on streamlining.

Many NGOs have pointed out that the streamlining of all UN reporting processes would greatly assist both NGOs and governments. For example, reports to the Conference of the Parties to the Biodiversity Convention and the CSD would have the same format. This should also apply to World Bank reports and to donor country report requirements. At present, developing countries are bombarded by the requests for reports on a wide range of topics, but without adequate consideration to the greater benefits which could be gained through co-ordination and consistency. The IACSD has yet to produce recommendations on such systemwide harmonization.

The IACSD and the CSD have developed an innovative structure to involve relevant parts of the UN system in monitoring and implementing Agenda 21. Relevant IACSD members have been designated as 'task managers' for particular chapters of Agenda 21. These UN bodies have been given responsibility for drawing up the Secretary-General's report to the CSD session. Reports must take into consideration information provided by governments, the UN system and major groups.

This approach has produced some interesting by-products: agencies are now answerable to another forum. This peer group review was apparent at the 1995 CSD session, when the Food and Agriculture Organization (FAO) (the task manager for forests) was not given the role as secretariat for the newly established Inter-Governmental Panel on Forests, which was located instead in the UN secretariat.

ANNUAL SESSIONS OF THE CSD

FIRST SESSION (JUNE 1993)

The first CSD session was timed to begin precisely one year after the climax of the Rio Summit. This symbolism was not lost on US Vice-President Al Gore, who called for each country to make a strong commitment to change. The main sticking-point during the two-week meeting was the lack of tangible financial muscle from Northern countries to back up the fine words. When challenged, the lack of progress towards the agreement at Rio to work towards a development aid target of 0.7 per cent of gross national product (GNP) was blamed on the world recession.

At the opening, Vice-President Gore succinctly summed up the potential of the CSD:

The role of this Commission is primarily catalytic – it can focus attention on issues of common interest. It can serve as a forum for raising ideas and plans. It can help resolve issues that arise as nations proceed in their sustainable development agendas. It can monitor progress. It can help shift the multilateral financial institutions and bilateral assistance efforts towards a sustainable development agenda.

There were more optimistic signs to come out of the session. Delegates and ministers recognized that impromptu financial initiatives were very unlikely at the time. Consequently, they began to put in place the means by which money could be used in future should circumstances change. Pragmatic co-operation characterized much of the meeting.

This was evident in the acceptance of the need for intersessional work to address sticking-points in finance and technology transfer. The Group of 77 developing countries (G77) waived their normal caveat that they do not sanction intersessional arrangements because these can stretch or exceed the capacity of G77 member countries. Northern countries anticipated this and were prepared to make practical commitments to fund the participation of developing countries' representatives in the meetings.

Chairing the first CSD session was Ambassador Razali from Malaysia who set the stage for a new kind of UN Commission. In particular, he helped to develop unprecedented access and involvement for NGOs, principally through *ad hoc* arrangements which led to a number of NGO statements in 'informal' sessions. Government delegates paid lip-service to the pivotal role that NGOs play in promoting sustainability, both nationally and in international fora such as the CSD.

The degree of dialogue between governments and NGOs was also significant. This applied both in CSD plenaries, where NGOs were given speaking slots at strategic points throughout all debates, and to informal negotiations over specific policies and initiatives.

The 1993 CSD:

- Agreed a three-year agenda through which the Commission would review about a third of Agenda 21 each year from 1994 to 1996, followed by a full assessment in 1997 and a General Assembly review of the whole of Agenda 21 later that year.
- Set up reporting processes to channel information on efforts to implement Agenda 21 into the CSD for review. The annual report process

would include submissions from national governments and from intergovernmental organizations. The CSD secretariat was to receive these, analyse them and then produce aggregated reports on Agenda 21 implementation at national and international levels. Scope was allowed for NGOs to contribute, both through their national governments' reports and directly to the secretariat.

- Planned intersessional meetings to prepare for the next CSD session.[3]
- Allowed a number of governments to offer to host meetings that addressed various parts of the CSD agenda.[4]
- Agreed other matters involving financial assistance and technology. Progress made by various parts of the UN system towards incorporating Agenda 21 into their operations was also addressed.

SECOND SESSION (MAY 1994)

Dr Klaus Töpfer, then German Environment Minister, chaired the second CSD session, which demonstrated the interest and involvement of politicians in the work of the Commission. It was not going to be just another 'talking shop'.

Probably the greatest success of the 1994 CSD was the work that Dr Töpfer did to bring forests back on to the international political agenda. He asked delegates and NGOs alike to 'give the issue air' just two years after the Rio Summit had failed to deliver a convention on forests. By doing so he succeeded in setting firm foundations for the setting up in 1995 of the CSD Inter-Governmental Panel on Forests.

The 1994 CSD:

- Recommended that relevant bodies should seek a legally binding status of the Prior Informed Consent Procedure.[5] OECD countries should ban exports of listed or dangerous substances to developing countries.
- Called for greater co-operation with governing bodies of international organizations, the Bretton Woods institutions and the General Agreement on Trade and Tariffs (GATT) and the World Trade Organization (WTO), and with major groups.
- Recognized that the overall financing of Agenda 21 and sustainable development fell significantly short of expectations and requirements.
- Agreed that additional efforts were essential in the area of transfer of environmentally sound technologies, co-operation and capacity-building.

- Acknowledged that additional measures needed to be taken to change contemporary patterns of consumption and production that are detrimental to sustainable development.[6]
- Emphasized the importance of the continuous exchange of information on practical experience gained by countries, organizations and major groups.
- Backed ongoing work on the elaboration of realistic and understandable sustainable development indicators that can supplement national reporting.
- Developed innovative ways of working. The need for a dialogue-oriented approach was recognized, including the use of panel sessions and other means by which information could be shared and the expertise of a wide range of actors could be sought.

There was much support for meetings hosted by governments and other organizations to address issues on the CSD's agenda. The need for effective intersessional work to prepare for the next session of the Commission was widely acknowledged. During the year of Dr Töpfer's chairmanship, there were over 140 government and NGO meetings which fed into the third session of the CSD in 1995.

One organizational problem which became apparent during the first two years was that CSD chairs were elected at the beginning of the annual session and served until the start of the session the following year. Initiatives developed by the outgoing chair would therefore reach their fruition under a successor who might not have the same commitment or interest, and who would be coping with the immensely difficult task of chairing a UN Commission session for the first time.

Attempts were made to persuade ECOSOC to change the normal arrangements and allow election of the chair and the Bureau of a UN Commission at the end of the annual session. But this was seen as a step too far by government representatives at the ECOSOC session and the less than satisfactory arrangements remained in place.

THIRD SESSION (APRIL 1995)

As many as 53 countries produced national reports and more than 50 ministers and secretaries of state attended the third session of the CSD. This included ministers for the environment, finance, planning, development co-operation, forestry, agriculture, labour and infrastructure. Ten countries made presentations on their national reports.

Another significant feature was the growing collaboration of the entire family of UN institutions, both during the preparatory phase and the session itself. The pervading atmosphere of optimism and expectation was apparent in the statement made by Under-Secretary-General Nitin Desai on the opening day:

> *We have to appreciate that the CSD is something unique among ECOSOC bodies. It has not only managed to mobilize the interest and active involvement of the UN system, including the development banks, but it has captured the attention of non-governmental groups and the public at large. The Commission has gotten this response because of the urgency of its subject matter and the open and transparent way it has conducted its business. The effort to be inclusive rather than exclusive has generated support for the Commission and commitment to its work programme.*

The 1995 CSD:

- Established an Inter-Governmental Panel on Forests which would report to the Special Session in 1997. Part of its remit would be to see if there should be a new convention on forests.
- Produced an analysis of the patterns of consumption and production, and the establishment of a work programme on consumption and production patterns.
- Called for a review of the mechanisms for transferring environmentally sound technologies.
- Agreed a timetable for the formulation of sustainable development indicators.
- Promoted an integrated approach to the planning and management of land resources.[7]
- Recognized the need to analyse the potential effects of environmentally related trade issues.[8]
- Recognized that poverty eradication is an indispensable requirement for sustainable development.
- Encouraged initiatives at national and international levels, including action to phase out lead in petrol.

One of the continuing areas of concern remained the financing of sustainable development, especially supporting national efforts in developing countries and economies in transition. Disappointment, but little surprise, was expressed by many at the continuing decrease in development aid, which declined both in absolute terms and as a percentage of GNP.

In 1994, the International Council for Local Environmental Initiatives (ICLEI) secured reference in the formal texts to the desirability of arranging an organized reporting process on the role of local authorities in implementing Agenda 21. During the 1995 session, negotiations were successfully concluded for the preparation and circulation of a collection of Local Agenda 21 case studies from all regions of the world, the mounting of a Local Agenda 21 exhibition during the CSD session, and the presentation of a local government case study from each region of the world on 18 April 1995. This 'Day of Local Authorities' was generally thought to be a constructive way to highlight concrete results at the local level through the contributions of specific major groups. This approach has been continued at subsequent sessions.

FOURTH SESSION (MAY 1996)

The 1996 CSD was in many ways a disappointment after its success in 1995. The Inter Governmental Panel helped to focus work on forests in one place. There was some speculation that the CSD would do the same in 1996 for management of the marine environment (Agenda 21, Chapter 17). The UK Prime Minister's Advisory Panel on Sustainable Development, chaired by Sir Crispin Tickell, raised the possibility of an Inter-Governmental Panel on Oceans as a way of moving forward in this area. This was subsequently taken up by the UK Government, but it did not prove possible to set up an equivalent structure under the CSD.

With the General Assembly review of Agenda 21 approaching, much of the CSD meeting was spent considering how the five-year review should be conducted, and what the priorities for consideration should be.

As in 1995, there was a day dedicated to the work of major groups – industry and trade unions worked together on a 'Day of the Workplace'. Some very impressive examples of how those major groups are involved in implementing Agenda 21 were presented.

At the CSD itself agreements were reached on the following subjects.

Oceans

A draft decision on institutional arrangements was formulated for consideration by the UN General Assembly on the Global Plan of Action negotiated at the Washington, DC, meeting on protecting the marine environment from land-based activities in November 1995. The Plan of Action gives a new and enhanced role to the UNEP in this field.

The Commission failed, however, to agree recommendations to the International Maritime Organization on the need for negotiation of a legally binding, global agreement on oil platform discharges and on 'user pays' fees for the upkeep of the straits used for international shipping.

Indicators

The Commission urged governments to pilot the 126 indicators developed by the CSD in conjunction with governments, UN agencies and major groups.

Changing Consumption and Production Patterns

The CSD reviewed the work programme and concluded that although eco-efficiency is a promising strategy for policy development, it is not a substitute for changes in the unsustainable life-styles of consumers. The Commission urged governments to look at their procurement policies to see if they could be 'greened'.

Trade and the Environment

The CSD addressed the relationship between World Trade Organization provisions and trade measures for environmental purposes, including those that are relevant to multilateral environmental agreements.

CHALLENGES FOR 1997

There was considerable debate among NGO representatives at the 1996 CSD session on the record of the Commission to date and on the issues which should be prioritized for the 1997 Special Session. There was general agreement that the CSD should be seen as a qualified success, but if it is really to get to grips with being the engine behind sustainable development at international level, it needs to do less and to do it better.

By 1995, it had become obvious that it needed an Herculean effort to move an issue forward within the CSD – an effort which worked for forests in 1995 but not for marine issues in 1996. Concentration on what Peter Padbury of the Canadian Council for International Co-operation terms 'road-block' issues would enable the CSD to spend five weeks a year making progress on just a few vital areas. It would also enable governments and major groups to concentrate their work in the intersessional period on those issues and would simplify the international agenda on sustainable development issues enormously.

Certain issues would require a two- to three-year preparatory period. This should also help the national reporting process: reporting to the CSD is particularly difficult because the guidelines are made available in July or August each year, leaving only three or four months for a government or organization to write its report and put it out for consultation.

The Special Session in June 1997 will have some very important work to do. This will include:

- Agreeing the next five-year programme of work.
- Reviewing what has been achieved over the past five years.
- Reviewing the outcome from the CSD Inter-Governmental Panel on Forests.
- Reviewing the implications of the report of the Stockholm Institute on freshwater resources.
- Reviewing the sustainable consumption and production patterns work programme.
- Reviewing the work of the major groups.
- Considering issues of institutional reform in the context of a follow-up to Rio.

THE FUTURE OF THE CSD

In any review of an organization, one of the questions that should be asked is whether it should continue to exist. The answer for the CSD is relatively simple. The issues it addresses are going to frame the 21st century and how we live our lives.

Norman Myers of Green College, Oxford was asked to present a paper on the 'Problems of the Next Century' at a UNED–UK seminar on 1997:

Perhaps the main message from our crystal balls is that we should not be surprised if we encounter one set of surprises after another, notably in the environmental sphere.[9]

We should bear this in mind for any attempt to define the issues which should be addressed over the coming years. It is still possible, however, to identify a number of areas which will require increasing international co-operation in future, and for which the CSD offers the most productive context for such work.

Any list of the challenges for the CSD and the Special Session has to be subjective. The following list is a synthesis of the major group and governmental positions as they were put forward in autumn 1996: finance, sustainable consumption and production, trade and sustainable development, freshwater, forests, oceans, urbanization, poverty, education, international co-operation, indicators of sustainable development, and the role of transnational companies.

The CSD has seen a large involvement of the major group organizations in its work. About 200 to 300 major group representatives have attended each Commission meeting at some point during the three-week period. The CSD has pioneered a greater involvement of the major groups in the work of an ECOSOC Commission.

None of the sessions is now closed – even the small working groups are held open for major group representatives to attend and in many cases to speak. Their increased involvement in implementing the UN Conference agreements has also meant increased involvement in framing them in the first place.

The Habitat II Conference expanded this involvement: at Istanbul and the preparatory meetings, NGOs were allowed to enter suggestions of text amendments. To do this they were required to organize themselves into a negotiating block and then the UN brought the NGO amendments out as an official UN document – A/Conf.165/INF/8. This was the first time that this had happened.

Following the Habitat II Conference, the Centre for Human Settlements – working with local authorities, NGOs and the business community – have drawn up a proposal to increase the size of the

Commission on Human Settlement. This will be to add 14 local authority seats, 12 NGO seats, and 8 for business and industry.

These precedents could be developed further to strengthen input from the major groups to the UN system as a whole.

INSTITUTIONAL REFORM AND THE CSD

The creation of the CSD as one of the operational outcomes of the 1992 Earth Summit came after a period of little change in the number and operations of ECOSOC commissions. Unlike most other functional commissions, the CSD was given a very broad mandate and programme of work.

Some governments argue that, with such an extensive agenda and schedule, the CSD could subsume the functions of most of the other commissions. Whether this would be to the detriment of the issues they currently address is another matter. US proposals that the CSD be moved to Geneva to 'facilitate interaction with the specialized agencies that are responsible for implementation of much of UNCED's programme of work' ('US Views on Reform Measures Necessary for Strengthening the UN System', February 1996) and 'absorb the functions of the Commission on Science and Technology for Development, the Committee on Natural Resources, and the Energy Committee' (Madeleine Allbright, US Ambassador to the UN, to the UNGA 1995) could be construed as a move away from the political focus that is apparent in the Commission's work to date, towards a more prosaic role that attempts only to co-ordinate programme activities within the UN system.

The International Conference on Population and Development in Cairo in 1994, the Copenhagen World Summit for Social Development in March 1995, the Fourth World Conference on Women in Beijing in 1995, and the Habitat II Conference all led to the agreement of plans of action to be monitored and promoted by the relevant ECOSOC commissions. The Commission on Population and Development, the Commission on Social Development, the Commission on the Status of Women, and the Commission on Human Settlements may all require slightly different mandates to make their annual sessions more accessible to the many organizations of civil society that followed each of their conference processes.

The format of the CSD's annual organizational session which has developed over the past four years is one which the above commissions may also want to incorporate. But this would require a commitment by governments to participate at the relevant ministerial level in these commissions, particularly at the high level sessions.

The CSD is at present the only commission that elects government ministers as chairs – the advantage of this is to politicize the work of the commissions. The required political commitment for substantial progress in the work of the commissions will be evident when others are able to do the same.

It will be necessary in future to find ways to bring into greater harmony the mechanisms that deal with the follow-up to the series of UN conferences and summits. Some of the suggestions outlined in the 'Synthesis Paper on NGO Priorities and Concerns for the 1997 General Assembly Special Session' by Tom Bigg and Peter Mucke on behalf of the CSD NGO Steering Committee should be addressed:

> *The relations between ECOSOC commissions addressing issues relevant to sustainable development is also important. ECOSOC in 1997 will review the work programmes of all such commissions and examine ways to achieve greater co-ordination. Practical proposals to enhance their work include:*
>
> - *Joint sessions of two or more commissions, especially the high level sessions.*
> - *Joint meetings of the Bureaux of the Commissions.*
> - *Possible merging of commissions or redefinition of work programmes.*
> - *Bringing into the Department for Policy Co-ordination and Sustainable Development the divisions that deal with Population and Development and Human Settlements.*[10]

These suggestions should be seen as strengthening the UN in the area of sustainable development. This requires a recognition that the UN should be given new and additional funds to ensure that it is effective.

CONCLUSION

The work of the CSD could prove to be effective in future in a number of different ways. Domestic pressure on government representatives to take Rio follow-up seriously in domestic politics – from major group organizations – could coincide with a realization that the Commission is the most suitable body to host international negotiations on how progress can be achieved towards specific objectives.

The hope of Dr Töpfer, Chair of the CSD from 1994 to 1995 and then German Environment Minister, that the CSD will come to function as 'an environmental Security Council' illustrates the dynamic role that its most active proponents feel the Commission could have.

This vision of the future would also entail steadily cranking up the CSD's ability to hold governments answerable to their peers and to their citizens for progress achieved. There are obvious problems with this, not least the difficulty of persuading governments to lay themselves open to such criticism and accountability.

Major group organizations have also begun to explore ways in which their own role in implementing Agenda 21, which is widely recognized as an essential component, can be assessed and reviewed by the Commission. This year, local authorities from around the world made presentations on their activities in this respect, and in 1996 business organizations and trade unions will do the same.

The CSD has become a central institution, positioned at the heart of all the disparate aspects of the follow-up to the Rio Summit. It also has the potential to wield considerable political influence over both national governments and international bodies whose functions are considered to be of relevance to sustainable development.

If the Commission did not exist, there would be a gulf between local and national implementation of Agenda 21 and global follow up. There would be much less possibility for the most significant bodies – including governments, international trade and financial institutions, etc – to be held accountable to representatives of civil society.

NOTES

1. It is interesting to note that both the UK and the USA now count the CSD as a success. When the UK was recently up for re-election to the Bureau of the Commission, the Secretary of State went as far as sending a letter to all governments asking for their support, which gives some indication of the importance placed on continuing to wield influence in the CSD's work.
2. Childers E and Urquhart B, *Reforming the UN System* (Dag Hammerskjold Institute, (1994), state that the objective is 'to ensure that capacities now

separated but in reality dependent upon each other are more efficiently harnessed, and that both the strategic attention to causes, and rapid response to consequences, are not impeded by structural flaws.

3. It was widely felt that two to three weeks per annum represented insufficient time to address adequately the number and extent of the problems in moving towards sustainability. Two intersessional working groups were established to tackle the issues of financial resources and matters relating to technology transfer respectively. These working groups were made up of governments which nominated participating experts. They met under the direction of the CSD's bureau of officers and were described as experiments in intersessional preparation rather than as permanent.

4. This has become an important aspect of the Commission's work. Often working in partnership, governments have taken responsibility for pushing forward international dialogue on specific issues. For instance, Anglo–Indian work on forests initiated in 1994 and a joint Canadian–Malaysian initiative on the same issue led to significant contributions to the CSD session in 1995 and to the creation of the CSD Inter-Governmental Panel on Forests. Approximately 120 government-hosted meetings have been held each year between 1994 and 1996 on issues relevant to the CSD's agenda.

5. The agreement on Prior Informed Consent was a key development set in motion by the CSD. It will be discussed at the Basel Convention Meeting in 1997 for final agreement as a legally binding agreement.

6. The Norwegian Government organized two workshops on sustainable consumption and production patterns, held in Oslo in 1994 and 1995.

7. This was presented as a cornerstone in combating deforestation, desertification and drought; promoting sustainable agriculture, rural and mountain development; the conservation of biological diversity and the sustainable management of all types of forests.

8. The Chairman's report states that the CSD 'recognized that there was a need to analyze the potential effects of environmentally related trade issues and in particular product-specific policies, such as eco-labelling and certain packaging and recycling requirements, especially as regards their potential impacts on exports, especially those of developing countries and countries with economies in transition; it was also necessary to strengthen mechanisms to improve transparency in the setting of such standards and to strengthen international co-operation which could create trading opportunities for developing countries in expanding markets for environmentally friendly products. In view of the impacts of trade liberalization on changing production patterns in exporting countries, the need for capacity building in developing countries and economies in transition to further integrating trade and environmental policies was stressed.'

9. 'Problems of the Next Century, Priorities for Earth Summit II, Norman Myers, UNED–UK, June 1996.
10. 'Synthesis Paper on NGO Priorities and Concerns for the 1997 General Assembly Special Session', Tom Bigg and Peter Mucke, CSD NGO Steering Committee.

3

A Changing Landscape of Diplomatic Conflict: The Politics of Climate Change Post-Rio[1]

Peter Newell

ABSTRACT

The Framework Convention on Climate Change (FCCC) is now five years old and a great deal of pressure is mounting to ensure that a legally binding protocol to reduce CO_2 emissions will be adopted at the Third Conference of the Parties to the Convention in Kyoto (December 1997). The path from the United Nations Conference on Environment and Development in 1992 (UNCED) has not been straightforward, and many policies and measures that were promised at the Rio conference have been dropped or watered down as the force of *realpolitik* has been brought to bear on the UNCED rhetoric. It is against a background of empty promises and increasing pressures to move the process forward (prompted by a potent combination of public concern, election year politics and increasing scientific consensus on the threat posed by climate change) that the negotiations up to COP3 will take place.

INTRODUCTION

Climate change provides one of the most serious and complex problems the international community currently faces. The scope of the issue means that it touches all areas of economic, political and social life. Yet although none are immune from the potentially devastating effects of climate change, which include increased incidence of extreme weather events, sea-level rise and desertification, those that contribute least to the problem will be hardest hit by its negative impacts. This makes climate change an issue of social justice. The combination of the magnitude of the problem in both physical and political terms conspire to present an unprecedented challenge to international cooperation.

Politically, the issue of climate change hit the international agenda in 1988, after a series of workshops established the importance of the issue in scientific terms. The Intergovernmental Panel on Climate Change (IPCC) was set up to advise governments on how best to respond to the issue, based on latest research on the science of the subject, its social and economic implications and what form policy responses might take. By 1990, the scientific group had produced a report that expressed certainty that current trends in the release of greenhouse gases would result in accelerated climate change.[2]

In February 1991, under the remit of the Intergovernmental Negotiating Committee for a Framework Convention on Climate Change, negotiations began towards an international convention to address this issue. Several negotiating blocs became apparent as discussions began on what constituted an appropriate response to the threat of climate change. At one end of the spectrum, the OPEC (Organisation of Petroleum Exporting Countries) states were resistant to the idea that any agreement on this issue was necessary, explained by their dependence on the exports of oil. At the other end of the spectrum, sat the AOSIS states (Alliance of Small Island States), those low-lying states most vulnerable to the prospect of sea-level rise associated with climate change. Their concern naturally was to secure far-reaching cuts in greenhouse gas emissions. In between these two polarities were positioned the US towards the OPEC position in down-playing the need for action, beyond what it described as 'no-regrets' policies (where only those actions are taken which are justifiable on other grounds than climate change alone) and the European Community which adopted a more progressive position, despite a failure to reach internal agreement on how they would achieve the goal of the Convention. For many states belonging to the G77 group of least-industrialised countries, climate change was an issue whose principal significance derived from the fact that it presented an opportunity to re-articulate the demands for a (NIEO) New International Economic Order and to press for the financial aid and technology transfer that had been denied them in other fora.[3]

THE CLIMATE CONVENTION

The agreement of the Climate Convention at the Rio conference in 1992, signed by more than 154 countries, was the outcome of one and a half years of hard negotiations over an array of difficult questions including whether or not a legally binding commitment was required, how to manage the thorny North–South issues which are so intrinsic to the climate change problem, and how to differentiate commitments. In the final months there was broad agreement that a convention of sorts was necessary, but consensus around content was lacking. Public expectation, driven by high media exposure of the Rio conference, forced the pace to quicken as the June deadline approached. One of the main stalling blocks to agreement, US President Bush, was forced to soften his position slightly in the run up to the Rio conference in the light of a looming presidential election and the loss of his advisor, White House Chief of Staff John Sununu, who fought a bitter bureaucratic battle against advocates of action of climate change within the administration.

The result of this hard bargaining was a framework convention which has as its aim, the prevention of dangerous interference with the climate system. Although no legally binding commitments to reduce emissions of greenhouse gases are included, parties are obliged to *aim* to reduce their emissions of CO_2 by the year 2000 set against emissions levels as they stood in 1990. The politics which brought the Convention into being centred around the need to bring the US on board, which was enabled by the shuttle diplomacy of Michael Howard, and an agreement that non-annex 1 countries (broadly-speaking the less developed country parties to the Convention) would not be required to take on obligations beyond broad reporting requirements. The principle underlying this separation of commitments is contained in Article 4 of the Convention which refers to 'common but differentiated responsibility', acknowledging the vast disparities between different nation's contribution to the problem. The Convention is to be brought into effect via national measures to be communicated to the convention secretariat through national reviews of policies and measures.

Post-Rio, a number of changes in the landscape of climate politics made a substantive outcome at the first meeting of the Conference of Parties in Berlin in March 1995 unlikely. Despite the election of

President Clinton in the US, his attempts to fulfill Bush's empty promise of a 'white-house effect to counter the greenhouse effect' were undermined by a Congress hostile to his BTU tax proposal. Within the European Union, the proposal for a community-wide carbon /energy tax, designed to be the centre-piece of EU climate policy, was also weakened by excluding energy-intensive industries and making the tax conditional upon the adoption of similar measures by industrial competitors such as Japan and the US. The weakening of the tax is explained by a potent combination of concerns over competitiveness, heightened amid global recession, and some of the fiercest lobbying ever seen against an EU proposal by the fossil fuel industries.[4]

THE FIRST CONFERENCE OF THE PARTIES

The main outcome of the First Conference of the Parties in Berlin March 1995 was the Berlin Mandate which requires the adoption of a 'protocol or other legal instrument' by the time of the third COP to be held in Kyoto in December 1997, containing commitments beyond the year 2000. The mandate also acknowledges the inadequacy of existing commitments. The issue of how states might implement actions jointly featured highly at Berlin, and the end result was a fudged compromise where parties' right to engage in actions implemented jointly was recognised, but no formal accreditation would be conferred upon the projects. Diplomatically, the conference also saw the emergence of a new grouping, JUSCANZ, made up of Japan, the US, Canada, Australia and New Zealand, united by their resistance to further action by annex 1 (the most industrialised country) parties in the absence of non-annex 1 parties also accepting further commitments to reduce their greenhouse gas emissions.

Institutionally, the Berlin conference created the SBI (Subsidiary Body for Implementation) and the SBSTA (Subsidiary Body for Scientific and Technical Advice) to oversee the compilation and review of national reports in the first instance, and to permit a more regular and institutionalised scientific input in the latter. And although the GEF (Global Environment Facility) is unpopular among many as the choice of institution to finance the implementation of the Convention, COP1 approved it as the continuing interim financial body.[5]

THE SECOND CONFERENCE OF THE PARTIES

The Second Conference of the Parties in Geneva in July 1996 was fore-shadowed by the publication of the Second Assessment Report of the IPCC Working Group 1, which identified a 'discernible human influence upon the climate system', and a report released by the World Health Organisation in the first week of the conference, which predicted grave and far-reaching implications for human health if the rate of climate change was not successfully abated.

Its functions were two-fold: to reaffirm existing commitments and to take stock of how well those commitments have been implemented to date on the one hand, and on the other, to map out a direction for the negotiations towards COP3. The conference agreed a Ministerial declaration which accepted the Second Assessment Report as a basis for further action, and acknowledged the need to create a legally binding instrument to bring about 'significant overall reductions'. There also appeared to be an emerging consensus, not explicitly articulated in the Ministerial declaration, that 550ppm (parts per million) of carbon in the atmosphere constitutes the all-important dangerous level of interference with the climate system, which it is the goal of the Convention to avoid.

The diplomatic landscape was subject to further change. The JUS-CANZ group seemed to have imploded. Australia's position moved further in the direction of the OPEC states, still emphasising uncertainties in the science and stressing the need for non-annex 1 countries to accept further commitments.[6] The US and UK both displayed a new progressiveness, with the US accepting the need for a legally binding instrument and refuting strongly the activities of the 'naysayers' who were seeking to discredit the climate science; a thinly-veiled reference to the lobbying activities of the fossil fuel lobbies. UK environment Minister, John Gummer, was also in strident mood declaring the 'after you Claude' lack of leadership in the negotiations to be at an end, outlining a number of specific policy proposals which his government intended to undertake.

The failure to agree rules of procedure was one of the failures of the Geneva meeting. As things stand, it is easy for blocking coalitions to stall the negotiations via a range of bureaucratic and procedural formalities. If these remain undecided, it may be tempting for the OPEC states and their attentive lawyers in the fossil fuel lobbies to employ these devices to the full in ensuring that agreement will not be reached by

Kyoto 1997. The lack of emphasis on the need to reduce levels of emissions below the 1990 baseline and absence of clear definition about what constitutes 'dangerous' may be considered further shortcomings of the conference.[7]

THE PATH TO KYOTO

Many important issues remain unresolved, and the pressure is on to reach a legally binding agreement to reduce emissions of greenhouse gases beyond the year 2000, by the end of 1997. The extent to which this is possible will be shaped in part by the evolving position of the US and whether the positive stance shown at COP2 will be maintained. Given the disproportionately high contribution the US makes to the problem, it is improbable that a protocol will be agreed without its approval. Eileen Claussen and Tim Wirth, key figures in the US negotiating delegation, are clear advocates of a responsible climate change abatement strategy, but they are acutely aware of the veto role that a Republican dominated Congress, where coal interests are strong, can perform if a protocol is agreed which they find unpalatable.

It is also notable that the EU remains largely without a climate policy strategy with only two member states on course to meet their stabilisation targets; both by default rather than resulting from an intentional greenhouse gas reduction strategy.[8] In the case of the UK, this was achieved through the demise of the coal industry. Germany has been able to call for a 25 per cent CO_2 reduction target by the year 2005, as a result of the re-unification process (the wall-fall effect) where manufacturing decline in eastern Germany has superficially strengthened the Kohl government's record on reducing greenhouse emissions. The credibility of the publicly proactive position of the German government on the climate issue is somewhat undermined however, by their destructive role in the EU energy council where they have been at the forefront in voting for cuts in the SAVE (Specific Actions to Vigorously increase Energy efficiency) programme designed to improve energy efficiency within the EU. The shape of the policies designed to meet the target is not encouraging. The SAVE II programme has suffered heavy budget cuts, energy efficiency standards legislation is unambitious and weak, and the fate of the carbon tax will be played out in Finance council meetings in which decisions on tax require unanimous backing. Many of the policies which had the potential to deliver an effective climate change strategy have been sacrificed at the altar of subsidiarity, where member states can claim that measures are best adopted at the national level.

The discrepancy between public pronouncements in international fora and the degree of implementation of measures directly intended to address the climate problem, is a recurrent theme in international climate politics. The lack of coordination of policy measures across different sectors within government is another. The agendas of Transport and Industry departments are often at odds with the greenhouse gas reduction strategies of Environment departments, so that whilst one department declares its aim to be stabilisation of concentration of greenhouse gases by the year 2000, another is seeking to build new roads or power stations with the effect of negating the effectiveness of the climate protection proposal.[9] EU plans for trans-European road networks, that will constrain the collective ability of the community to set tough targets, provide just one example.

The disarray which currently characterises EU climate policy is all the more disturbing when it is recognised the EU's position is still the most advanced among OECD parties. If the EU is failing to provide leadership, it is pertinent to ask where it is going to come from. There is also deadlock over who acts first; annex 1 (industrialised) or non-annex 1 (less industrialised) parties? While there was a clear expression of support for annex 1 parties to take further action at COP2, there are still a number of parties who want to see tougher commitments from the 'south' before going further themselves..The argument runs that China, India and Brazil will, in the future, provide the bulk of emissions growth against a background of rapidly expanding populations in the context of India, and vast reserves of coal in the case of China, and therefore there is little point in OECD countries acting when the beneficial effects of keeping their own emissions in check will be offset by rapid growth elsewhere. At the moment, the emissions of the OECD countries exceed those of these emerging areas. The question is whether it is reasonable to permit China and India to greatly expand their use of fossil fuels without taking on annex 1 status and therefore being bound by annex 1 party commitments. One powerful argument is that unless OECD countries demonstrate a willingness and ability to reduce their own emissions, they can hardly expect commitments from others who have historically contributed very little to the problem.

The balance of political power in the negotiations is shifting and this extends beyond inter-state bargaining and into the world of NGOs, where particularly on the business side, the hegemony of the perspective of the fossil fuel industries seems to be waning as the 'sunrise' (renewable) energy industries, and increasingly the insurance industries, begin to mobilise. The task for environmental NGOs is to try to craft a 'green' group of states willing to take further action, supported by these coalitions, such as that which was able to bring the Berlin Mandate into being at COP1.

THE ROAD AHEAD

There are a number of proposals on the table which will help to structure the debate in the coming months. The AOSIS protocol, based on a 20 per cent reduction in CO_2 emissions by the year 2005, is now seen by many as unworkable. EU proposals, given their preference for longer time frames and less ambitious reduction goal (10 per cent by 2005 and 15–20 per cent by 2010), may offer more scope. Perhaps the best that can be hoped for in time for the Kyoto meeting, is a reduction goal(s) with a menu of possible policies and measures, by which the commitments may be implemented. As has been pointed out before, the problem with menus of measures, is that some parties may choose not to eat.

The strategies that will bring any new agreement to life will require elucidation. A range of instruments have been suggested, ranging from tradable permit schemes to the further consolidation of joint implementation schemes. There is a lack of precedent for permit trading schemes on an international scale, but many see in them the opportunity to simultaneously address concerns over equity, efficiency and effectiveness. Joint implementation schemes retain the advantage that they can be initiated immediately (indeed a number of schemes are already up and running) but problems of creating a comparable index and apportioning credit remain. Environmental NGOs are alert to the possibility that the former strategy is being advanced as a strategy because it will open up a controversial debate over how permits should be allocated that will delay the negotiation process, and the latter as a means by which the largest polluters can avoid having to take action 'at home' by investing in countries where it is cheaper to reduce emissions. These issues will not go away and will need to be addressed at some point.

Whether it is constructive in view of the tight timetable ahead to open up such a difficult debate at this stage, given that special pleading over national circumstances could delay agreement of new commitments by years, is an important question.

There is evidently much political ground to cover before a post-Convention agreement, that will command the support of all parties, can be adopted. The scientific basis for a meaningful, legally binding protocol which addresses head on the threat posed by the climate change issue is there. Whether the voices of those concerned about the magnitude and impacts of the issue are sufficiently loud to drown out the demands for political expediency will become clear in the months ahead. One by one the excuses for delaying action are being removed as scientific assessments about the severity of the issue confirm cause for concern, and economic forecasts about the impact upon countries GDP of acting responsibly on climate change, highlight the vast potential for energy-saving, and the advantages to be gained by stealing a lead in the production of energy-efficient technologies and investment in the emerging markets in renewables. Unfortunately, none of these things provide guarantee of an effective or just response. What they may do is help to expose the diplomatic stalling for what it is; naked self–interest disguised as a serious attempt to address the issues.

NOTES

1. I am grateful to Dr Matthew Paterson for comments on this chapter.
2. Houghton, J, Jenkins, GJ and Ephraums, JJ (eds) (1990) *Climate Change: The IPCC Scientific Assessment* Cambridge: Cambridge University Press.
3. For more details on the nature of these negotiating blocks see Paterson, M and Grubb, M (1992) 'The international politics of climate change' *International Affairs* Vol 68 No 2, pp 293–310.
4. *The Economist* (1992) 'Europe's industries play dirty' May 9th.
5. For useful assessments of the Berlin conference see both Grubb, M and Anderson, D (eds) *The Emerging International Regime for Climate Change: Structures and Options after Berlin* London: RIIA, and Arts, B and Rüdig, W (1995) 'Negotiating the Berlin Mandate: Reflecting on the First Conference of the Parties to the UNFCCC' *Environmental Politics* Vol 4 No 3 Autumn, pp 481–488.
6. There is perhaps evidence however of a softening in the OPEC position, notable at the AGBM meeting in Geneva, December 1996, where the strategy seems to have switched from emphasising scientific uncertainties to

underlining more prominently the economic costs of climate change action and the need to compensate areas heavily dependent upon the export of fossil fuels. See the NGO bulletin *ECO* produced at this conference for other information on this.

7. For a more detailed assessment of COP2 see Newell, P and Paterson, M (1996) 'From Geneva to Kyoto: The Second Conference of the Parties to the UN Framework Convention on Climate Change' *Environmental Politics* Vol 5 No 4, Winter, pp 729–735.

8. For more on individual positions of EU Member States see *Independent NGO Evaluations of National Plans for Climate Change Mitigation: OECD Countries* (1996) Fourth (Interim) Review June, Brussels: Climate Network Europe.

9. See O'Riordan,T and Jäger, J (1996) *The Politics of Climate Change: A European Perspective* London: Routledge.

4

The Convention on Biological Diversity

Fiona McConnell

The year 1987 produced two important landmarks in the bringing to-gether of the environment and development issues. First came the pub-lication of the Brundtland Commission's report, *Our Common Future*, which set out the common concerns, challenges and endeavours which would be involved in achieving sustainable development. One of the report's recommendations was for a convention that would require rich countries to pay for action to slow down or prevent the extinction of species – most of which were in poorer countries – and the destruction of their habitats.

Secondly, there was the Montreal Protocol, perhaps the first inter-national agreement to adopt concrete measures for tackling a global environmental problem, with provisions for regular review and for tak-ing account of the special needs of developing countries.

In the same year, two other noticed signposts were erected during the Governing Council (GC) of the United Nations Environment Programme (UNEP). First, there was a Swedish proposal for a major event to mark the 20th anniversary of the 1972 Stockholm Conference on the Human Environment; surprisingly, this generated very little interest at the time. Secondly, the United States proposed a convention under the heading of biological diversity, a term soon to be shortened to biodiversity. The idea was to combine the patchwork of existing interna-tional nature conservation agreements dealing with endangered species (Convention on International Trade of Endangered Species – CITES),

47

wetlands—Wetlands of International Importance, especially Water Fowl Habitat (Ramsar, 1971), migratory species (Bonn) and so on. A group of scientific experts would 'investigate ... the desirability and possible form of an umbrella convention to rationalise current activities in this field'.

The Swedish proposal gathered support during the next two years, but the scientific experts made little headway in addressing the broad topic of biodiversity. UNEP's 1989 GC spent much of its time trying, unsuccessfully, to find a better definition of sustainable development than that of *Our Common Future*, but eventually agreed to recommend to the UN General Assembly that there should be a 1992 UN Conference on Environment and Development (UNCED) to take account of achievements since Stockholm 1972. The UN General Assembly then agreed that UNCED should be held in June 1992 in Rio de Janeiro.

Also at the 1989 GC the US still championed an umbrella convention, but forcefully resisted proposals that it should include biotechnology. Developing countries made it clear that without biotechnology, they would oppose any new convention. They put forward arguments that would be developed skilfully during subsequent negotiations: most of the genetic resources that provided raw materials for biotechnology in agriculture and pharmaceuticals came from developing countries, which received virtually nothing for them. If these basic resources were to be conserved, there should be a more equitable sharing of the benefits. Those who claimed that the planet's living resources were 'global commons' were preaching a new form of colonialism, because the resources, in fact, belong to the countries in which they are found.

Eventually the GC decided to authorize work on 'an international instrument for the conservation of the biological diversity of the planet'. An account should also be taken of 'the full implications of the new biotechnologies' and 'adequate machinery for financial transfers from those who benefit from the exploitation of biological diversity... to the owners and managers of biological resources'.

The scene was set, the main arguments had been tentatively expounded, and the agenda was more or less decided negotiations could now begin for the Convention on Biological Diversity (CBD).

Considerable delays took place, however, before 'real' negotiations began. International environmental attention was more concerned with the climate change convention. UNEP's scientific experts did not report on the proposed scope of the CBD until well into 1990, and even then could not agree whether or not to include biotechnology. It was therefore a remarkable statement of faith when, at the first UNCED Preparatory Committee in August 1990, Secretary-General Maurice Strong announced that he envisaged agreement at Rio on a legally binding convention on biodiversity as well as on climate change. Negotiations had not even begun.

The challenge of developing a CBD in less than two years did not lead to noticeably swift progress. There were to be seven formal negotiating sessions beginning in November 1990. The first two got no further than agreeing rules of procedure and electing a chairman. The next four were characterized by suspicion and acrimony: North versus South on finance, especially the role of the newly established Global Environment Facility (GEF), technology transfer and conservation obligations. There was also G77 and the European Union versus the US on biosafety, as well as opposing views within EU member states, especially on financial obligations and global priorities, and simmering resentment between African and Latin American countries. Nevertheless, the general shape and content of the CBD gradually emerged, albeit in text festooned with square brackets and alternative, often contradictory language.

Tentative agreement was reached on giving equal weight to conservation and sustainable use, and eventually to benefit sharing. The emphasis would be on action at national level by the contracting parties, rather than on supranational regulation. There would be articles on traditional conservation measures, both *in situ* and *ex situ*, on access to technology, including biotechnology, on national strategies and action plans, and on setting up a subsidiary scientifc body.

Compromise language was introduced to mollify those who could not accept firm commitments – 'as far as practicable' or 'in accordance with national legislation or policies, as appropriate'. And there was much confusion about whether protecting intellectual property rights would help or hinder the CBD. The need to address financial matters and technology transfer was acknowledged, but without resolution, particularly in the light of parallel negotiations on these issues on climate change and in UNCED preparations. The US maintained throughout that biotechnology should not be singled out from other technologies. Matters were further complicated when countries who had failed to get their way in the CBD tried to reintroduce their ideas into Agenda 21's chapters on biodiversity and biotechnology.

It is scarcely surprising that prospects for the CBD at the time of the seventh session in May 1992 were not good. Even after the seven days allocated by the UNEP for completing the work on the text, there remained significant problems, notably with the CBD's principles of biosafety and finance. But three days were set aside for a Final Act Conference to celebrate completion of the convention and to propose how it should be implemented. There was also UNEP's Executive Director, Dr Tolba, who used the three days to impose his personal will on delegations and to force negotiations to an improbable but successful conclusion.

By sheer force of personality and irresistible pressure, Dr Tolba isolated the most active 20 or so delegations and, throughout most of the three days and nights set aside for the Final Act Conference, he relentlessly chipped away at their objections.

Principle 21 of the Stockholm Declaration was accepted verbatim, as were the CBD's Principle (Article 3), although it caused the UK and some others considerable anxiety. The US did not try to veto Article 19's call for consideration of 'the need for and modalities of a protocol' on biosafesty. Article 20 on financial resources was painfully agreed, line by line, leaving only Article 21 on the financial mechanism.

The fundamental point at issue was the extent to which the CBD should be authorized to control the GEF, or any other funding mechanism, or to decide how much money should be levied from donor countries. Under pressure from Dr Tolba, the donor countries one by one agreed on an ambiguous form of words in Article 21 in return for which the G77 – but with Malaysia still objecting – gave way on a separate Article 39, giving the GEF a temporary role until the first Conference of the Parties (COP). By now the US had virtually washed its hands of the CBD and the UK was the last delegation to give way on Article 21. There were bitter complaints by France that its demands for global decisions on species and habitats were ignored. The CBD was concluded.

There remained less than four hours for a hastily convened Final Act Conference at which the text of the CBD would be 'initialled' before being sent to the UNCED, where it would be open for signature. There was no time for congratulatory speeches. Resolutions were agreed on the work that was needed before the first COP. Statements were made on difficult issues: the UK and most potential donor countries recorded their interpretation of the text of Article 21. France was so annoyed at losing out on global lists that she refused to sign the Final Act. Malaysia also refused to sign owing to the CBD's acknowledgment of the GEF. The US deplored the unseemly haste of the negotiations. Switzerland and Spain put in lengthy bid and counterbid to house the CBD secretariat. By now it was very nearly midnight on Friday 22 May 1992 – less than ten days before the Earth Summit.

Up to this point the CBD had generated little public interest. Environmental NGOs had been conspicuous by their absence during the negotiations. Only the WWF and the World Conservation Monitoring Centre had been concerned enough to attend all the negotiating sessions, although the World Conservation Union (IUCN) seconded a legal adviser to work with the UNEP secretariat. The business community took no formal part, although in the US in particular it strongly lobbied against any mention of biotechnology. Media attention had focused on climate change, but suddenly switched to the CBD.

Tens of thousands of people poured into Rio de Janeiro at the beginning of June – politicians, diplomats, officials, experts, NGOs, businessmen, opera singers, film stars. The world's press and television arrived in force looking for a story. They found it in the refusal of the US to sign the CBD and the possibility that others, such as the UK, Japan and France, might follow suit. From 1 to 8 June the CBD became front page news in *The Times* in the UK and a regular feature in CNN's global newscasts.

Journalists became overnight experts on the shortcomings of the CBD, supported by some of the NGOs – once they had tracked down a copy of the text – which were scathing about the convention's vagueness and lack of mandatory targets and commitments. But within a few days, the NGOs decided that an instrument that could so greatly upset the US must have *something* good about it. Not wanting their heads of state or government to arrive in Rio with negative baggage, most of the waverers agreed to be among the 150 plus nations to sign the CBD.

Only the US held out. President Bush was dismissive of a flawed convention that 'threatens to retard biotechnology and undermine the protection of ideas'. At the same time he was careful to stress that US efforts to conserve biodiversity would be strengthened and would almost certainly exceed the requirements of the convention.

After Rio, the media circus moved on to find other stories but the CBD was now firmly on the political and environmental map. By UN standards, the required 30 ratifications were quickly achieved so that the convention could come into force in December 1993. At present

(October 1996) over 150 countries have ratified. This figure does not include the US, although under the Clinton administration they have at least become signatories.

As attention turned to implementation, the UNEP convened expert panels to point the way forward on key issues, such as finance, technology transfer and the possibility of a biosafety protocol. The panels gave way to a more formal Intergovernmental Committee (IGC) whose purpose was to prepare for the first Conference of the Parties (COP1). The IGC meetings were remarkable for having 80 NGOs in attendance, only a handful of whom were from the business sector, and for being covered by the Earth Negotiations Bulletin (ENB). (The ENB's factual reports on the proceedings, established during the UNCED process, allow non-participants to find out speedily and with confidence what is happening in a range of post-Rio meetings; they are also helpful to participants who need to know what happens in working groups or plenary sessions that they are unable to attend.)

By the time of COP1 in Nassau in November 1994, more than 100 NGOs were attending as observers, almost exactly matching the number of government parties. COP1 was not a lively event, in spite of demands by some campaigning groups for a protocol on the protection of forests and for a moratorium on releases to the environment of genetically modified organisms (gmos). These proposals were sprung on governments too late for serious consideration, but they succeeded in alarming the small contingent of business NGOs. They were also unhappy about grandiose ideas for a clearing-house mechanism, set up by Article 18, that would somehow organize technology transfer.

COP1 did manage to clear many procedural and budgetary matters. It agreed a rolling work programme and the basis of a subsidiary body of scientific and technical experts (SBSTTA). It established a CBD secretariat but without deciding where it should be located, it extended the GEF's interim role, and it reaffirmed that national plans and strategies would be the mainspring of implementation. It could not agree whether financial decisions should be based on unanimity or majority voting, and scarcely touched on the possibility of a biosafety protocol.

By the time of COP2 in Jakarta in November 1995, clearer progress could be discerned. The secretariat would be based in Montreal. SBSTA's work was more clearly defined, albeit with increasing political supervision. Agreement was also reached to start work on a biosafety protocol, and the GEF's interim role was again extended in spite of misgivings by many developing countries and NGOs. The continuing disagreement over financial procedures did not seem quite so divisive, and there were signs that the business sector had got over the shock of COP1 and was trying to look at the CBD as an opportunity for demonstrating good practice rather than as a serious threat to commercial activity.

Progress, however, has been more clearly marked by actions taken at national level. In the UK, the most immediate action was putting into practice Prime Minister John Major's undertaking at Rio to establish 'the Darwin Initiative'. This is a scheme to enable poorer countries that are rich in biodiversity to benefit from British skills; it is currently given government support of £3 million a year and has so far attracted matching private sector funding of some £2 million.

In 1994 the UK government published its Biodiversity Strategy setting out the framework for a range of conservation actions in Britain. To take this forward, a Biodiversity Steering Group – made up of government officials, agencies, academia, collections, environmental NGOs and businesses – published a Biodiversity Action Plan in 1995, with costed targets for saving the most endangered species and habitats. This plan proposed that interested groups and organizations, including businesses, should assume the role of 'champions' for specific species or habitats – an innovative idea that has won much support in the UK and which is likely to be taken up by other countries. With government endorsement of the main proposals of the plan, the group is now charged with monitoring the implementation of its own proposals and with producing a Millennium Report on progress.

It can be reasonably expected that The United Nations General Assembly (UNGA)'s 1997 review of progress since Rio will find that many other countries have set out their biodiversity plans and are beginning to put them into practice. There will be disappointment, no doubt, that insufficient progress has been made in almost all areas of the CBD, but the UN General Assembly Special Session will have the benefit of a report from COP3 (Buenos Aires, November 1996) which, it is hoped, will record some major steps forward, such as:

- Agreement on financial matters, especially voting procedures.
- A better understanding of the role of the GEF in supporting biodiversity projects.

- The main terms of a biosafety protocol.
- Increasing co-operation from the business sector.

It should also be borne in mind that the 250 parties to the CBD continue to regard the US as a major player in the implementation process, notwithstanding domestic obstacles to formal ratification.

The Special Session should be able to reflect that the concept of biodiversity – and the fact that it embraces bugs and bacteria as well as elephants and pandas – is becoming much better understood. There are even, in the UK at least, local biodiversity action plans linked with the Local Agenda 21 process.

In terms of fulfilling the three objectives in the convention's Article 1, most of the action so far has focused on 'the conservation of biological diversity'. Attention is now being turned increasingly to 'the sustainable use of its components', but it looks as if it will be a long time before practicable measures are agreed by the parties on 'the fair and equitable sharing of the benefits arising out of the utilisation of genetic resources'.

The CBD cannot yet claim to be a major success story. The imprecise nature of its provisions and the emphasis on national implementation make it difficult to decide how far it has directly stimulated action. And, in any event, there is still far more rhetoric than action. Five years is probably too short a period to detect any significant slowing down in the continuing destruction of habitats and loss of species. Perhaps the picture will be clearer in ten rather than five years.

5

The Desertification Convention

Camilla Toulmin

The drylands are estimated to make up one-third of the world's land surface and to provide a home to some 900 million people. The cradle of ancient civilizations and at the hub of trading routes for many centuries, dryland areas have been the source of many valuable crop and animal species. They have always been subject to marked fluctuations in rainfall and occasional drought, bringing variability in associated crop and livestock production, and the risk of harvest failure.

The severe droughts in Africa in the 1970s and '80s generated particular concern for the future of dryland peoples, and the worry that many of these areas were being degraded by 'over-cultivation' and 'overgrazing' to such an extent that they would soon no longer be able to maintain the populations which depended upon them. Recent research shows that such levels of alarm are often not warranted and that the land-use practices of many farmers and herders often provide the best starting point for the evolution of more sustainable patterns of land use.

Dryland degradation has been encapsulated in the term 'desertification' which is defined in Article 1 of the International Convention to Combat Desertification as: 'Land degradation in arid, semi-arid, and dry sub-humid areas resulting from various factors, including climatic variations and human activities'.

Desertification as a term has generated considerable confusion owing to its association with the idea of desert advance. Although sand-dune movement is certainly a problem in certain locations where, for example, shifting sands threaten valuable infrastructure, such as a road or railway track, there is no evidence to show a progressive advance of desert areas into neighbouring lands. Instead, one sees the desert frontier shift according to the rainfall received from one year to the next. When rains are good, vegetation flourishes in areas which formerly were bare; when rains fail, however, desert-like conditions expand as grasses fail to germinate.

Desertification includes a range of processes, such as the loss of soils through water and wind erosion, declining soil fertility, a loss of vegetative cover, increasing vulnerability to drought and a general impoverishment in the diversity of plant and animal life. However, the incidence and significance of such degradation processes vary greatly from place to place, depending on the nature of the resources, such as soil type and slope, pressures on land use, and the institutions which regulate access to and control over resources.

In some places, farmers seem to have established relatively sustainable systems for using their land and producing enough food. Field-level work has demonstrated the existence of a much broader range of technical options which can bring significant and rapid returns to farmers. But elsewhere, there are serious problems of soil erosion and depletion of soil nutrients, leading to the heightened risk of harvest failure. In such cases, land users may be either unaware of, or unable to address such problems.

Several factors seem to explain successful patterns of adaptation by farmers and their ability to manage land effectively. A growing scarcity of land makes each plot more valuable and, as a result, it becomes more worthwhile to invest in its improvement and conservation. Rising population density renders land more scarce and also provides the additional labour required for the often highly labour-demanding processes involved in agricultural intensification, such as the transport of manure and the construction of soil conservation structures.

Having access to markets for the sale of crops is another important element which helps to increase the value that farmers place on their land, and their consequent willingness and ability to invest in its improvement. The security with which people hold the land on which they depend is also critically important to their incentive to care for it and to invest in improving it. Customary systems can often provide such assurances. Where parallel and often contradictory systems of tenure exist, however, this can lead to very damaging land-use practices as farmers seek to assert control over large tracts of land through its clearance, even though they have no intention to farm it.

The highly diverse conditions found in dryland areas, and differences in how people are managing their resources, argue against the design of 'blanket' approaches to dryland management. Rather a local approach is needed which supports a process led by herders and farmers to identify the problems of and the opportunities for improving their livelihoods.

A History of International Action

The need for a tailored approach to suit the circumstances of different settings poses a great challenge for any global initiative aimed at promoting better resource management in drylands. The International Convention to Combat Desertification is one such attempt in a sequence of international initiatives.

The UN Conference on Desertification (UNCOD) in 1977 was the first formal effort by the international community to examine the desertification problem and to come up with recommendations for action. It followed the harsh droughts of the Sahel and Ethiopia of 1973–74, and generated a Global Plan of Action to Combat Desertification, for which the UNEP was given responsibility. Considerable attention was paid to drawing up national action plans to combat desertification in affected countries, and surveys to assess the extent of desertified land. A funding mechanism – DESCON – was established to finance anti-desertification activities, for which donor support was sought.

Progress with the Global Plan of Action was very disappointing, for which the UNEP has been held partially responsible. National plans were drawn up, but often bore little relation to the conditions which were being met on the ground nor to the practicality of achieving the aims set. The data generated through the various surveys undertaken were given little credence by donors, and bilateral agencies avoided DESCON, preferring instead the traditional channels of funding their own projects.

The experience of trying to tackle dryland development through a global approach helps to explain the muted enthusiasm with which the donor community received the proposal for an International Convention to Combat Desertification (CCD) in the run-up to the Earth Summit.

This call had come from the Africa group during the preparatory sessions for the Rio summit, and it reflected their sense of frustration with the emphasis and direction taken by the debate, with its focus largely on climate change and biodiversity – both issues of much greater interest and importance to the richer nations. They felt that their priority concerns regarding poverty, drought and food insecurity were not receiving the attention they deserved. The OECD countries promised, as a consequence, to start negotiations for a Desertification Convention as a means of keeping African governments engaged in the Rio process.

Negotiations for the Convention began in Nairobi in May 1993, and were followed by four further sessions of the International Negotiating Committee on Desertification (INCD) in Geneva, New York, Geneva and Paris where, in June 1994, agreement of the Convention text was achieved.

The Convention runs to 40 articles spread over 32 pages, and is supplemented with four regional annexes to cover Africa, Asia, Latin America and the northern Mediterranean area. A central element within the text is the commitment by affected countries to devise National Action Programmes to Combat Desertification, which are intended to map out a set of priorities to include policy change, training and research needs, economic incentives, drought preparedness and clarification of tenure rules.

Delegates also agreed to a resolution on urgent action for Africa, which urged governments of affected African countries to begin the process of implementing the Convention immediately, even though the treaty would not enter into force for two or three years, given the time taken for the Convention to be ratified by the signatory governments.

Negotiations have continued throughout the interim period, focusing on a number of issues that were either left unresolved during the first five sessions, or where the wording of the text is left somewhat unclear. For example, which organization should take responsibility for housing the global mechanism proposed in the text and what should such a mechanism actually do?

Equally, these sessions have sought clarification of the functions expected of the Committee on Science and Technology, whom it should comprise, and where the permanent secretariat for managing the Convention should be sited. The amount of time and effort spent on these issues and the heat they have generated suggest the importance which certain organizations place on acquiring the mandate for leading international action on desertification, a mandate which is seen to have particular importance in an era of stagnant or declining funds.

The 50th ratification of the Convention was announced by Chad in September 1996, leading to the treaty entering into force in December 1996. The first Conference of the Parties is due to be held in October 1997 in Rome.

WHAT HAS THE CONVENTION ACHIEVED?

As with all conventions, the balance sheet of several years' negotiations looks quite mixed. On the positive side, more promising approaches to the development of dryland areas have received widespread coverage and generated a fair degree of consensus regarding what constitutes best practice. Thus, the early sessions of the INCD provided an excellent training opportunity for delegates who were plunged into debates about the importance of decentralized land management, and of maintaining a mobile pastoral sector, and the existence of simple but effective methods for conserving soils.

The text of the Convention contains many valuable guidelines for development practice and constitutes a code of conduct for both recipient and donor governments. Several key principles underlie the approach set out in the CCD which include:

- The importance of involving local people in planning and designing any proposed interventions.
- The call for better co-ordination between organizations involved in the same field, whether at national or local levels, to avoid duplication and contradictory approaches.
- The need to build on local knowledge and skills, through a partnership between local people and outside researchers or extension staff.

Another positive aspect has been the high degree of involvement by NGOs in the negotiations. This means that they have been able to suggest improvements to the text and lobby for mention of contentious issues, such as terms of trade and debt relief. NGOs have been able to develop strong links among themselves through the network established during the INCD, now called the *Réseau International des ONG sur la Désertification* (RIOD). This constitutes a potentially useful set of

NGO alliances for future work and possibilities for exchanging ideas and experience on drylands management worldwide.

The fact that the Convention is a legally binding document, to which parties are committed under international law, means that countries will now theoretically be answerable for their actions. It provides therefore a point of leverage for members of civil society to press their governments for changes in how business is done, to conform more closely to the principles enshrined in the Convention. The significance of this legal aspect will vary from country to country, depending on the desire of a given government to be seen to comply with international law.

PROBLEMS

On the downside, the process of drawing up the Convention has absorbed very considerable sums of money and the time of large numbers of people, which might well have been better spent elsewhere. With ten sessions of negotiations, each involving many hundreds of people, it is likely that the bill will approach US$100 million, even before the first COP has taken place. For such expenditure to be justified, it must be hoped that the CCD will bring major improvements to address the needs of dryland areas.

Despite a recognition of the need for a local focus to tackle dryland development, a new series of National Action Programmes to Combat Desertification has been proposed, to be supplemented by subregional and regional action programmes. Although these are called 'programmes', not 'plans', and are meant to initiate processes rather than constitute a shopping-list of projects, there is little doubt that many of the mistakes of past planning exercises will now be repeated. Already there are turf battles between different ministries in a number of countries regarding who should have the mandate for taking forward the National Action Programme, since any such responsibility will carry, it is hoped, a sizable budget to match.

Donor agencies are competing with each other to be the lead organization or *chef de file* in a given country, and 'participatory' planning processes are being bogged down in a welter of meetings which are intended to be representative, but where such legitimacy is often lacking and, hence, the outputs lack authority.

Much of the text of the Convention embodies an approach which assumes a centrally important role for the state and other agencies to play. There is much less recognition that powerful forces exist and processes are under way over which governments have little or no control, such as prices, land-use practices and population movements. Although governments may wish that they had mastery over these fields, past experience shows the very limited and sometimes damaging results from attempts to control prices or tell farmers how they should be using their land. The ambitions of government administrations are expressed within the articles of the Convention, but past experience might have led them to be more cautious about their hopes.

The guiding principles behind the Convention challenge those responsible for its implementation. The high-minded terms found within its pages will be much more difficult to carry out in practice. 'Participation, partnership, co-ordination, decentralization...' – each of these words sounds very appealing, yet their translation into practical action requires a much clearer assessment of the interests of different groups who see this as either a potential threat to their livelihoods or an opportunity to acquire greater power.

Not surprisingly, a sensitive issue such as power cannot be tackled directly by a consensus document such as a Convention, but its neglect risks the promotion of policies which assume a degree of harmony which is unrealistic. The text of the Convention is based on an idealized view of how society operates and evolves, and neglects the conflicting interests which inevitably are found within it, and the likelihood that there will be winners and losers in any process of change.

It is widely admitted that decentralization of land management, for example, is a good thing, because it permits decision-making to take place at a level much closer to the land user. Certainly it was completely inappropriate for central government to take responsibility for land management and conflicts over land, since local bodies should be much better informed about conditions in their neighbourhoods and the history surrounding particular disputes. However, those who are members of the state administration at both central and local levels are not always entirely disinterested. Thus, 'decentralization' may involve merely the transfer of control and influence from central government to local élites, with the ordinary farmer or herder no better off.

One of the fundamental problems associated with the CCD concerns the unbalanced pattern of interests between the different parties.

This was evident from when the Convention was first proposed and has dogged the negotiations ever since. Essentially, the question of degradation in dryland areas is different from global environmental problems such as climate change or ozone depletion.

In the latter two cases, joint action is needed at global level to encourage governments to reduce harmful activities by their citizens which ultimately will affect everyone. By contrast, although the problem of dryland degradation may be widespread throughout the world, it does not have the same kind of impact on the global environment. Attempts have been made to show that continued degradation of dryland areas will have a significant and aggravating impact on global warming, but the evidence to date is not convincing.

As a result, there is no overall global interest in tackling desertification. The parties to the Convention are split into two main camps – recipient-affected countries and donor countries, some of which are affected to a lesser or greater extent, such as the US, Australia and the countries of the northern Mediterranean.

Affected recipient countries hope for improved aid flows which are more flexible and longer term, while donor countries have tended to emphasize the importance of seeing proof of recipient countries' willingness to take seriously the commitments outlined in the Convention before they will come up with the funding. As a result, the drawing up of a National Action Programme to Combat Desertification is being taken as the hurdle which recipients must leap before they can qualify for the finance they are seeking. And in order to qualify properly, such programmes have to conform to the qualities expressed in the text, in terms of their participatory and consultative approach.

Thus, the very rapidly drawn up plans which some countries have presented for funding have not found favour with donors. Where recipient countries are more sophisticated in terms of understanding and handling their donors, the participatory approach and language is being followed as the price to pay for getting renewed funding. However, these programmes may be seen as a means to an end and the result of donor exigencies, rather than having an intrinsic merit.

All this has meant also that there has been less interest and lobbying from the NGO movement in developed countries for governments to ratify and implement the CCD than has been the case for climate change, where interest within the media and political groups has been higher.

One of the fundamental difficulties surrounding initiatives such as the CCD is the relatively narrow circle of people who know much about it. There is a serious problem in making it better known among national governments, donor agencies, NGOs and other relevant organizations. Those involved directly in the negotiations represent a tiny minority of government servants from a given country. Where a country is represented by someone from the Ministry of the Environment, for example, there may be no knowledge of the commitments being entered into in the Ministry of Agriculture or other relevant government departments. Hence, when it comes to implementation, very few people may have either an interest in or an understanding of how to adhere to the commitments. This leads, overall, to a lack of respect for international law because such treaties are signed and ratified without a clear understanding of the implications.

WAYS FORWARD

With the first Conference of the Parties to the CCD not due until after the Special Session in June 1997, it is perhaps too early to cast judgement on the possible benefits it may bring. However, as noted above, there is a serious cause for concern about the marginal benefits conferred by further action programmes being drawn up, and the web of conflicting interests and agendas appearing at national and international levels which may absorb much funding and prevent a great deal happening on the ground.

The CCD contains a host of challenging commitments. There is some doubt about the knowledge and readiness of the different parties to carry through what they have formally agreed, since many people do not know or understand the nature of the commitments which their governments have signed up to. These commitments will not be easy to meet, as can be seen by looking at the call for better co-ordination among donors – a plea which to date has been more honoured in the breach than in the practice.

A certain level of competition between government structures and donor agencies is probably inevitable. The transaction costs of meeting and deciding how to allocate tasks may be considerable, so that perfect co-ordination is a pipe-dream.

The administrative structures of recipient and donor governments frequently find it difficult to incorporate new approaches and procedures into the way they conduct business. If the CCD is to bring a more flexible, longer term and more co-ordinated approach to development funding, it must tackle entrenched systems for firmly organizing the funding of programmes and accounting methods. But the Convention alone is unlikely to achieve such changes.

It is thus unrealistic to expect that the CCD will bring radical change to the conditions and prospects faced by dryland peoples. In some countries, however, it should add weight to arguments in favour of a more sensible approach to working with local farmers. And elsewhere, NGOs may be able to use the leverage presented by their government, having ratified the CCD to push for changes in policy.

Whether such marginal improvements can justify the time and cost involved in the process of negotiations is much less clear. The international community should be trying to learn lessons from global approaches to tackling local issues, such as dryland degradation.

6

The Forest Principles and the Inter-Governmental Panel on Forests

Carole Saint-Laurent

The UNCED Earth Summit failed to make significant headway on forests. Their efforts on forests failed in the midst of a North–South negotiating divide and resulted in the weak and defective Statement of Principles and Agenda 21 chapter.

The tortuous negotiations on forests reflected all that was wrong with the UNCED process, including the failure to deal adequately with underlying causes of environmental degradation and the reluctance of Northern countries to take responsibility for their wasteful patterns of consumption.

Since the UNCED, two primary intergovernmental initiatives related to forests have come into being. The first is the Inter-Governmental Panel on Forests (IPF), created by the Commission on Sustainable Development (CSD) in 1995 to give added impetus and focus to the UNCED follow-up on forests. While the creation of the IPF could be viewed as a step in the right direction, it is too early to tell what success it will have.

In parallel to the deliberations of the IPF and CSD, the Conference of the Parties (COP) to the Convention on Biological Diversity (CBD) began its deliberations on forests in 1995 and will give particular attention to terrestrial biodiversity, including forests, beginning in 1996. The CBD was opened for signature at the UNCED and came into force in December 1993.

The meetings of the Conference of the Parties to the CBD, as well as the IPF and CSD, are part of a process leading up to the UN General Assembly Special Session (UNGASS) that will see governments taking decisions on the form and content of international deliberations on forests for years to come. In 1997, governments will also need to demonstrate that they have achieved progress on the UNCED commitments. It will not be enough merely to identify issues that need further consideration by the international community. Without specific action and commitments, governments will have little of value to show to the UNCED on forests for five years of follow-up. The acid test for the follow-up process will continue to be whether it has evolved enough and can generate enough political momentum, to find solutions to the types of impasse that plagued the UNCED.

In addition to these intergovernmental initiatives, innovative partnerships between industry and non-governmental organizations – in particular, the Forest Stewardship Council and the forest products buyers' groups – are contributing in concrete ways to the conservation and sustainable use of forests.

This paper will examine the context for current initiatives on forests and propose a range of options for moving forward in 1997 and beyond into the next five to ten years of international deliberations on forests.

BACKGROUND

The loss and degradation of the world's forests, both temperate and tropical, continues. Natural, old-growth and semi-natural forests are being destroyed rapidly. Even where forest cover remains constant, quality is lost through the effects of industrial forestry operations, pollution damage, human settlement, introduced pests and diseases, and changes in fire incidence. Many important forest eco-systems are protected inadequately. Biodiversity, environment, climate and people all suffer as a result.

International response led to the establishment of the International Timber Organization (ITTO) and the Tropical Forestry Action Plan (TFAP), initiatives whose scope is restricted to tropical forests and whose prospects for slowing deforestation are marginal. These limitations are the result of mandates that set neither forest conservation nor the concerns of people who live in or depend on forests as central objectives.

Nor have they addressed the need for a full valuation of the range of goods and services that forests provide.

What is clear is that the international community's efforts in the 1980s and early 1990s to stem the loss and degradation of tropical forests were ineffectual. It also became evident that temperate forests were more severely degraded than was often imagined and that immediate efforts were needed to reverse the continuing trend of destruction of the remaining old-growth temperate forests. There remained, therefore, an urgent need to go beyond existing initiatives.

UNCED

On June 14 1992, the United Nations Conference on Environment and Development (UNCED) completed an ambitious negotiation process lasting two years and involving delegates from 170 countries, many intergovernmental bodies and thousands of non-governmental organizations. The success or failure of the UNCED must be assessed on the basis of its progress on issues that are fundamental to conservation, sustainability and human welfare. These include:

- Fair and environmentally sound terms of trade.
- Equitable debt, aid and structural adjustment policies.
- Clear recognition of the responsibilities of business and industry.
- Reductions in wasteful consumption.
- Full valuation of natural resources.
- Fair and equitable access to technology and its benefits.

Without progress on these issues, it will be difficult to deliver meaningful long-term progress on sectoral issues such as forests, biodiversity, toxic chemicals and agriculture.

Analysis of the root causes of environmental problems, such as loss of biological diversity and deforestation, leads directly to key development issues. Tropical forest destruction, for example, is driven by such causes as:

- Unsustainable and environmentally unsound development.
- Inequities in trade relations which lead to 90 per cent of the value of tropical timber accruing to consumer countries.

- Pressure to export unsustainably produced commodities to pay off foreign debt and to meet excessive consumption demands.
- Failure to value fully the environmental and social benefits that forests provide.

UNCED AND FORESTS

The UNCED failed to recognize the interconnections between forests and issues such as biodiversity and climate change. Nor did it acknowledge the role of forests within the broader land-use context. Instead, the Statement of Forest Principles adopted at the UNCED is regressive in some areas. This is particularly so when it is considered in conjunction with the Agenda 21, Chapter 11 on combating deforestation – a document that too closely resembles the 'top-down' interventionist policies laid down in the flawed TFAP.

Chapter 11 attempted for the first time to look equally at all the world's forests – to create a level playing-field that would make countries feel a joint responsibility. However, it failed to do this. The chapter does not contain a clear statement that unsustainable use of forests must be stopped. Reference is made merely to promote sustainable use. Eventually, Chapter 11 betrays itself and the UNCED in paragraph 11.36 which mentions 'accelerating development' rather than UNCED's stated goal of 'sustainable development.'

None the less, in Chapter 11, governments agreed to undertake a number of actions, including:

- To establish, expand and manage protected area systems which include systems of conservation units.
- To act to maintain and expand the existing vegetative cover.
- To rehabilitate degraded natural forests to restore productivity and environmental contributions.
- To promote adequate legislation and other measures to control conversion to other types of land uses.
- To ensure the sustainable use of biological resources and conservation of biological diversity.
- To apply appropriate market mechanisms and incentives to help to address global environmental concerns.

CSD AND FORESTS

The first organizational session of the CSD recommended that their pro-gramme of work should be based on clusters of the chapters of Agenda 21. The forests issue was included in cluster 7: land, desertification, forests and biodiversity, mountain eco-systems and sustainable agricul-ture (Chapters 10–15).

The third session of the CSD in April 1995 was meant to review progress on 'combating deforestation', and the management, conserva-tion and sustainable development of all types of forests – as dealt with in Chapter 11 of Agenda 21 and the non-legally binding Statement of Principles on Forests. The CSD meeting in 1995 was widely hoped to be a crucial step forward in addressing global forest problems. But non-governmental organizations feared that the meeting would result in a position that was so weak that it would make very little difference, and would encourage further delay in implementing effective action.

IPF

In the end, the Commission delayed immediate action but encouraged further deliberation by establishing the Intergovernmental Panel on Forests (IPF). The IPF will provide its final conclusions and recommen-dations for future action to the CSD in April 1997. These will be trans-mitted to Earth Summit 2 (UNGASS) for its overall review of the implementation of the UNCED decisions.

In establishing the IPF, the CSD said that it considers 'further con-crete actions...to be an urgent priority' and that the panel should pro-mote multi-disciplinary 'action'. The following programme of work was adopted:

- National forest and land-use plans.
- Underlying causes of deforestation.
- Traditional forest-related knowledge.
- Afforestation, reforestation, restoration, fragile eco-systems, deserti-fication, drought and pollutants.
- Countries with low forest cover.
- The transfer of finance resources and technology.
- The assessment of multiple benefits of forests.

- Criteria and indicators for sustainable forest management.
- Trade and the environment.
- Institutions and instruments.
- Legal mechanisms.

The IPF has so far given limited attention to conservation concerns, particularly forest quality, biodiversity, protected areas and the restoration of forests. Recognition of the contribution that can be made by the Convention on Biological Diversity, particularly on national forest programmes and the development of criteria and indicators, is helpful, but effective collaboration and integration between the IPF and CBD has not been achieved.

Implementation of the specific commitments contained in Chapter 11 of Agenda 21 seems to be largely forgotten, while other issues, such as promoting trade in forest products, are receiving a disproportionate amount of attention. In short, the focus on 'action' that was made so clear by the CSD in setting up the IPF has so far been replaced by a focus on 'process'. For example, in developing recommended guidelines for the preparation of national forest plans, the IPF has been preoccupied with the procedures for developing these plans rather than with the substantive content – that is, the principles and criteria for the conservation and sustainable use of forests.

CBD

While the CSD gave the IPF a comprehensive mandate on forests, it is not the only forum that is relevant to forests. The Convention on Biological Diversity (CBD) deals with the conservation and sustainable use of all types of biodiversity, including forests. It has a role to play, therefore, whatever the outcome is of the IPF process.

The Convention contains provisions that relate to both the sustainable use of forest biological diversity and to the fair and equitable sharing of benefits arising from the use of forest genetic resources. It contains specific commitments regarding, *inter alia*, the establishment of protected areas and the development of incentives for the conservation of biodiversity.

The second Conference of the Parties (COP2) to the CBD held in November 1995 provided to the IPF information on indigenous and local communities and forests, and a statement on the links between biological diversity and forests calling for a dialogue between the COP and the IPF. The statement also indicated that *in situ* forest conservation activities, including protected area networks, have an important role to play in achieving sustainable forest management, and should be integrated into national forest and land-use plans.

In September 1996, the Subsidiary Body on Scientific, Technical and Technological Advice (SBSTTA) to the CBD recommended that:

- Biodiversity considerations be integrated fully into the IPF recommendations and proposals for action.
- National forest plans should be based on an eco-system approach incorporating conservation measures.
- The conservation of biodiversity and the maintenance of forest quality should be included in the deliberations on criteria and indicators.

These points could provide the basis for a programme of work on forests for the CBD. The third Conference of the Parties in November 1996 determined what future action should be undertaken on forests under the auspices of the CBD.

LINKS BETWEEN THE IPF AND THE CBD

There is some confusion about the respective roles of the IPF and the CSD on forests versus the role of the CBD. One important clarification is that the CBD is a legally binding agreement, while the IPF is a political forum which arrives at recommendations with political but not legal weight. Another clarification is that the CBD only applies to its parties – this includes more than 150 countries, but not the United States – while the IPF is open to participation by all countries. Unfortunately, this confusion has contributed to the lack of immediate action on forests with some governments using the existence of one forum as an excuse for no action in the other, and vice versa.

INNOVATIVE NON-GOVERNMENTAL PARTNERSHIPS

While governments are tied up with lengthy negotiations that may or may not bear fruit in terms of real action on forests, other sectors of society are spawning solutions. One example is the Forest Stewardship Council (FSC) which was formed in response to the need for a credible and honest system for identifying sustainably managed forests as acceptable sources of forest products.

The FSC was founded in 1993 by a diverse group of representatives from environmental institutions, the timber trade, the forestry profession, indigenous people's organizations, community forestry groups and forest product certification organizations from 25 countries. It is an independent, non-profit, non-governmental organization.

The FSC supports environmentally appropriate, socially beneficial and economically viable management of the world's forests. The FSC intends to promote good forest management by evaluating and accrediting certifiers, by encouraging the development of national and regional forest management standards, and by strengthening national certification capacity by supporting the development of certification initiatives worldwide.

The FSC has defined ten principles of sustainable forest management, including:

- Conformity with those of national law and international agreements.
- Respecting the right of local populations to own and exploit their land.
- The conservation of biodiversity, resources, fragile eco-systems and landscapes.
- The evaluation of management methods and their social and environmental impact.

By June 1996, more than 2.3 million hectares of natural forest had been certified by four approved certification bodies. A steadily increasing number and variety of forest products are already available to the public.

Another effective initiative is the 'buyers' groups' founded by the World Wide Fund for Nature (WWF), which bring together enterprises which are active in the wood trade – importers, wholesalers and retailers. These undertake to produce and buy wood which is certified as coming from a sustainably managed source. Such groups already exist in Great Britain and Belgium; others are forming in Austria, Germany, Australia, Cameroon and North America.

PRINCIPLES AND OBJECTIVES

No matter what direction the international community takes on current and future action and deliberations on forests, it is possible to identify a few key principles and objectives:

PRINCIPLES

- Forests face serious problems throughout the world. Although attention has focused on the threats confronting tropical moist forests, many other forests – including those in dry tropical, subtropical, temperate and boreal regions – are also at risk, albeit sometimes from different threats.
- Quality is as important as quantity in considering forest status. A focus on the losses of total forest cover, particularly in the tropics, has tended to obscure an equally serious loss of forest quality in temperate and boreal areas. Loss of quality can result from factors such as inappropriate management, air pollution, spread of exotic species and an unnatural incidence of fire. Quality issues are becoming increasingly important in the tropics as well.
- First priority should be given to the maintenance of biodiversity as a means of maximizing all the goods and services that the forest can provide. Forests and their products can contribute to sustainable development, poverty alleviation, and local and national economies. Most forest management now focuses narrowly on the timber harvest and the non-consumptive benefits of forests – for example, water catchment protection and soil stabilization are often disregarded.
- The global forest crisis must be addressed with urgency. Governments are already five years into a process that must result in the development of sustainable stewardship of the global forest estate. But the amount of high quality forest which survives long enough to provide long-term benefits is limited. So decisions taken in the next few months will be critical.

OBJECTIVES

- To establish a network of ecologically representative protected areas. This objective addresses the issue of protected forest areas for the conservation of biodiversity and the maintenance of ecological processes. The focus is consequently on preserving sufficient forest to allow natural ecological dynamics to continue indefinitely. Local involvement in both planning and co-management is essential for success.

● To set up environmentally appropriate, socially beneficial and economically viable forest management outside protected areas. This objective is concerned with improving forest quality in forests outside areas fully protected for biodiversity. Management should meet Forest Stewardship Council principles and criteria or their equivalent. Management must ensure that forest dwellers do not suffer physically or culturally as a result of the mismanagement of forests, or of bad planning decisions relating to them.

● To develop and implement ecologically and socially appropriate forest restoration. This objective aims to re-create near-original forests and restore representative forest areas in those places that have been degraded or deforested, such as in much of Europe, and generally to increase the area of semi-natural forest. Forests should be restored under criteria and standards of high forest quality, stressing multiple use and the restoration of natural dynamics and biodiversity. Human needs, particularly those of indigenous and local people, should be included in all forest restoration plans.

● To reduce forest damage from global change, including a decrease of pollution below damage thresholds for forest eco-systems, as measured by critical loads. This objective aims to reduce and, where possible, eliminate the impact of a range of global change effects, including atmospheric and water pollution, ozone depletion, global warming and human-induced forest fires. A major factor will be the elimination, generally at source, of pollution damage from local and long-range atmospheric pollution, water pollution, soil contamination and toxic waste.

● To use forest goods and services at levels that do not damage the environment, including the elimination of wasteful consumption, to attain a level of use of the forest goods and services within the regenerative capacity of the forest estate. This objective aims to establish levels of consumption of forest products that minimize environmental effects, bearing in mind:
– The effects of the over-consumption of forest products.
– The potential for forest products to substitute for other products.

– The potential for substituting other products in place of forest products, and the need for greater equity in the availability of forest products.

PRIORITY AREAS FOR ACTION

The magnitude of the task involved in moving towards well-managed forests worldwide can sometimes appear overwhelming. Any international process, therefore must avoid dissipating its effort in too many different directions. For this reason it is important, based on the principles and objectives outlined above, for the UNCED follow–up process to focus on a few key and realizable priorities, particularly:

- To agree to a definition of forest quality and consequent criteria for forest management, including the conservation of forest biodiversity.
- To identify the means whereby local participation in decision-making about management and the distribution of benefits from forests could be increased.
- To promote the establishment of a network of ecologically representative forest reserves.
- To promote policies for increasing the forest cover, including ensuring that a high quality of forest is achieved.
- To agree to mechanisms for transferring financial resources to deliver on the actions needed and to continue to press for progress on other cross-sectoral issues.

FOREST QUALITY

Sustainable forest management should aim to create and maintain high quality forests which address the following needs:

- Authenticity: a measure of how closely the composition and processes of forests correspond to the natural forest of the area. In many countries, the original natural forest has been lost irretrievably.
- Forest health: an assessment of forest health with respect to disease or pollution damage, and robustness in the face of global climate change.

- Environmental benefits: a gauge of the role that the forest plays in bio-diversity conservation, soil and watershed management, climate, etc.
- Other social and economic values: including a broad array of values to humans, ranging from commercial considerations through to spiritual and religious values.

INDEPENDENT CERTIFICATION

Independent timber certification can play a key role in the promotion, development and financing of sustainable forest management and high forest quality. It provides a market incentive for improved management. Certification is seen as a 'soft', non-regulatory, policy tool that can help to bring the forest sector into line with the principles of sustainable forest management.

Among other advantages, credible certification based on performance standards can help countries to regain their lost market share and to avoid future losses. Experience in Belgium, the UK and Scandinavia suggests that rapid progress towards certification is possible.

PEOPLE

Experience has shown that a 'top-down' approach to forest management is seldom effective in achieving long-term improvements. The participation of local communities, in planning, decision-making and management, and in access to the various goods and services which the forest provides, are important prerequisites for success in forestry and have been recognized as such in the UNCED Forest Principles.

Recognition of the land rights of local communities and indigenous people should be given high priority. Effort should also be geared towards the provision of assistance to communities in the development of sustainable use projects and practices, and building the capacities of communities to undertake these projects.

PROTECTION

A well-designed and well-managed network of protected areas is an essential part of the forest estate. As a priority, protected areas should be established in forests that are near to the natural state and display authenticity of both the biodiversity and natural ecological dynamics. Ecologically representative areas of forest – that is, sufficient areas of each forest type – should be protected to ensure that the ecological processes can continue.

Reserve networks covering at least 10 per cent of the country have been agreed in principle or have been achieved already in countries such as Cameroon, Australia, Canada, Costa Rica and Ecuador. Cameroon is committed to protecting 30 per cent of its forests, Australia 15 per cent and Canada 12 per cent. Costa Rica has protected 25 per cent and Ecuador 18 per cent. Currently about 6 per cent of the world's forest area is protected legally.

Reaching a target of 10 per cent can be achieved either by setting aside 10 per cent in each country or by concentrating on areas with the best opportunities for protection, leading to a worldwide result of at least 10 per cent. If the latter option is chosen, some method of achieving equity in paying for the setting aside of land must be found.

RESTORATION

Chapter 11 of Agenda 21 recognized the importance of forest rehabilitation and regeneration in restoring the ecological balance, and expanding the contribution of forests to human needs and welfare.

Forest restoration balances responsibility between those countries which still possess large areas of high quality forest and those which have undergone substantial deforestation or forest degradation. In countries where natural forests have disappeared or been reduced to fragments, conservation options are more limited. In these cases there is often a need to restore areas of once forested land to a more authentic state.

Large-scale forest restoration will become increasingly important in Europe, East Africa, and northern Asia. Major reforestation successes have been achieved already in South Korea, Finland and parts of Pakistan.

FINANCIAL RESOURCES

The importance of addressing cross-sectoral issues – particularly financial resources – was highlighted by the UNCED, but practical steps to address these have proved more elusive. If anything, the financial resources situation has worsened since the UNCED.

Discussions in the CSD have developed a useful framework for identifying new sources of funding. There are already a number of innovative and effective initiatives. At the moment, the expansion of these initiatives offers the most promise for generating new and additional funds.

One approach lies in the reduction of subsidies to release financial resources, at the same time as reducing pressure on the environment. For example, government support for below-cost timber sales, tax incentives for foreign timber companies and the use of mechanisms, such as transfer pricing, all result in the undervaluing of forests and act as disincentives for sustainable forest management.

A continuing challenge for the UNCED follow–up process has been to wrestle with the integration of cross-sectoral issues into the implementation of the individual chapters of Agenda 21 which relate to sectoral issues. It is clear that efforts must continue to make progress on financial resources, as well as on trade, technology transfer, and other issues that underpin progress on forests.

INSTRUMENTS AVAILABLE FOR IMPLEMENTATION

The primary tools available and the appropriate forums for addressing priority action areas are as follows:

1. Implementing existing agreements – Agenda 21 and the CBD. It has been clear for some time what action governments need to take on forests. Some of these are contained in Chapter 11 of Agenda 21, others in the Convention on Biological Diversity. Implementation of these agreements has been poor. Neither a new forum nor a new convention is needed as existing agreements, including Agenda 21, the Forest Principles and the CBD, provide an adequate framework and commitments to enable governments to take action on forests now, no matter what the outcome of the IPF process.
2. Adopting by the IPF of a programme of action. To give further impetus to the implementation of existing agreements and to go beyond them, the Inter-Governmental Panel on Forests could adopt at its final session in February 1997 a programme of action focusing on a

few key and realizable actions. This practical and politically important option is being promoted by Manuel Rodriguez of Colombia, Co-chair of the IPF. Among other things, it would help governments to save face in 1997. Such a plan of action should contain actions to be taken by the UNCED follow-up process, as well as by governments directly along the lines indicated in this paper.

3. Setting up a high level intergovernmental forum. Some governments have called for a continuation of the IPF as it is. Others want it to be succeeded by a ministerial level political forum. While ministerial level participation could lead to greater political commitment and involvement, in at least some countries the question would arise of which minister would represent the country – trade, environment or natural resources. This obviously could affect the positions taken by a government on particular issues. None the·less, the notion of a high-level forum to generate political will for action on forests merits further consideration.

4. Drawing up a new international legal instrument. Proposals for a new convention on forests have existed for many years without garnering the necessary support. At the moment, Canada and the European Union are its strongest proponents. There are different views of the main purpose of such a convention, ranging from the need to take a holistic view of forests to securing market access for a country's timber products in exchange for commitment to some definition of sustainable forest management.

It is not clear at all what place conservation could or should occupy in the convention, particularly given the existing remit of the Convention on Biological Diversity. It is also unclear whether it would be better to restrict a convention to those aspects of the forest issue that are not dealt with elsewhere – for example, trade in temperate forest products, or whether a holistic convention that would cover all aspects of forests would be better.

Another alternative which should be explored is a convention that would link the components which are relevant to forests from existing conventions, particularly the Convention on Biological Diversity and the Framework Convention on Climate Change.

Pressure for a convention is premature without consensus on a few fundamental factors, including identification of gaps in the implementation of existing agreements, recognition that a new instrument should not undermine existing agreements, and clarification of the

role of each agreement and institution with a forests mandate. The real question is how would a new legal agreement on forests promote implementation of the UNCED agreements or go beyond them.
5. Partnerships and NGO initiatives. While the international community continues its deliberations on forests indefinitely, in one forum or another, independent non-governmental initiatives, such as the Forest Stewardship Council and forest products buyers' groups, will continue to operate and to garner increasing support and participation. Governments can contribute to such initiatives by providing a supportive policy environment in which such initiatives can have a chance of developing and operating.

AN ACTION PLAN FOR GOVERNMENTS

Notwithstanding – or perhaps because of – the ongoing international negotiations on forests, specific and concrete action against which progress may be measured has been limited. There remains an urgent need to act. Immediate action should not be precluded by the negotiation of a new legal instrument or by the establishment of a new or improved forum on forests. Specific action is needed by governments to demonstrate commitment to the conservation and sustainable use of forests, and to build confidence in intergovernmental initiatives.

The WWF has set the following international targets for forests:

- To achieve high quality and sustainable management of forests, including no net deforestation, by the year 2000.
- An ecologically representative network of protected areas, covering at least 10 per cent of the world's forests, by the year 2000, demonstrating a range of socially and environmentally appropriate models.
- Voluntary independent certification of timber, under the auspices of the Forest Stewardship Council, from at least 10 million hectares of forest by 1998.
- Restoration of representative forest areas in those places that have been deforested or where forests have been degraded, and generally an increase in the semi-natural forest area.

The adoption of such targets by governments would stress the urgency of the transition to sustainable forest management (SFM) and would provide a useful focus for the identification of specific actions. These targets translate into the following concrete and achievable actions by governments:

- To prepare national forest plans, within a broader land use context, and to include principles and objectives, as well as targets.
- To include in national forest plans a commitment to increase protected areas through the establishment of an ecologically representative network of protected areas.
- To identify and adopt measures to ensure the full participation of indigenous people and local communities in forest planning, conservation and management.
- To examine successful attempts at ecologically and socially sensitive forest restoration and to replicate successful models.
- To recognize the role of non-timber forest products, biodiversity and human cultural values in forest restoration programmes.
- To review national experiences with timber harvesting subsidies and their reduction to learn from innovative approaches.
- To support the independent, voluntary certification of timber.

These actions can be undertaken by governments and have merit whichever intergovernmental process on forests they may most relate to. Agenda 21, the CBD, the CSD and the IPF all have the necessary mandates to support such an action plan.

CONCLUSION

The preparations for the UNCED marked a high point in terms of hopes for the future of the world's forests. The outcome of the UNCED was disappointing, however. Hopes were raised again when the CSD was established with a mandate to monitor, among other things, progress on the implementation of the Statement of Principles on Forests and Chapter 11 of Agenda 11.

The response of the CSD was to establish the Inter-Governmental Panel on Forests. Again, hopes were raised that this forum could bring the necessary focus to forests issues. The Convention on Biological Diversity was signed and ratified and came into force. It is not clear whether the full potential of the Convention and the IPF will be fulfilled. At present the signs are not encouraging: implementation of the former is less than impressive and negotiations in the latter seem more concerned with process than substance. But the opportunity still exists in the lead-up to Earth Summit 2 to improve the prospects for both forums.

Meanwhile, deforestation continues and previously stable or untouched forest areas are being lost. However, the news is not all bad since the UNCED and some progress has been made, including:

- An international forum focusing on forests.
- Rapid progress towards independent certification of forest products.
- Changes in forest practice by some major forest products as a result of consumer pressure.
- Increasing support for sustainable forest management among buyers, consumers and business people.
- Agreement to protect forests in a number of countries.

Interestingly, much progress has resulted from non-governmental orga-nizations working with industry, rather than from governments or inter-national bodies. Developments such as the Forest Stewardship Council and buyers' groups, and efforts to promote certification in countries such as Belgium, Sweden and the UK, provide a framework and impe-tus for changes in forest management.

Achieving forest quality and sustainable forest management will benefit both people and the environment. Governments, the interna-tional community, industry and civil society all have a role to play in meeting this challenge.

7

The Rio Declaration

Philippe Sands

States and people shall co-operate in good faith and in a spirit of partnership... in the further development of international law in the field of sustainable development.

Principle 27, Rio Declaration on Environment and Development

The Rio Declaration on Environment and Development and the other agreements from the Earth Summit in 1992 contain a large number of general principles. It is, perhaps, too early to be certain of the impact of these agreements on domestic and international law, although the early indications are very hopeful. I was a little sceptical after Rio about what the impact of Agenda 21 and the Rio principles might be – the conventions seemed to offer the best opportunity to move forward.

As we review our progress over the last five years, I now think that we can be much more optimistic. The agreements from Rio are starting to affect our lives in so many different ways. This essay will focus on the Rio principles and how they are being used – in particular the elaboration of these principles into either national or international law in the field of sustainable development.

The following issues will be considered:

1. How have these principles come about?
2. The principles under consideration will be identified.

3. Their status in international law will be described, as well as the implications that status has for domestic implementation through court action or through domestic codification.
4. The question of what principles are will be asked because it requires elaboration to avoid confusion. One point that is very clear is that common law lawyers have a very different approach to principles from continental lawyers, which can have very significant implications for domestic implementation. Principles are treated very differently, depending on the legal culture in which we find ourselves.
5. The legal consequences will be discussed in hard, practical terms of applying principles, both in international law but also in domestic law.

In the run-up to the Earth Summit, there were discussions within the negotiations of the Biodiversity Convention and the Climate Change Convention about the provisions in those treaties that were called 'principles' – in particular, Article 3 of the Climate Change Convention which is called 'Principles'. The article was very strongly opposed by most of the OECD members, in particular the United Kingdom and the United States who considered that it imposed requirements that were too broad and incapable of practical application. The G77 was strongly in favour of an article on principles. Their approach was strengthened by the opposition of two very important countries. It was taken that if they were so strongly against 'principles', there must be something very good about them.

A monumental battle took place right up to the adoption of the treaty in May 1992 about whether Article 3 should be in it at all. The provisions ended up in the text, subject to some drafting amendments to reflect the concern about the nature and legal consequence of the principles.

There is a very rare footnote in Article 1 of the Convention under 'Definitions' which provides that titles are only inserted to assist the reader: it does not say what it is to assist the reader with. It was proposed by the United States legal adviser who wanted to ensure that Article 3 'Principles' could not create actionable obligations.

The second aspect of the drafted change that sought to give effect to that requirement was the introductory *chapeau* to Article 3, which states that parties in their actions to implement the Convention shall be guided by the following principles. Of course, the effect of that *chapeau* is to restrict the principles that follow within the scope of the Convention only, not to create general principles of international law.

By contrast, the Biodiversity Convention also has an Article 3 called 'Principles'. It reflects Principles 21 and 2 of the Stockholm and Rio Declaration respectively. This article does not have an introductory *chapeau*; it simply says that states have sovereignty over natural resources and responsibility not to cause damage to the environment in the areas beyond jurisdiction. That language was problematical for a number of states and some, including the United Kingdom, put in an interpretive declaration indicating that the principle was only intended to apply to the implementation of the Biodiversity Convention and did not create a general international legal principle. Other countries took a different view and understood this to be the establishment of a general obligation in international law.

This is mentioned because it reflects the fundamental concern that underlies the issue of the codification of the Rio Principles into domestic law. What legal consequences should principles have? What legal effect should they have in the development of national laws, and in the interpretation and application of those laws before the courts? There are widely differing views about what role principles should have. Is there a broad consensus on what the operational principles are in the field of the environment and sustainable development? Is there agreement as to what these principles mean in practice?

One example is the second nuclear test case between New Zealand and France. This was before the International Court of Justice (ICJ) in September 1995. Both sides broadly agreed that Principle 21 of the Rio Declaration reflects customary international law, that there is a precautionary principle which has a certain status, and that there is an obligation to carry out an environmental impact assessment. Both countries took that view. Where they disagreed, however, was what these 'principles' really meant in practice. France said that it would carry out and apply the precautionary principle and, of course, Principle 21. The ICJ did not deal with the merits.

Similar situations arise that relate to the two advisory opinion questions concerning the legality of the use of nuclear weapons, in which countries discussed all sorts of principles for and against the legality of their use. Principles are also at issue in the Hungary–Slovakia dispute, concerning the construction of a dam on the Danube. States at the international level therefore are thinking very seriously about these issues, although it is clear that they do not necessarily agree about what all the issues mean in practice.

Similar considerations apply in the European Court of Justice. It has become clear in the area of codification in the national context that the Rio Principles and Agenda 21 are being used.

The Environmental Protection Committee of the National People's Congress of China has recently been drafting two new pieces of environmental law – a general framework law and a law on water pollution management. What is remarkable in the drafting of these new laws is that when the six drafters from the National People's Congress could not agree about what particular rule or principle to include, the drafters would bring out the Chinese language version of Agenda 21 and lift the language directly from the Agenda and incorporate it into the draft text. This was the international language which the People's Republic of China had signed up to, even though the principles and rules of Agenda 21 are so vague in most cases that they are unenforceable.

So, in terms of international experience, there seems to have been significant case law and practical development.

THE EMERGENCE OF PRINCIPLES

The roots of the Rio Declaration can be traced back in international treaties and conventions 50,60 and even, in some cases, 100 years. There is nothing new about them.

What is new is the attempt co-ordinate them and bring them together into a coherent whole. Thus, you will find the principle of future generations stated in the International Whaling Convention of 1946 and the principle of sustainable management of fisheries in the Pacific Fur Seal Arbitration of 1893.

It is true that there is now broad agreement as to what the principles mean in practice. We now need to identify individual principles and rules which are capable of being given practical effect. For example, the precautionary principle is now incorporated into the 1995 Straddling Fish Stocks Agreement in a way that gives it a more precise meaning. Similarly, the UN Economic Commission for Europe is engaging in an effort to negotiate what will be the first convention on public participation, access to information, and so on – in effect, it will be implementing Principle 10 of the Rio Declaration. These are more sensible and practical ways to go forward.

CATEGORIES

There are two broad categories of principles. In the first category, there are what one might call the core principles, which are inherent in the concept of sustainable development. In the second category, principles are drawn from other areas of international law which provide assistance in the achievement of sustainable development.

In the first category, there are four core principles:

- The integration of the environment and development.
- The application of equity between present generations.
- Consideration of the needs of future generations.
- The non-exhaustion of renewable resources.

The second category includes the principle that is reflected in Principles 21 and 2, the principle of good neighbourliness and international co-operation; the principle of common but differentiated responsibilities; the principle of precaution, and the principle of governance – namely, participation by civil society in the decision-making and the polluter pays principle. The principle of environmental impact assessment has not been included in the core list of principles because it is a rule, rather than a principle: it comes from the core principle of the need to integrate the environment and development, taking into account environmental impact when a development project is being implemented.

LEGAL STATUS

Different principles have different legal statuses. Some bind treaties, and in that context they obviously have a different application in national legal systems. It is very important to distinguish in domestic implementation between those principles or rules which apply as a matter of treaty law and those which states are legally bound to implement. On the other hand, there are principles of customary international law and those which are not binding at all.

As we have seen, in the United Kingdom there is a reluctance in the Dudderidge case to treat principles as actionable. Even when a principle has a clear legal status – for example, where it is referred to in article 130R(2) of the Treaty of the European Union – it does not mean that national courts will implement and apply it in a given case. They will find ways if they can to avoid doing so in certain jurisdictions. In other jurisdictions, judges might be nervous about relying on general principles and applying them to the facts of a particular case.

The European Commission is enforcing some of these principles against member states but not applying them internally. There are a number of cases before the European Court of Justice where individuals and non-governmental organizations are seeking a judicial review of the European Commission for the failure to take environmental obligations into account. At the European Court it is being argued that principle 10, for example, creates an obligation to interpret Article 173 of the EC Treaty in such a way as to allow a judicial review by individual and environmental associations, in particular in circumstances where their interests are affected. The pleadings of the European Commission make for dismal reading when compared to the Commission's public commitments to the Rio Declaration.

Most experts agree on a broad list of principles that reflect customary international law, but this is of little practical meaning unless agreement is reached at the international level on what the practical effect of a principle might be in particular cases. That did not happen in the nuclear test case, it may or may not happen in the case of the nuclear weapons Advisory Options which are currently before the International Court of Justice, and it may or may not happen in the Gabcikovo–Nagymaros case, which is clearly about sustainable development.

THE MEANING OF PRINCIPLES

What exactly do we mean by principles and rules? This is something that lawyers need to think about, in terms of general international law and also national legal systems.

In general international law, the position is fairly clear: distinction can be made between a principle and a rule. There is not absolute agreement about what the distinction means, but the discussion of this can be traced back. There are some interesting arbitral awards and some interesting opinions from the International Court. For example, in the case between Italy and Venezuela in 1903, the Umpire stated:

A rule is essentially practical and moreover binding, that there are rules out there as there are rules of government, while the term principles expresses a general truth which guides our actions, serves as a theoretical basis for the various acts of our life, and the application of which to reality produces a given consequence.

Principles have a softer status. They assist in the integration and implementation and application, but they do not create substantive obligations that are actionable in their own right.

This approach is shared by most lawyers in the United Kingdom, reflecting that in common law tradition it is not enough just to create principles. By creating principles the judiciary may be at risk of having a broad discretion to apply its own intuitions to the facts of a particular case, so the tendency in both the United States and the United Kingdom is to be cautious. A principle for a lawyer in one country is not the same as a principle for a lawyer in another country.

LEGAL CONSEQUENCES

It is clear that the way you take the narrow common law construction, or the broad rules-orientated construction of principles, can have different practical consequences, both at the national and international level.

Approaching it as a common lawyer, principles provide a useful aid to constructing and interpreting legal instruments. After they have been implemented in national legal systems, they can be given practical application in that way. That is, for example, the approach taken by the European Court of Justice in its 1992 judgment of the Wallonian waste case (European Commission v Belgium), where the issue was whether or not Belgium or the Wallonian region was entitled to ban all non-hazardous waste from being imported into the Wallonian region. There was no clear rule in European Community law: there were no directives and the matter had to be decided by reference to the rules of the free movement of goods.

What the Court did to justify its conclusion was to refer to two sets of principles: the first principle in Article 130R(2), which states that environmental damage should be rectified at the source, and the principles of proximity and self-sufficiency which are implicit in the Basel Convention of 1989. These principles asserted in its conclusion that Belgium was entitled in the absence of a Community rule, to ban the importation of non-hazardous waste into the Wallonian region.

It was a particularly difficult judgment for a number of reasons, not the least of which was the fact that at the time of the judgment the Basel Convention was not in force, had not been ratified by the European Community, and did not really express the principle exactly as the

European Court understood. But this indicates the way that courts are sometimes willing to apply principles.

Secondly, a further legal consequence of the principles is the establishment of substantial obligations in their own right. With reference to the distinction made earlier between principles and rules, Principles 21 and 2 work as a rule. They create substantive obligations, and that was the manner in which they were relied upon by New Zealand in 1995, and by New Zealand and Australia as long ago as 1974.

Thirdly, principles at the international and national level can contribute to the development of new rules – for example, the Straddling Fish Stocks Agreements. Principles can also contribute to the development of new rules where there are gaps in the law.

Fourthly, the principles fill in the gaps and build bridges between different areas of international law – for example, the expert working group which was brought together to look at whether international law required GATT panels when interpreting GATT in the context of the Tuna Dolphin case and other similar cases. The group was not very firm about how far we should go in saying that the Vienna Convention on the Law of Treaties required GATT panels to take principles into account. In this way principles might provide a bridge.

In conclusion, there is a final comment on codification and implementation. It is important to return to the basics of the cultural and legal differences to understand how principles and rules can be applied in different national contexts and how they can be applied in the international context.

It is also important to bear in mind that the relationship between the national and the international is a two-way process. Some of the principles that have emerged, such as the precautionary principle, came first in national law, bounced their way up into international law and then returned in various different legal cultures. Similarly, national legal practice can then define international obligations.

On 30 July 1994, the Philippine Supreme Court, in a landmark decision, recognized the standing of citizens and non-governmental organizations to sue on the right to the environment as an intergenerational right. How we can extend the right to petition to the international arena concerning the Rio Principles should be one of the key issues that will be dealt with at next year's UNGASS.

Part II

MAJOR GROUPS

8

Non-Governmental Organizations

Peter Mucke

Non-governmental organizations (NGOs) were allowed to participate to an unprecedented extent in the UNCED meeting, both in the official intergovernmental conference and the parallel NGO summit, Global Forum '92. Agenda 21 established that level of NGO participation as standard for the future. Chapter 27 of Agenda 21 – 'Strengthening the Role of Non-Governmental Organizations: Partners for Sustainable Development' – states:

> *Non-governmental organizations play a vital role in the shaping and implementation of participatory democracy. Their credibility lies in the responsible and constructive role they play in society. Formal and informal organizations, as well as grass-roots movements, should be recognized as partners in the implementation of Agenda 21. The nature of the independent role played by non-governmental organizations within a society calls for real participation; therefore, independence is a major attribute of non-governmental organizations and is the precondition of real participation...*
>
> *Non-governmental organizations, including those non-profit organizations representing groups addressed in the present section of Agenda 21, possess well-established and diverse experience, expertise and capacity in fields which will be of particular importance to the implementation and review of environmentally sound and socially responsible sustainable development, as envisaged throughout Agenda 21...*
>
> *To ensure that the full potential contribution of non-governmental organizations is realized, the fullest possible communication and co-operation between international organizations, national and local governments and*

non-governmental organizations should be promoted in institutions man-
dated, and programmes designed to carry out Agenda 21. Non-govern-
mental organisations will also need to foster co-operation and
communication among themselves to reinforce their effectiveness as actors in
the implementation of sustainable development...

But is there any need at all for these three-ring negotiating circuses?
What happens after the curtain falls? Sceptics have calculated the environmental damage that conferences have caused as a result of air travel,
air-conditioned conference buildings and inconceivable amounts of
paper used to publish the respective conference results: is it worth it?

NGOS COMING OF AGE

Global problems demand global solutions. Many non-governmental
organizations are accordingly aware that their participation is vital.
Now that NGOs have gathered five years' experience with summit
mania, the discussion of the pros and cons – including new or more
developed forms of their participation in international negotiations – is
gaining momentum.

It is a virtually undisputed fact that citizens' action groups, grass-
roots movements and the organizations which grow out of them are
being assigned increasingly important societal and political roles. Civil
society's growing weight is also reflected in the UN's treatment of
them: in 1948, the UN's Economic and Social Council granted consultative status to only 41 NGOs. This number rose to 978 by 1993 and
has been augmented by an additional 550, which were granted consultative status by the Commission on Sustainable Development (CSD) following the Earth Summit in Rio.

In September 1994, UN Secretary-General Boutros Boutros-Ghali
emphasized the important role that NGOs play:

Non-governmental organizations are a basic form of popular representa-
tion in the present-day world. Their participation in international orga-
nizations is, in a way, a guarantee of the political legitimacy of those
international organizations.

But based on their experience to date, many NGOs are demanding that
the nature of NGO participation be re-examined, consequences be

drawn and changes be made in the currently practised forms of NGO participation. They consider the present situation in which they are allowed to attend, but not to participate in any serious way, is unsatisfactory and not commensurate with the expense involved. Jens Martens, an expert on the UN, has remarked regarding the future role of NGOs in the United Nations:

The future relationship between the United Nations and NGOs should be shaped not only by consultations but by true participation as well. This point was already stressed by the world's governments in 1992 in Agenda 21 and its chapter on strengthening the role of non-governmental organizations, and then emphasized once again in the programme of action adopted by the International Conference on Population and Development in Cairo.

The NGOs' new understanding of their place in the UN process sees them not as mute observers or a mere vehicle for providing information, but rather as material political players.

INTERNATIONAL CO-ORDINATION

Today's far-reaching global problems in the environmental and development fields mean there has to be a close exchange and clearly defined co-ordination between local, national and international levels. On the one hand, international-level discussion often suffers from a lack of information about local conditions, problems and needs. On the other hand, international exchanges and discussion processes can provide new stimuli for local and regional work, and can even lead to new forms of action or to co-operation between various sectors, such as the ecology movement and unions. When participating in international negotiations, NGOs should pay special attention to these processes. This will inevitably require the assistance of local organizations.

LEGITIMATION

As the non-governmental sector grows and becomes better represented, the question of who they represent becomes increasingly crucial. And what about legitimation? English conference jargon already goes so far as to differentiate between NGOs (non-governmental organizations), NGIs (non-governmental individuals) and QUANGOs (quasi-NGOs which are dependent in some way upon the state or industry).

NGO representatives will have to take a stance on this issue and find a solution to the legitimation problem, because the growing number of options for participation and having a say in decisions will also increase the frequency with which official representatives will want to know specifically who they are dealing with.

As much as people like to speak of the 'international NGO community', there is no such thing. The standpoints and interests of these many groups are simply too heterogeneous for them to form a community. The first step we need to take is to abandon this illusion.

NETWORKS

Continued co-operation is more effective when it is incorporated into a well-defined and transparent framework. Understanding this has led to the establishment of international networks which at present are generally geared to specific fields, such as biological diversity, climate or agriculture. Earlier efforts to set up an international network for the entire environmental and development sector failed to produce any lasting results.

In response to this problem, a convention was held in Manila in December 1995 to co-ordinate the existing national environment and development networks. A loosely organized international 'union' with this type of basis has the advantage of being able to build upon existing processes for reaching a national consensus and the democratic legitimation connected with these processes.

International networking will become considerably more important in the future. One of its presumed advantages is this: when it is possible to reach a national consensus on specific positions before a conference, the number of participants could be reduced through 'combined' representation. Past experience has shown, however, that efforts to reach a national – much less an international – consensus on a position generally leads to agreement on the well-known smallest common denominator. In other words, it is likely that positions will be watered down.

This cannot be the point of co-operation. We must make sure that positions remain intact and clearly defined.

An example of an established and effective mechanism through which NGOs have worked together since 1994 has operated around the UN Commission on Sustainable Development (CSD). The CSD NGO Steering Committee was formed by representatives of NGOs and other 'Major Groups' present at annual sessions of the CSD. Members of the Committee are elected by region, issue and Major Group. The system of regional representation helped to ensure that there were more Southern than Northern NGO representatives on the Committee. Two co-Chairs – one from the north and one from the south – were chosen by all the Northern and Southern-based NGOs present. These co-Chairs took on responsibility during CSD sessions to organize Steering Committee Meetings, and also to act as the focus for the Steering Committee in the intersessional period. It was agreed that they should be New York based so as to enable them to have regular meetings with officials from the UN as well as relevant UN Missions.

Key roles identified for the Steering Committee included sharing information with organizations around the world and making necessary arrangements to strengthen NGO input to official processes. The Committee has also overseen the work of caucuses meeting to focus on specific issues. This has allowed for selection of NGO spokespeople in key areas, which has in turn enhanced input to the intergovernmental process.

The Steering Committee had three overall working objectives when it was set up – to be transparent, accountable and democratic. Each year elections to the committee from the various caucuses take place and two co-Chairs are elected or endorsed by the whole body of NGOs. Since 1993 the Committee has grown as Major Groups, International Networks and issue based caucuses have joined. At present the Steering Committee membership includes organizations such as the International Confederation of Free Trade Unions, the International Chamber of Commerce, the International Council for Local Environmental Initiatives, Greenpeace International, the Women's Environment and Development Organization, Third World Network, the World Conservation Union (IUCN), the Habitat International Coalition and many others. Staff have been taken on in New York to prepare for the '97 UN General Assembly Special Session through the financial support of the Ford Foundation and the Dutch Government.

Because the Steering Committee's remit is not to formulate policy but to co-ordinate development of common NGO positions it has gained the support of a wide range of organizations, who appreciate that greater dialogue and co-operation is in the interest of all non-governmental participants in sessions of the CSD.

COMMUNICATION

Communications structures and opportunities are of vital importance to international conference activities. The use of new communications methods – at present, e-mail and the Internet in particular – will increase and become extremely important for the rapid exchange of opinions and information.

Communications structures can be combined and improved in two different ways. First, an information network can be put to effective use during periods between international meetings by deploying it for the direct transmission of information and material originating in, for example, UN offices in New York and Geneva. This requires 'feeders' who devote part of their working day to this task. Information that they feed into the system is generally transmitted via e-mail to regional nodes which have been established throughout the world and operate reliably. These nodes, in turn, use existing communications systems to forward the information they have received to interested parties in their region who do not have access to e-mail facilities. Of course, such a network would have to be set up to allow information to flow in both directions.

Secondly, during conferences – particularly when comments on individual points or texts under negotiation are needed – the opinions of experts who are not present but part of the network can be quickly obtained via e-mail or fax. A good example of productive co-operation is provided by the worldwide Climate Action Network, which has set up effective information structures for the climate discussion, along the lines described in the first point.

FUNDING

NGO participation in negotiations is often unbalanced. Whoever has the requisite personnel and financial resources participates. Everyone else stays at home – in particular, organizations from developing countries or from Eastern Europe, and local and regional grass-roots initiatives. But it is precisely these groups that could have the necessary expertise and knowledge of what is specifically needed in a certain area. Governments should therefore improve at least the regional balance between conference participants by setting up a fund which would provide the financial means that is necessary for participation.

DECENTRALIZED DISCUSSIONS

As mentioned above, UN bodies are including the civil society increasingly in their activities. NGOs have become an integral part of conference activities over the years. Today, they have options that clearly extend beyond their formally established rights.

In the meantime, it has become common practice for NGO representatives to make statements at conferences and committee meetings. Under-Secretary-General Nitin Desai forcefully confirmed this when he said:

> *Non-governmental organizations have been a part of the United Nations since 1945, and their involvement in the work of the UN and its family of organizations and programmes has grown tremendously over the years. The Economic and Social Council, in particular, as well as its functional commissions and other bodies, have benefited very significantly over the years as a result of the active participation of NGOs in consultative status who represent a valuable corps of representatives dedicated to the goals of the United Nations, as well as to the causes they espouse.*

To date, discussion processes have been delegated to the UN's central bodies. However, to make sure that participation is broader, discussions should be conducted to a greater degree on a decentralized basis as well, such as at regional conferences or through hearings.

CONTINUITY

A focus on continuity must supersede the current focus on summits. Large international conferences have the advantage of arousing a considerable amount of public interest, of mobilizing people and groups who are interested in the particular topic and of ensuring that work is completed by the deadline set by the opening of the conference. But they also leave behind an all-too familiar feeling of uneasiness, which can last for months in some cases.

Solutions to environmental and development problems are definitely not to be found in unrealistic discussions that lead to nothing. UN Secretary-General Boutros Boutros-Ghali emphasized in his statement to the 48th Annual DPI/NGO Conference in 1995 that:

> *Non-governmental organizations provide a framework for citizens to face practical challenges and situations. They provide a means for individuals and groups to mobilize for common purposes and common ideals. They make it possible for complex aspirations to take concrete form and to flourish. Following the international conferences in Rio, in Vienna, in Copenhagen, in Cairo and in Beijing, there is an important role for NGOs in making sure that the commitments reached at these conferences are honoured. You must watch. You must speak. You must insist. You must act.*

This is the reason why the NGOs' primary fields – independent, non-governmental work aimed at benefiting society and the environment, and impartial, critical analysis of existing obstacles and mistakes on the part of the respective government – are of vital importance. Lobbying will always be an ancillary activity, particularly if it is to be credible, because NGO competence evolves out of independent work. In this context, international conferences constitute only one element of lobbying.

9

Local Authorities and Agenda 21

Jeb Brugman

Local authorities around the world have accepted the challenge of Agenda 21, and they have done so with a recognition that their performance for sustainability is far from perfect. Facing up to this fact has meant working actively with local residents, community organizations, NGOs, businesses, unions, and other groups to begin the local process of sustainable development, covering Agenda 21 from Chapter 1 to Chapter 40. Furthermore, they have been fundamentally reforming the process of local governance along the way.[1]

As many as 14 chapters of Agenda 21 directly relate to areas of management where local authorities play a primary policy or service role. Chapter 28 endorses the proposal made by local authority associations during UNCED that local authorities should produce a 'local Agenda 21' in co-operation with local residents and institutions. The resulting efforts are changing the way that local authorities go about their day-to-day business and make their long-term investments.

This chapter will look at worldwide progress with the implementation of Chapter 28. Proposals and plans for expanding and strengthening the initiative in the coming years will then be presented.

THE STRUCTURE OF THE LOCAL AGENDA 21 INITIATIVE

The Local Agenda 21 Initiative, which was launched by the International Council for Local Environmental Initiatives (ICLEI) in 1991 on the eve of the Earth Summit, has engendered one of the most extensive follow-up programmes to Agenda 21. A recent survey made by the ICLEI and the Commission on Sustainable Development (CSD) reveals that, since 1992, more than 2000 local authorities in 51 countries have established Local Agenda 21 planning processes.

Such a breadth of response in a matter of a few years could only be achieved through the mobilization of existing capacities in the local government community – namely, through the independent contributions of national and international associations of local government.

A closer review of Local Agenda 21 activities demonstrates that the follow-up has been greatest where these associations have established national campaigns (*see* Box 1). As of June 1996, national campaigns were underway in nine countries. National municipal associations had established campaigns in Australia, Denmark, Finland, the Netherlands, Norway, Sweden and the United Kingdom. National governments had established campaigns in China and Japan. These campaigns correlate with more than 70 per cent of the estimated total of Local Agenda 21 planning efforts.

BOX 1: THE LOCAL AGENDA 21 INITIATIVE

In preparation for the 1992 Earth Summit, the International Council for Local Environmental Initiatives (ICLEI) convened three meetings in 1991 of their international municipal experts group to develop the concept for Local Agenda 21. This concept was presented to heads of selected national government delegations and UNCED secretariat staff in a meeting prior to the UNCED's third preparatory meeting. As a result, a specific recommendation to endorse the Local Agenda 21 concept was proposed in Agenda 21 and adopted at the Earth Summit in Rio de Janeiro.

During the period of June 1992 to June 1996, more than 1500 communities from 51 countries have undertaken Local Agenda 21 planning activities. Most of these communities have been mobilized to action by national associations of local government, through their national Local Agenda 21 campaigns. In addition, a few national governments, such as China and Japan, have established national campaigns. By June 1996, national campaigns were active in Australia, China, Denmark, Finland, Japan, the Netherlands, Norway, Sweden and the United Kingdom. These campaigns accounted for approximately 79 per cent of the total Local Agenda 21 activities. New campaigns were being established in Brazil, Colombia, Ireland, Germany, Greece, Peru, South Korea, and Turkey.

Even where national campaigns have not been established, individual local authorities, sometimes in concert with international assistance programmes, have initiated Local Agenda 21 planning in Austria, Belgium, Canada, Croatia, Ecuador, France, Hungary, India, Indonesia, Italy, Kenya, Latvia, Morocco, Mozambique, Nepal, New Zealand, Papua New Guinea, Peru, the Philippines, Poland, Portugal, Romania, Russia, Senegal, Slovenia, Slovak Republic, Spain, South Africa, Switzerland, Tanzania, Thailand, Uganda, Ukraine, United States and Zaire.

The ICLEI has established an international research collaboration with 14 local authorities to test and jointly evaluate the methods and tools being used in Local Agenda 21 planning. The preliminary results of this project have been published in *The Local Agenda 21 Planning Guide: An Introduction to Sustainable Development Planning* (ICLEI/IDRC/UNEP, 1996).

Source: ICLEI

As of the same date, new national campaigns were being established by national associations of local government – with or without central government involvement – in additional countries: Brazil, Colombia, Ireland, Germany, Greece, Peru, South Korea and Turkey.

National associations of local government have been able to achieve this because of their long-standing legitimacy with local government leaders and their institutional capacity to provide country-specific training and technical support. A typical national campaign is overseen by a multi-stakeholder steering committee that is staffed by the national association. The campaign manages a recruitment effort, prepares guidance materials, organizes a series of training workshops, operates special projects on activities such as indicators development, and liaises with the central government.

Parallel with and, in some cases, in service to these national campaigns, international associations of local government and UN agencies have established their own Local Agenda 21 programmes. In some instances, regional campaigns, such as the European Campaign for Sustainable Cities and Towns, have been established to support further national association involvement in Local Agenda 21. They also serve to co-ordinate regionwide experience-sharing among participating municipalities and associations.

The ICLEI has focused its efforts since 1992 on supporting the development of the Local Agenda 21 process in developing and transitional countries. The ICLEI's Local Agenda 21 Model Communities Programme[2] is a 14-city applied research effort to test a framework for sustainable development planning, suitable to developing country contexts. This programme, and a parallel project in Central and Eastern Europe, has produced Local Agenda 21 planning guides providing the technical basis for new initiatives in these contexts.

A variety of UN and donor agency programmes have also field-tested participatory action planning frameworks that support Local Agenda 21 implementation. Primary among these are the Sustainable Cities Programme of UNCHS, the Urban Environmental Guidelines Project of the German Agency for Technical Co-operation (GTZ), and the Rapid Urban Environmental Assessment Project of the Urban Management Programme. These projects have successfully supported the efforts of individual cities. To date, they have not been linked with the larger Local Agenda 21 movement.

LOCAL IMPACT

The true test of Local Agenda 21 is the impact of the process at the local level. Since 1992, the ICLEI has undertaken a detailed, comparative review of local practice with dozens of case studies.[3] Their primary conclusion is that the greatest impact of Local Agenda 21 during its first years has been to reform the process of governance at the local level so that the key elements of the sustainability concept can be factored into local planning and budgeting.

The application of the sustainable development concept in local communities challenges traditional structures and procedures of local government.[4] Sustainable development requires:

- Integrated consideration of social, economic and environmental conditions, and this has been inhibited traditionally by the organization of municipalities into separate, sometimes competing disciplinary departments.
- Public participation and partnership approaches to problem-solving, and such approaches have been inhibited traditionally by public–private sector role distinctions, lack of municipal recognition of 'informal' communities, administrative culture, and municipal labour contracts.

- The consistent implementation of long-term strategies which have been compromised traditionally by their lack of integration with the statutory development, land-use and other plans which govern near-term municipal behaviour.

In short, without institutional reform, Local Agenda 21 planning is an academic exercise. It can never change the key investment and policy decisions of local institutions.

In response to this challenge, most Local Agenda 21 efforts have:

- Set up a representative, multi-sectoral planning body or 'stakeholder forum' as the co-ordinating and policy group for developing and monitoring a long-term sustainable development action plan.
- Carried out some kind of assessment of existing local social, economic and environmental conditions.
- Implemented a consultation programme with community groups, NGOs, business, churches, professional groups and unions to identify proposals and priorities for action.
- Developed and implemented an action plan, often with specifically defined targets for achievement.
- Set up monitoring and reporting procedures which hold the local authority, business and households accountable to the action plan.

As the cases of Cajamarca, Peru (Box 2), Lancashire County, United Kingdom (Box 3), and Kanagawa Prefecture, Japan (Box 4) illustrate,

---

BOX 2: LOCAL AGENDA 21 IN CAJAMARCA, PERU

The provincial municipality of Cajamarca in Peru ranks among the poorest communities in the world. In 1993, the infant mortality rate was 82 per cent higher than the Peruvian national average, and 30 per cent higher than the average for the world's low income countries. The province's main river has been polluted by mining operations and untreated sewage. Farming on the steep Andean hillsides, overgrazing and the cutting of trees for fuel has resulted in severe soil erosion.

That same year, the mayor of Cajamarca initiated an extensive Local Agenda 21 planning effort for the province. This effort had two main components. The first was a dramatic decentralization of the provincial government so that local government decisions would reflect the needs of the province's many small and remote communities. Cajamarca City was divided into 12 neighbourhood councils and the surrounding countryside into 64 'minor populated centres' (MPCs), each with their own elected mayors and councils. The provincial council was reconstituted into a body with 48 mayors from the MPCs, 12 Cajamarca city mayors, 12 district mayors and the provincial mayor.

The second element of the initiative is the creation of a Provincial Sustainable Development Plan. An Inter-Institutional Consensus Building Committee was established with representation from the province's different jurisdictions, NGOs, private sector and key constituency groups. Six 'theme boards' were established under this committee to develop action proposals in the following areas: education, natural resources and agricultural production, production and employment, cultural heritage and tourism, urban environment, plus women's issues, the family and population.

These theme boards were charged with creating a strategic plan for their respective areas. Training workshops were held in the new local authorities to gather local input, and educational notebooks were prepared for the local mayors to use in discussing proposals and ideas with their constituents.

The plans prepared by the theme boards were integrated into a Provincial Sustainable Development Plan, which was submitted to the provincial council in August 1994. Having received approval, after a series of public education workshops about the plan, it was submitted for public approval through a citizens' referendum.

Source: The Provincial Municipality of Cajamarca and UNDP/CSD/ICLEI,
The Role of Local Authorities in Sustainable Development,
New York, April 1995

BOX 3: LOCAL AGENDA 21 IN LANCASHIRE COUNTY, UK

Lancashire County's Local Agenda 21 effort began in 1989 in an effort to bring key stakeholders together to develop shared solutions to coastal water pollution problems. Later, the initiative was expanded to include the full range of environmental and municipal service areas in the county.

The process began with the establishment of an environmental forum made up of 200 representatives from over 80 organizations, including national government departments, industries and utilities, local government, health agencies, public interest groups and universities. The first task of the forum was to collect and share information to complete the

the findings of the Green Audit, the forum was engaged in a process with a newly established County Environmental Policy Unit to create a Local Environmental Action Plan (LEAP).

The LEAP process involved four specialist working groups in the following areas:

- SWG1: Air, energy, transport and noise.
- SWG2: Water, waste, land and agriculture.
- SWG3: Wildlife, landscape, townscape and open space.
- SWG4: Education and public awareness.

Parallel to the county's external LEAP planning effort, a Better Environmental Practices Strategy (BEPS) committee was established from county departmental representatives, called environmental monitoring officers. The purpose of BEPS is to upgrade the local authorities' own environmental performance. Their mandate involved the establishment of an environmental management system for the county council, which involves periodic internal audits of council performance.

Lancashire's LEAP was approved by the council in 1993. It will be revised every five years following an updating of the county's Green Audit. Indicators are being developed to monitor county progress towards sustainability in the intervening period.

Source: Lancashire County Council and UNDP/CSD/ICLEI, *The Role of Local Authorities in Sustainable Development*, April 1995, New York.

Box 4: Local Agenda 21 in Kanagawa Prefecture, Japan

In 1993, Kanagawa Prefecture in Japan adopted a civic charter for global environmental protection called the Kanagawa Environment Declaration, as well as a local action plan called Agenda 21 Kanagawa. Agenda 21 Kanagawa was developed through an intensive process of dialogue that involved thousands of local residents and businesses, as well as the local authorities within Kanagawa.

Kanagawa Prefecture is the home of some eight million residents who live primarily in the Yokohama and Kawasaki metropolitan areas in the eastern part of the prefecture, along Tokyo Bay. With a gross domestic product equivalent to that of Sweden, Kanagawa is also one of the most highly industrialized regions of the world. Through its policies and actions, the prefecture and its local municipalities can have an impact on the global environment.

In the late 1980s and early 1990s they became aware that the focus of environmental concern had shifted away from end-of-the-pipe industrial pollution problems to the more complex and issues of consumer life-styles, the structure of urban space and the gradual loss of natural lands to urbanization. Furthermore, the impact of local activities on the global environment, as demonstrated by Kanagawa's contribution to the ozone depletion problem, played a part in this changing awareness.

Agenda 21 Kanagawa was formulated by a new Inter–departmental Liaison and Co–ordination Committee, made up of the heads of every department within the prefecture and chaired by the Vice Governor. A working level committee made up of section chiefs from each department was established to review detailed proposals. A secretariat within the Environment Department managed the public consultation and internal review processes.

Public input was provided through three sectoral 'conferences' or committees: one for citizens and non-governmental organizations, one for private enterprise, and one for local municipalities in Kanagawa. In addition, neighbourhood consultative meetings were organized and a direct mail package and questionnaire was sent to thousands of residents.

The final Agenda 21 Kanagawa is a detailed and comprehensive document. The 1994 budget for the 52 environmental protection projects implemented within the framework of the Agenda totalled US$149 million. Initiatives to date include:

- Building 100 'eco-housing' units which make use of rain water and recycled materials and are highly energy efficient.
- Setting up a prefecture-wide system to recover and destroy ozone-depleting CFCs. Subsidies are provided for the purchase of non-CFC equipment.
- Setting a target to reduce consumption of tropical timber in public projects by 70 per cent over a three-year period. The prefecture is also working with the local construction industry to reduce the widespread practice of using such timber for concrete mouldings.

In terms of management reforms, a new Kanagawa Council for Global Environmental Protection has been established to continue the interdepartmentalism initiated through the Local Agenda 21 development effort. Finally, in each prefectural section, an individual employee has been assigned to manage in-house environmental performance and to educate prefectural staff.

Source: Kanagawa Prefecture and UNDP/CSD/ICLEI, *The Role of Local Authorities in Sustainable Development*, April 1995, New York.

the implementation of such a Local Agenda 21 approach requires local authorities to decentralize governance, to reform their current departmental structures, and to change traditional operational procedures.

Most Local Agenda 21 efforts have started their planning activities by creating new organizational structures to implement planning. On the one hand, new stakeholder organizations are being created to co-ordinate community-wide involvement and partnership formation for sustainable development. On the other hand, municipalities are instituting internal reforms, such as the creation of interdepartmental planning units, or the establishment of neighbourhood or village-level government units.

These activities generally consume the first years of the Local Agenda 21 effort. Such institutional reforms may not produce immediately concrete improvements in development or environmental conditions, but they are changing the fundamental approaches and policy focus of hundreds of local authorities. As a result, these local authorities are becoming more open, participatory and dedicated agents of the sustainable development agenda.

QUALIFYING THE LOCAL AGENDA 21 SUCCESS STORY

The primary success of the Local Agenda 21 movement to date has been to build the prerequisite local institutional capacity for sustainable development in hundreds of communities and dozens of countries. This has been accomplished with surprisingly little external support from donor agencies and central governments. Progress has probably been fuelled in many countries by the recent introduction of decentralization policies. But it could be argued that Local Agenda 21 is doing more to facilitate the successful implementation of these policies than the policies are supporting the Local Agenda 21 effort.

A smaller number of communities – primarily those that started work before 1992 – have actually completed their Local Agenda 21 plans and begun full-scale implementation. Nevertheless, the potential impact of these plans can be observed in the dozens of cases where work is underway.

The case of Kanagawa Prefecture, Japan, where 52 projects are being implemented with a US$149 million budget, gives some indication of what is possible in rich countries. In developing countries, implementation tends to begin by addressing a few priority problems. For instance, the Local Agenda 21 effort in Quito, Ecuador, is focusing on the stabilization and protection of the many ravines in that city's low income South Zone. The Local Agenda 21 effort in Santos, Brazil, is establishing community solid waste management schemes in selected low income neighbourhoods.

Whether in rich or poor communities, the steady implementation of a comprehensive plan to change the fundamental development trends of a community will face numerous new challenges. In the first instance, these plans will need to be supported by national government policies and programmes, and few existing Local Agenda 21 efforts are linked to national-level strategies.

There are exceptions. In South Africa, for instance, Local Agenda 21 has been adapted as a mechanism to implement that country's Reconstruction and Development Plan. In Colombia, Local Agenda 21 is being linked to a major World Bank-funded, Ministry of the Environment project to improve the environmental management capacities of local government.

Implementation of the action plans that have been prepared by stakeholder groups will also require the integration of these plans into the separate, statutory planning processes of local government. This will require further local government reform. For example, as a first step, in Hamilton–Wentworth, Canada, departmental staff are now required to demonstrate the consistency of any new proposed action with the community's 'Vision 2020' action plan. But further efforts will need to be made to amend the existing land-use, transportation and capital-budgeting plans of the municipality so that they are consistent with the objectives of Vision 2020. Actual performance in implementing the plans, therefore, cannot be evaluated.

Another area of uncertainty is the relationship between Local Agenda 21 action plans and the global objectives of Agenda 21. Of necessity, a Local Agenda 21 must address established local priorities. While Local Agenda 21s in rich countries tend to include actions on issues such as climate change and the protection of global biodiversity, these issues may not receive much attention in communities of the developing world. This being said, the Local Agenda 21 process does at least educate local residents about the linkages between local and global problems.

As communities now begin to focus their energies on the implementation of Local Agenda 21 action plans, local government associations will need to invest greater resources to support the establishment of the Local Agenda 21 process in more developing countries. The experiences from existing Local Agenda 21 efforts and national campaigns appear to be applicable in a diversity of settings. Transferring and adapting these experiences in new countries should not be compromised by the preoccupation with implementation.

FUTURE PROSPECTS

The Local Agenda 21 movement launched in Rio in 1992 is entering its second phase. As highlighted above, this phase of development will be characterized by the implementation of action plans on the one hand, and by the expansion of Local Agenda 21 activities into new countries on the other. For this purpose, the local government community will need to organize new kinds of support.

For its part, the ICLEI is working to establish regional Local Agenda 21 campaigns in Africa, Asia and Latin America. These regional campaigns will work with national associations of local government and other country-level partners to establish strong national Local Agenda 21 programmes. At the same time, work will be undertaken with selected cities to prepare country-specific guidelines for Local Agenda 21 planning.

Meanwhile, existing national campaigns, in partnership with their international associations such as the ICLEI, have begun to set up procedures for measuring the impacts and evaluating the overall performance of the Local Agenda 21 effort. Most of these activities are taking place in developed countries, but the tools being tested, such as indicators and auditing schemes, will undoubtedly be of future value to the campaigns in developing countries when they reach the implementation stage.

In conclusion, the local government community remains committed to Local Agenda 21. Having renewed the United Nations' commitment to the Local Agenda 21 process at the UN Conference on Human Settlements, local government associations are preparing for the expansion of the Local Agenda 21 movement. The growing centrality of this movement in the local government world has engendered increasing support from bi- and multilateral development agencies.

The continued success of Local Agenda 21 will mean that new resources will have to be deployed in keeping with the principles of

Local Agenda 21 itself. In other words, it must retain the partnership with the national, regional and international associations of local government that initiated Local Agenda 21 and that have made it such a success for the United Nations and, for a growing number, the cities and towns around the world.

NOTES

1. For a review of local government responses to all chapters of Agenda 21, *see* Brugmann, J (1996), 'Local Authorities and Agenda 21' in *Human Settlements: People Making a Difference*, San José, Costa Rica, Earth Council, ICLEI *et al*, pp 11–17. Some paragraphs of this article are excerpted from this report.
2. This programme is supported by the International Development Research Centre (IDRC), the UN Development Programme (UNDP), the Dutch Ministry of Foreign Affairs, the US Agency for International Development, and the New Zealand Ministry of Foreign Affairs and Trade.
3. For example, see ICLEI (1996), *The Local Agenda 21 Planning Guide: An Introduction to Sustainable Development Planning*, Toronto, ICLEI/IDRC/ UNEP and ICLEI/UNCSD/UNCHS (1995), *The Role of Local Authorities in Sustainable Development: 14 Cases on the Local Agenda 21 Process*, UN Department for Policy Co-ordination and Sustainable Development, New York.
4. For a more detailed consideration of this topic, *see* Brugmann, J (1994) 'Who Can Deliver Sustainability? Municipal Reform and the Sustainable Development Mandate' in *Third World Planning Review*, Vol 16, No 2, pp 129–146.

10

The Business Charter for Sustainable Development

Björn Stigson

This chapter will focus on the work of the World Business Council for Sustainable Development (WBCSD) and how the issue of sustainable development is addressed, the progress made since Rio and opinions of the UNCSD process. A view of industry will be given from the WBCSD's perspective, but the organization does not represent all of industry, only its members. Today, the WBCSD is in a transitional phase between an earlier long era where the debate on environmental issues had been dominated by awareness creation by the green NGOs. They have done a very good job and have put industry in a defensive position, where industry has had to respond to the agenda set by other parts of society. Now society is more aware that we are entering a new phase, a phase of solution seeking. Solutions require more than awareness: they require knowledge, access to technologies and leadership. All these elements can be found within industry, and solutions therefore require the participation of industry.

WHAT IS THE WBCSD?

The World Business Council for Sustainable Development is a coalition of 125 leading international companies. Its mission is stated in its Articles of Association and contains certain key words:

- To provide business leadership.
- A catalyst for change towards sustainable development.

- To promote eco-efficiency.
- Environmental and resources management.

The history of the WBCSD goes back to 1 January 1995 when the World International Conference on Environmental Management (WICEM) and the Business Council on Sustainable Development (BCSD) merged to create the present organization. The BCSD's history goes back to 1990 and the preparation for the Rio Summit. The WICE was founded by the International Chamber of Commerce (ICC) in 1993 to respond to the conventions emanating from Rio. The reason for the merger was to create one strong business voice on the issue of business and sustainable development.

OBJECTIVES

The objectives of the WBCSD can be defined by four key points:

- Leadership.
- Policy development.
- Best practice.
- Global outreach.

These will be outlined below.

Leadership

The focus of the WBCSD is on international and cross-sectoral issues and this is also evident in the make-up of the organization's membership. Its members live in 35 countries, including OECD countries, developing countries and countries in transition. The organization spans the different sectors of industry and business.

Besides the members in the World Business Council, it has also a network of national and regional BCSDs in developing countries and countries in transition. In these organizations, there are approximately 700 leading local businessmen as members. These national BCSDs are independent and self–financed, working under the World Business Council umbrella. They have their own individual work programmes.

The work in the World Business Council is led by its members, two of whom lead each working group, which also includes representatives from other interested members. The result of its work programme is spread via participation in conferences, through its communications programme, and through education and training. The WBCSD is not a lobbying organization, rather it acts as an advocate for business and speaks on behalf of businesses on the different issues surrounding sustainable development.

Policy Development

In its policy development work, the World Business Council focuses on sustainable development subsystems and the framework conditions for business to contribute to sustainable development. It actively seeks partnerships and co-operation with other organizations that share its views and objectives.

Best Practice

The WBCSD publicizes case studies of best practice from its members and other companies. It encourages its members to inform the council about their achievements. It supports the ICC Charter as a general guideline for environmental performance in companies.

Global Outreach

The network of national and regional BCSDs in developing countries and countries in transition is a very important element of the WBCSD's structure and adds to its credibility.

SUSTAINABLE DEVELOPMENT FROM THE PERSPECTIVE OF INDUSTRY

Sustainable development from an industry perspective is built on three pillars: economic growth, ecological balance and social progress. Industry's contribution to sustainable development comes through eco-efficient leadership. This contribution can be more or less effective, depending upon the framework conditions in operation. There is also the important element of uncertainty with regard to sustainable development.

SUSTAINABLE DEVELOPMENT

Sustainable development is development and not a stable state. The World Business Council also recognizes that it is not the same for everyone. There are big differences between countries, and between global and local issues. It is very difficult to define with any certainty how much development the planet can sustain. It is also difficult to quantify sustainability in financial terms. In its cost calculations and investment calculations, business uses a discount factor for future income, and costs to reflect the time value of money and the risks in the future. Assuming a capital cost of 10 per cent, plus a risk factor of 5 per cent, all effects more than six to seven years in the future have zero value today in financial calculations, unless what is foreseen to happen in six to seven years' time is of infinite proportions. An important issue for society, therefore, is who will pay today for the future long-term uncertainty? Industry's role in society is to make a return on capital and it cannot be expected to invest with zero expected return.

In its work programme the WBCSD is trying to define sustainable subsystems. Of special interest is the Sustainable Paper Cycle project which is unique because it is the first time that such an extensive study has been carried out. It looks at all aspects of the cycle from growing the fibre to the final product and its recycling. As this subject is very sensitive and highly emotive, the council realized that whatever the conclusions it came to as an industry, they would be highly criticized by other parts of society. Therefore it contracted the International Institute for Environment and Development (IIED) in London to do the research and to present an independent report. The project has cost US$1.5 million and the cost has been met by its members and other organizations.

The IIED study will be finished at the end of 1996 and the output will be a research report and a short booklet. The input from the Council's side has been through an advisory group to the IIED consisting of the sponsors of the project. There is also an advisory group of eminent persons with special knowledge on the subject. It has also included extensive discussions with NGOs and other parts of society.

ECO-EFFICIENT LEADERSHIP

'Eco-efficient leadership' is the business contribution to sustainable development. This term has two elements: the first is eco-efficiency which is about simultaneously improving environmental and financial performance; the second is about leadership, having visions, being proactive, transforming organizations and people. In everyday speech, eco-efficient leadership is how to do more with less, bring more value to your customers and come out looking great.

A very important element of the contribution by industry to sustainable development comes from innovation, and technical innovation especially. Many parts of society underestimate the enormous potential for technical development in the future. It is not a question of a few percentage points of improvement in resource use or energy efficiency; rather, substantial improvements can be made – possibly as much as factor 4 or factor 10. It is not possible to judge whether these numbers are realistic today, but the potential for improvement is very substantial.

It is imperative that industry demonstrates how much technology contributes to sustainable development and the WBCSD plans to publicize these gains.

It is important that life-cycle analysis is built into product development work and is not added at the end as an issue of recycling. Progressive companies nowadays have very elaborate computer systems to calculate environmental land units (ELUs) of ongoing research and development projects.

The WBCSD has three working groups that have been addressing this issue: one is studying eco-efficiency, another is making an assessment of the environment, (a report on the subject will be released soon), and the third is concentrating on Central and Eastern Europe. A very extensive training programme in Russia, which will start at the beginning of next year, is being prepared (1996–99). Based in St Petersburg, 600 Russian managers will be trained by the WBCSD over a three year period. The programme is a combination of theory and education, with internships in its member companies in the West. Each participant will be provided with a mentor, a manager from member companies, for a period of one year. In total, this project has a budget of US$ 10 million, of which half is provided by the Nordic governments and half comes from the in-kind contribution from members in the form of teachers, mentors and internships.

Framework Conditions

The contribution from industry to sustainable development through eco-efficient leadership can be more or less effective, depending on the framework conditions under which industry operates. This deals with government policies and regulations. These should be enabling, not hindering, although this is not always the case. It is recommended that the frameworks are established in consultation with businesses, with particular attention being paid to the consequences for the future. Framework conditions include elements such as open and competitive markets, internalizing environmental cost, the role of financial markets, etc. Some of these are discussed below.

Financial Markets

Financial markets represent an important driving force for sustainable development and they will probably be the most important driving force in the future. Requirements from lending institutions for higher interest rates on higher risks of an environmental nature is putting pressure on environmental performance.

The insurance industry has experienced the negative consequences of environmental exposure to a very high degree. There will be difficulties in insuring certain environmental risks and this will be reflected in higher insurance premiums.

A third player of importance in the financial markets will be the auditors who sign the annual reports confirming that the balance sheet is clean. In future, they will need to take into account environmental considerations and they will come under pressure to do so. At the start of 1997, *Financing Change* will be published, discussing this subject as it relates to 'Changing Course'. It is written by Stephan Schmidheiny and Federico Zorraquin, with a Foreword by Jim Wolfensohn, now head of the World Bank, who was previously a member of the Business Council for Sustainable Development.

Joint Implementation

Joint implementation, also known as actions jointly implemented, carries certain values. Whatever the term used, the issue is the same –

namely, how can we get more value, in the form of improvement in the environment from the resources that we have to invest? In business, the WBCSD strongly believes that it makes a great deal of sense to invest in improving industrial processes in developing countries and countries in transition. For the same investment, greater improvements are gained in these countries compared to developed countries.

Percy Barnevik, ABB, has assessed that 80 per cent of future environmental problems are in the developing countries, 15 per cent in Eastern Europe and 5 per cent in OECD countries. His view was that ironically industry spends 95 per cent of its time on OECD problems rather than on the problems in developing countries and countries in transition.

The term 'joint implementation' does not refer only to the planting of forests; rather, it is concerned with improving energy generation, energy transmission and industrial processes in the high energy-consuming industries, such as metals, pulp, paper, etc.

In 1996 the WBCSD started a project called ABACK – International Business Action on Climate Change – which will focus on matchmaking between companies to transfer environmentally friendly technologies to developing countries as part of a first pilot phase.

At this point two points need to be stressed. First, there are *no* clean technologies but there are certainly technologies that are more environmentally friendly than others. Secondly, the speed of technology dissemination is a key issue to improve environmental performance. For example, power generation plants are on average 30–40 years old, with an efficiency rate of 26–28 per cent. If these were replaced with new plants, then the efficiency would increase to 56–58 per cent. If they were combined with district heating, efficiency could be increased to 95 per cent – a considerable improvement!

ENVIRONMENTAL SHAREHOLDER VALUE

In 1996, the WBCSD began a new project which will study environmental shareholder value. It will analyse whether the Stock Market correctly differentiates between good and bad environmental performers in its valuation of companies. The hypothesis is that it does not make this differentiation and that there is a need to educate financial analysts on the matter.

ECOLOGICAL BALANCE

The WBCSD has focused on climate and energy issues to which the organization has much to contribute. Other important issues have not yet been addressed but there is an obvious need, probably in partnership, with other organizations to look at what industry can contribute.

Biodiversity is one area the WBCSD has been discussing in a joint project with the IUCN. Another issue is access to water. Industry is a small user of water compared to some other sectors of society. Industry accounts for about 10 per cent of the world's water consumption compared with 70 per cent for agriculture. The problem with the use of water by industry is that often it draws water from the same sources which supply the public. A potential conflict could arise in the future between the public and industry with regard to access to water.

INDUSTRY ACTIONS BEFORE AND AFTER RIO

I have had the privilege to be associated with industry and environmental issues since the early 1980s. In 1982 I became Chief Executive for the Flakt Group – a Swedish-based multinational that was the world's biggest environmental control technology supplier. However, at that time there was little interest in environmental issues and we described ourselves as an air technology group. In 1985 we became 'Air Technology for Quality of Life' and in 1988–89 we changed our name to 'Environmental Technology for Quality of Life'. Although our products and systems were still the same, the environment had become an important issue.

In 1990 I took part in the preparations for Rio in Bergen where we saw the first real industrial environmental meeting. In 1992, WICEM II in Rotterdam was a further step. Since Rio, the actions implemented in industry to improve environmental performance have been substantial. Does the rest of society realize the extent to which industry has changed and is changing to become more environmentally efficient and thereby also more competitive?

I wish that all parts of society were changing as quickly and as much as industry. The WBCSD intends to document how industry has responded to the Rio challenges and will have a report ready in 1997 for the five year anniversary of Rio.

THE PERCEPTION OF NATURE

Another element of the post-Rio world is the changed perception of nature and industry. Historically, the view was that if industry was to gain, nature had to lose and vice versa. Today, the WBCDS realizes that this picture is not true. There is not a conflict between industry and nature. It is possible to improve both the financial performance of industry and the ecological performance in the form of resource efficiency – known as eco-efficiency. The council no longer sees nature as an endless resource. Instead, it sees the necessity of high environmental standards as a condition for staying in business, whether it is clean or closed. As mentioned earlier, the Council sees that the financial community is also starting to be an important driving force. Overall, this leads to a perception of environmental performance as an opportunity, as a source of competitive advantage.

DRIVING FORCES FOR ENVIRONMENTAL PERFORMANCE

The driving forces for environmental performance have changed dramatically in recent years. Historically, it was dominated by legislation, but today the picture is more complex.

UNCSD

How does this relate to the UNCSD? In the process leading up to Rio, the organizers of the Rio summit saw the necessity for increased involvement by industry and took the initiative to create the Business Council for Sustainable Development. The need for private sector involvement in responding to the challenges from Rio is even greater than the need was in the process leading to Rio. However, the involvement asked for in the UNCSD proceedings from the private sector is limited and is not in proportion to the challenges we are facing in finding solutions to the environmental problems.

Edward Woolard, Chairman of DuPont, wrote the following in an open letter to the Harvard Business Review in reply to a comment on an article by Michael Porter: 'The green economies and lifestyles of the 21st century may be conceptualized by environmental thinkers, but they can only be actualized by industrial corporations.'

First, there is too little private sector involvement and it is not being asked for by the UNCSD. Secondly, the structure of the UNCSD needs reconsideration. The chairmanship of the UNCSD is a one-year mandate. The chairman resigns at the beginning of the annual UNCSD meeting which he has helped to prepare. It is a very strange set-up because a process like the UNCSD needs a strong chairman who represents important stakeholders – the national governments – and who takes a lead role in setting the agenda for the UNCSD. The one-year term for the chairman is too short for this purpose. The chairman should have the chance to stay for a minimum of two years and should lead two annual conferences during that period.

The UNCSD process is a complicated and difficult one. However, for better or worse, it is a process that we have today within the international community to respond to the Rio challenges. We are willing from our side to bring our resources and competence to support the UNCSD process in whatever way possible. We hope, though, to be given more possibilities to do so in the future. We believe that we can contribute to many of the issues of sustainable development.

The major leadership challenge for industry today is to adopt eco-efficiency as the business norm for the 21st century. It is a global challenge – as pertinent for companies in the US, Europe and Japan, as it is for those in other regions of the world, especially the fast-growing economies of Asia and Latin America, and in the emerging economies of Central and Eastern Europe.

Eco-efficiency certainly begins in the workplace, spurred by a top-management vision to create a corporate culture for eco-efficiency, and followed by an action programme to inculcate that culture throughout the corporation. But while it is up to business to make the change on the ground, other players need to play their parts in accelerating the process.

The fact that the sustainable development agenda is now about delivering solutions, not about identifying the problems, throws the spotlight more closely on the non-governmental organizations and their role. The time is right for NGOs to get involved in co-operating with industry in implementing practical solutions. Fortunately, this is beginning to happen.

The general public cannot exempt itself from the reform process, either. All of us – producers and consumers – share a responsibility for the world's environmental problems and for solving them. Political leaders worldwide have the means to promote and accelerate the process of change.

The reality is that the success of the post-Rio agenda is as critical to industry's own future as to society's. The question now is to know how can business capitalize on its progress and move forward in its pursuit of eco-efficiency and towards a sustainable future?

Encouragement is the key. Leading businesses need to advocate the benefits to industry of such action, and governments need to provide the policy frameworks to ensure that markets reward eco-efficiency. This is, of course, much easier to say than to do. Action is even more difficult because of the confusion about the exact role of business in sustainable development. What can or can not business do?

There is considerable debate about the relative roles of business and government in society. In those regions where government is less mature, there are often demands for business to take on the traditional jobs of government and to provide many of the social services. In some parts of the world where government is strong, there are demands for it to relinquish control in countries where business is thought to do things better.

The discussion about the respective roles of government and business – where they meet and where they diverge – is set to run for some time. But what is clear is that business cannot move beyond society. Business is a part of society and evolves within it.

Clearly, business can contribute to the process of change in a way that will benefit both itself and the whole of society, and WBCSD member companies would like to be part of this change towards sustainable development.

MAJOR GROUPS

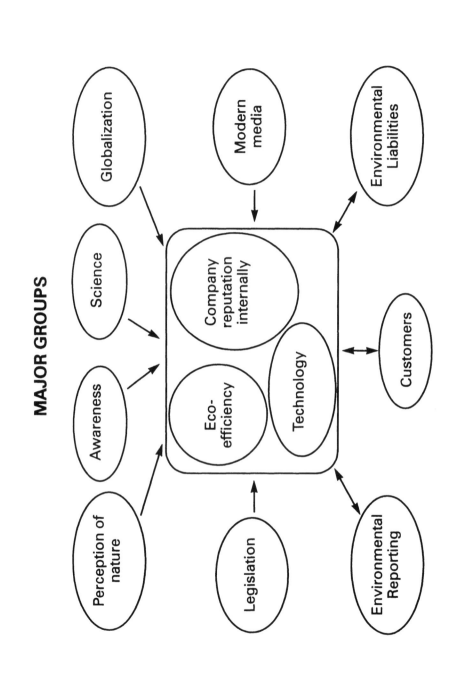

11

Trade Union Action: A Paradigm for Sustainable Development

Winston Gereluk and Lucien Royer

A trade union evaluation of the Commission on Sustainable Development (CSD) is possible only in the context of an understanding of the role that workers have played in promoting sustainable development. In particular, widespread use of the terminology related to 'sustainability' since the Earth Summit has created the impression that the concepts and the promotion of sustainable development are recent phenomena.

In fact, the movement for sustainable development can be traced back beyond the Industrial Revolution, when workers first engaged in action to mitigate the worst effects of unsustainable production. They did so by forming trade unions, the first manifestations of workplace democracy and probably the first organized groupings in history to promote sustainable development – a role they proudly carry forward today.

Unions have therefore taken up the challenge of Agenda 21 as part-and-parcel of their struggle for safe working conditions. Environmental protection is seen as an extension of the rights they had already won for occupational health and safety. In the process, they have embraced local initiatives that have provided new dimensions to health and safety, and have raised their profile in the community. They have also been taking part in partnerships with employers that have pushed back the traditional boundaries of industrial relations.

125

WORKPLACE HEALTH AND SAFETY

It has now been over 200 years since workers in Britain formed the first recognized trade union, overcoming centuries of brutal and uncompromising repression of the right of workers to organize themselves over fundamental issues.

The final impetus for this historical breakthrough was provided by unprecedented increases in productivity that marked the Industrial Revolution – a dramatic restructuring of industrial, economic and social relations that resulted in inhuman working conditions, unsafe plants and the emergence of waged employees as cogs in a dirty, polluting industrial machine that was spreading throughout the world.

The shadow thrown by this industrial transformation is now recognized as unsustainable development. Trade unions may have been the first so-called non-governmental organizations in history to promote sustainable development. This is why trade unions have taken Rio 1992 and the CSD so seriously.

Throughout history, production has always entailed risk to the health and safety of direct producers – be they slaves, serfs, independent producers or waged employees. Early Greek and Roman societies understood the dangerous and debilitating nature of work in their mines and foundries, so they reserved it for their slaves. Pliny, the ancient Roman historian, referred to the use of transparent bladder skin as respirators against the inhalation of dust, in order to extend the productive working life of the slaves. They wove asbestos into cloth, providing one of the first recorded illustrations of the 'loss-control' slogan that safety pays.[1]

In the 16th century, the German physician Georgius Agricola identified miners and smelters of gold and silver as particularly likely to die an early death from a work-related disease identified only as 'consumption'. During the 17th and early 18th centuries, the Italian physician Bernardo Ramazzini provided an inventory of the diseases that were peculiar to various trades in his famous book, *Diseases of Workers*. He was the first to insist that doctors take a patient's occupation into account when recording their medical history.

The relationship between unhealthy, unsustainable workplaces and their surrounding environment was noted early in 1832, by C. Turner Thackrah, a physician in the English industrial borough of Leeds. He conducted one of the first sophisticated comparative studies of disease as it related to industrial activity. His disturbing investigation uncovered a much higher incidence of death in the manufacturing centre, due to 'injurious agents [which] might be immediately removed or diminished', noting that 'evils are suffered to exist, even where the means of correction are known and easily applied'.[2]

Added to the scourge of industrial pollution were mechanization, 'continuous flow operations', and 'machine pacing'. By extending the length of the working day and intensifying the work process, employers increased the pace of work and reduced skill requirements. One result, repetitive strain injury (RSI), is today one of the fastest growing occupational illnesses.

Workers in offices and the service industry alike suffer the effects of work on electronic and electrical assembly lines, which have also contributed to stress and intensified monitoring of workers. This history is important because it shows that the role of the CSD stems from a long struggle to confront unsustainable practices and that workers are central to its outcome.[3]

In short, workers have been the first victims of unsustainable practices, as evidenced in over 120 million work-related incidents around the world, which kill more than 220,000 workers – over 500 per day – and injure many times that number. Between 65 and 160 million workers also contract work-related diseases. The sickness, pain and personal deterioration which starts at the workplace is soon manifested in the family, the community and – most persistently – in the eco-system.

Shocking as these body counts are, they cannot obscure the likelihood that the majority of cases are never reported. Studies by the Bureau of Labour Statistics in the United States indicate that for every disabling injury which is reported, another ten are not. This finding is consistent with other countries.

Problems associated with workplace pollution are even more extensive, as evidenced by cancer statistics alone. The National Cancer Institute in the United States has estimated that at least 20–40 per cent of all cancer is related to the workplace. The 40,000 cancer deaths every year in Canada, for instance, would mean that at least 10,000 cases are work-related – which figure alone would dwarf official compensation statistics.

PREVAILING THEORIES AND OBJECTIVES

The risks faced by workers are related to the industrial relations of the workplace and the way that decisions are made. The objective of trade union movement in occupational health and safety, for example, is to involve all aspects of the worker's life, just as the modern concept of sustainable development extends to every sector of economic and social life.

This view is consistent with the definition of occupational health provided in 1963 by a joint committee of the International Labour Organization and the World Health Organization:

> *The promotion and maintenance of the highest degree of physical, mental and social well-being of workers in all occupations, the prevention among workers of departures from health caused by their working conditions, the protection of workers in their employment from risks resulting from factors adverse to health; the placing and maintenance of the worker in an occupational environment adapted to his physiological and psychological condition.*[4]

Prevailing law, custom and policy in most countries poses an opposing agenda, however – one that is based on a 'contractarian' framework which dictates that work-related risks are freely contracted by workers and remain, in one way or another, under their control. This 'market-based' explanation is now being used to respond to the concerns over the environment.[5]

Workers and citizens faced with harsh economic circumstances quickly recognize the fallacy behind mainstream doctrines like 'voluntary choice' or 'voluntary assumption of risk'.[6]

Unions have also pointed out the limitations of a cost-benefit response, which clearly ignores the inequality of power in the employment relationship. They have also taken issue with the proposition that health and safety resources should be allocated at work according to the willingness to pay for hazard reduction.

In most societies, the majority of 'damage costs' related to illness and injury have been either socialized or imposed directly on workers, their families and communities. Individual employers seldom have to absorb the costs associated with the losses they have caused.

The doctrine of 'free contracting' has also affected risk assessment, producing higher allowable levels of exposure to specific hazards in the workplace than for the general public. It presumes that control measures are triggered when workers demand risk premiums or some other form of compensation in return for exposure to hazardous work environments.[7] Environmental cost-accounting, as a market-based policy instrument, tends to rest on much the same assumptions.

Trade unions have also learned that, even where standards are high and regulatory tools adequate, enforcement tends to be inadequate. This is because there are typically too few enforcement officials, and even these are given mandates which preclude an aggressive stance towards enforcement, favouring conciliation-oriented approaches over prosecution.[8]

Finally, trade unions have had to counter challenges from the business and legal community – supported by scientists and physicians – who contest claims that a hazard exists at all, in absence of proof 'beyond a reasonable doubt'. Too often, the absence of strong, conclusive, positive evidence is used to justify inaction. This resistance is based on the realization that conversion to healthy, safe and environmentally friendly production will be costly, primarily because most workplaces and process have been designed without these in mind. This is why employer control measures so often concentrate on individual workers and work practices, rather than on structural factors, making workers more 'safety conscious', and even leading to medical screening, genetic testing and 'medical removal' of workers.

THE MEANING OF WORKPLACE DEMOCRACY

In many countries, unions have succeeded in eradicating the most blatant economic inequities of 19th and early 20th century *laissez-faire* capitalism. Their true achievement can best be measured against the places where there are now no inequities compared to where the worst excesses are still evident.

But organizing trade unions has never been a simple affair. From the earliest days, there has been persistent resistance from employers, revealing the structural antagonism of interest that is inherent in the employment contract. The state has usually added its own hurdles. In fact, many jurisdictions still maintain legal prohibitions against free association for wage labour.

Unions have proved to be the only reliable vehicle through which workers have been able to win a measure of democracy in the day-to-day operation of the workplace, as they transform a mythical 'freedom to contract' under the individual employment contract, into a more meaningful 'collective freedom to contract'.

Safer workplaces and sustainable development are a direct result, as workers who have won the right to engage in this joint rule-making have often moved on to become leaders in the movement for 'public participation', as contemplated by Agenda 21.

Unfortunately, despite encouraging pronouncements made by delegations to the CSD, 'public participation' still remains a distant dream for most of the world's workplaces and communities. In fact, workers have paid a terrible price for promoting it: at least 378 workers were murdered in 1995, 1,900 were injured and over 68,470 others were improperly dismissed because of their activities.

Many of these workers were on front line battles to fight unsustainable practices. For example, between 1964 and 1992, 1,681 rural workers in Brazil were murdered over land-use disputes – many in the Amazon where they were trying to stop destructive logging practices.

Concrete steps to strengthen workers' rights to meaningful association are a key part of the effort to enhance their ability to participate in the long journey toward sustainability. Two cases best illustrate this. It is likely that neither the 1985 Bophal disaster in India nor the more recent 1993 Kader toy factory fire in Thailand would have occurred if workers had been allowed to participate meaningfully in decision-making. The failure to guarantee the right to participate through unions continues to be a major bar to progress towards sustainable development.

PRODUCTION, CONSUMPTION AND EMPLOYMENT

Unions have learned that policies for sustainable development go hand-in-hand with policies for sustainable employment, and that there is no inherent trade-off or conflict between jobs and the environment. In fact, they have found that jobs are at risk where industry fails to anticipate and adapt to change, or where governments fail to integrate environmental with labour market strategies.

Immediate adjustment problems do arise, but the net effect of sustainable development on employment, working conditions and the quality of work can only be positive, provided it is properly co-ordinated and directed.

Unions are particularly well suited to address these short-term impacts because they can point to growing evidence that current production patterns are producing 'jobless growth', job insecurity and environmental damage. They have engaged in strategies to show how sustainable patterns can achieve the triple dividend of employment growth, environmental protection and lasting wealth creation.

For them, Agenda 21 reflects the historical quest of workers around the world for full employment – sustainable livelihoods in safe, clean and healthy environments, at work and beyond, as opposed to the chronic unemployment and underemployment that contribute directly to negative environmental effects.

Unfortunately, even though the CSD has recognized that poverty has to be eradicated before it can achieve its goals, it has fallen short of recognizing 'employment' as a key economic indicator for determining progress towards sustainable development. Reference to 'employment' is usually appended as an afterthought, not as a central part of a strategic implementation plan.

MAKING DECISIONS AT THE POINT OF PRODUCTION

As they exist at the point of production, workplaces are properly becoming the focus of Agenda 21 strategies. Cleaning up production practices, eliminating waste, changing consumption habits and developing positive patterns of development at the global level has to involve a fundamental change to workplace activities and attitudes. So much of our consumption and production occurs in the world's workplaces and are determined by the employment relationships which arise there.

An integrated and co-ordinated partnership approach to environmental protection is called for. It must build on the joint knowledge and expertise of management and trade unions to develop guidelines and best practice about how to integrate health and safety with environmental management, and other risk management systems and practices.

Unless this happens, the ability of countries and sectors to meet targets successfully will be severely limited, as Bill Jordan, General Secretary of the International Confederation on Free Trade Unions (ICFTU), warned in his address to a conference organized in late 1995 by the ICFTU and the DGB in Germany. He noted that a major reason why industrialized countries have failed to meet targets for reducing gas emissions is the 'wide gap between the people who set these targets and the people who work at the source of the emissions'.[9]

Unfortunately, politics of avoidance have submerged workplace issues in the CSD debate. References to 'workplaces' are typically excluded from adopted texts, in favour of references to production processes or consumer behaviour, as though the experience of workers and the behaviour of consumers were separate issues.

Analysis of about 1000 pages of text adopted in the last three years shows that the following constructions appear no more than 30 times in total, and then usually only as side notes: workplaces and conditions of work, workers and trade unions, employment and employment programmes, health and safety as linked to the environment.

Workplace action leads inevitably to social change, because changing sustainable patterns of production and consumption will require the active participation of the public and closer co-operation between industry, trade unions, NGOs and government. In many countries, trade unions provide the only realistic route to participation in industrial and government policy-making. With their experience in health and safety and collective bargaining, and because their members actually perform the work, unions have the expertise to engage others in necessary strategies.

Environmental protection has proved to be a rallying point for new alliances and coalitions that trade unions can rely upon to stop the erosion of health, safety and environmental protection because of restructuring and globalization. Union environmental initiatives have enhanced the potential of trade unions to organize, to gain the support of other groups and to play an important role in the lives of their communities.

THE MEANING OF PARTNERSHIPS

Production at the workplace depends on a pact between workers – or their representatives, and the employer. Employers do not contract productive labour; they contract only the 'capacity to work'. The process whereby this is transformed into productive labour involves an 'agreement to work' and is the focus of human resource management.

Unions and worker groupings have proved to be invaluable vehicles for achieving these agreements. But cleaner production and sustainable development at the workplace will bear fruit only if unions are given a place in the decision-making process. This is why trade unions have taken seriously the current debate within the CSD about the need to change world patterns of consumption and production.

Because of this, trade unions are willing to enter into 'partnerships' to achieve Agenda 21 objectives, even though the concept itself has been used traditionally to obscure the true nature of industrial relations. Just as employers and unions already co-operate to produce goods and by-products, they can co-operate to change production and to eliminate the wastes.

Such co-operation is happening in both simple and complex ways. At times, workers and their unions are consulted directly. At others, they work through a *mélange* of consulting firms, management techniques and reporting mechanisms. Too often, however, these measures lead to more 'efficiencies' which are then exploited to increase production and consumer demand. To participate meaningfully in the process of change, workers must be shown how their consumption is related to sustainable production.

Workers and their unions must be involved in co-operative ventures if they are going to understand problems, design solutions and implement change. If that includes strategic decisions about the tools used for analysis, consulting firms to be hired, records to be maintained, behaviour to be examined, evaluations of data and recommendations for changes – the potential for progress is tremendous.

Partnerships can also collaborate to encourage changes in consumption patterns as a part of the process. Excluding trade unions in the process would make the necessary quantum changes impossible.

Traditional collective bargaining structures by themselves may create problems, as explained by the representative of the German chemical workers' union, the IG Chemie, in its presentation to the 1996 CSD 'Day of the Workplace':

> *IG Chemie sees little point in forcing through environmental objectives within the context of collective bargaining. Attempts to do so could very quickly raise the wrong kind of questions, focusing attention on neo-liberal interests, such as offsetting material benefits with regard to wages and social security against environmental protection. The union views environmental action much more as an element of a programme of complete economic and social restructuring, and believes that any change in production-related and consumer habits can entail improvements in the quality of life where they are most urgently needed: in other words, where people live and work. The underlying message is aimed at 'community well-being', and in practical terms, involves society's and people's orientation toward the principle of solidarity in all areas of social life. Consequently, IG Chemie's strategy*

*focuses on obtaining voluntary agreements from employers on matters relat-
ed to environmental protection.*[10]

Workplace parties in Germany have fashioned a system of co-operation
based on works councils, which are elected by the entire body of
employees to involve them in the administration of company welfare on
the basis of co-operation and integration, which is primarily governed
by the works constitution. These councils have extensive authority over
modifications in the workplace, including technical changes, installations, or changes to the process, and may assert co-determination rights
where these are in conflict with the latest technological findings. They
also have co-determination rights over vocational training, with the
right to integrate environmental training at company level.

A milestone was reached on 20 August 1987. It was then that
chemical companies and the IG Chemie broadened the mandate of
works councils. Their declaration provides a framework for joint action
towards sustainable development; it empowers works councils to make
company agreements on environmental protection that extend their
mandate, with more access to information on environmental questions
and to a greater right to participation.

This unique ability to work through the sovereign 'rule-making'
bodies based on union-management agreement was illustrated by other
labour representatives at the 1996 'Day of the Workplace':

- Finland: A union in the hotel and restaurant industry participated
  with selected tourist enterprises in a pilot project which demonstrated the value of the eco-audit as an environmental management tool
  for this sector.
- Australia: The central trade union organization formed partnerships
  with the country's leading environmental group, as well as a number
  of companies and industrial associations, in a nationwide programme
  to identify and develop 'green jobs'.
- North America: The Labourers' International Union (LIUNA)
  showed international leadership in an emerging environmental
  industry by forming training partnerships to provide its members
  and associated employers with a competitive edge in hazardous waste
  clean-up and remediation.
- The Philippines: The San Miguel Corporation, an industry leader, has
  negotiated an environmental protection clause into the collective

bargaining agreement with the Congress of Independent Organizations – Associated Labour Unions (CIO–ALU) to establish labour-management co-operation for environmental protection.

- Sweden: A professional employees' union, the Confederation of Professional Employees (TCO), is working with environmental organizations, consultants and companies to set up environmental standards and environmental labelling to influence everyday decisions and affect purchasing, work and the environment.
- Zimbabwe: Trade unionists identified problems and co-operative sustainable development solutions for local authority workers and communities facing environmental degradation, unplanned urbanization and extreme poverty.[11]

IMPLEMENTING CHAPTER 29

The 'Day of the Workplace', held on 30 April 1996 at the Fourth Session of the CSD, represented a milestone in the growing commitment which the world labour movement has to Agenda 21. In preparation for the day, the ICFTU published case studies on progress towards sustainable development made in the six countries mentioned above, four of which were presented, along with a visual display to a special session of the CSD. They also published a pamphlet which contained summaries of 20 positive cases.

The ICFTU is able to engage in projects like this because it has access to about 2½ million worksites around the world through its affiliates, and has developed a close relationship with leading NGOs. Through them, we know of the gains that have been made towards sustainable development through collective bargaining, accords and special agreements with employers and industry associations. In addition, most international trade secretariats (ITSs) are encouraging their affiliates to expand the focus of collective bargaining beyond the workplace to include the general environment and sustainable development.

This action is helping to turn Agenda 21 objectives into reality. The question for the future of the CSD beyond 1997 is how this agency can promote further progress.

In this evaluation, attention must be given to the International Labour Organization (ILO) and the contributions it has made to our efforts. One outstanding example is the ILO's project entitled 'Worker Education and the Environment', that was initiated in the early 1990s with assistance from the Norwegian government. It helps trade union officials to develop strategies for preparing training processes and materials designed to increase environmental awareness, and cleaner, healthier and safer production practices. It has already trained hundreds of union leaders and staff, often under difficult circumstances.

Just as importantly, ILO initiatives proceed from a principle of social justice, recognizing that it is not possible to promote sustainable development in many regions or countries without meeting basic social and economic development objectives – that is, poverty and environmental degradation go hand-in-hand.

The ILO has shown how that trade union movement can engage wealthier industrialized nations in the battle against poverty, disease and social injustice as a prerequisite to sustainable development. It has encouraged unions to operate as social development organizations, and to provide grassroots worker education as a vital component in environmentally friendly policies at the workplace.

JUST TRANSITION

Workers have gained an understanding – based on hard experience – that any conversion towards more sustainable patterns of production and consumption will have an immediate impact on terms and conditions of employment. Historically, workers have borne the brunt of displacements that result from changes to the modes of production, especially where they are excluded from decision-making.

Trade unions will not allow workers, their families and communities to bear all of the cost of the transition to sustainability, which is why they are beginning to press for 'Just Transition' programmes to facilitate the transition involved in national plans. Full union participation in decision-making will become a precondition for co-operation with employers, environmentalists or governments on environmental issues, and any resulting programme must include at least the following:

- Income protection.
- Access to new jobs.
- Educational assistance.
- Support for affected communities.

Corporations must be willing to accept responsibility in return for the profits that society has allowed them, by funding the Just Transition programme through a tax on environmentally damaging production.

But unions have also learned that economic instruments as an 'eco-tax', when used without proper forethought and participation, can have significant social and distributive impacts. These must be understood fully and offset with measures to make sure that social costs are minimized and shared equitably, and that the revenues gained from market-based measures are used to compensate for regressive effects on income distribution and for environmental purposes. Failure to provide such guarantees means that there will be resistance from the workplace parties and the public.

THE WAY FORWARD

The case studies presented at the CSD 'Day of the Workplace' indicate that trade unions are serious about the concept of workplace partners and will continue to press employers to develop joint approaches to workplace and community sustainable development.

Delegates at the 16th World Congress of the ICFTU held in Brussels on 25–29 June 1996, reaffirmed that environmental issues were vitally important to them. They approved a draft policy statement on trade union action entitled *Trade Unions and the Environment: Action for Safe Workplaces and Sustainable World Employment*.

The policy paper builds on Agenda 21, and particularly Chapter 29, by committing the ICFTU to a programme for the following issues at global, national, regional and local level:

- Preventing the transfer of ecologically substandard products and production systems and hazardous waste by multinationals to developing countries where legislation or enforcement is weak.
- Reducing risk, preventing pollution and introducing cleaner technologies in the workplace.
- Promoting the ratification of the recently adopted ILO Convention 170 on Safety in the Use of Chemicals at Work and Convention 174 on the Prevention of Industrial Disasters.
- Environmental auditing companies, with the participation of workers and their representatives.
- Making nuclear power stations safer and cleaning up the environmental despoliation in Central and Eastern Europe.

- Making the international toy-manufacturing industry safer.
- Setting international standards for workplaces.

The Challenge of Internal Responsibility

As governments engage in a worldwide retreat from traditional regulatory roles, the control of the workplace will depend more than ever on
voluntary corporate action and self-imposed restraint. A world order is
also emerging in which transnational corporations and investors are
more than ever allowed a free hand in making their own rules, to set one
community – and even one country – against the other in an attempt to
achieve the lowest possible production costs.

So it has become increasingly important that unions assert themselves in 'internal responsibility' policies to give discretionary powers to
employees and enforcement officials. In most local economies, they will
provide the only effective response to increasing corporate control and,
in the absence of government intervention, the only centre of strength
capable of asserting the interests and priorities of workers and their
communities.

The ICFTU resolution notes that the union movement must respond
in a timely and appropriate manner to make sure that increasingly influential international standards reflect a broader agenda than that of international organizations that represent business and employers. Based on
the premise that proper labour relations are a prerequisite for effective
environmental management, the resolution takes the International
Standards Organization (ISO) to task for turning its back on ILO conventions which contemplate trade union participation in this area.[12]

The ISO trademark of quality environmental management cannot
become a credible standard unless it guarantees full involvement and
co-determination by workers and their union representatives.

Training is the Key

Upgraded union communication and education are crucial in the new era
of voluntarism. At a 1995 conference in Sofia, UK Environment Minister
John Gummer referred to the steep learning curve that is
required for these changes to occur.[13] Workers can bring about these
changes if unions provide the training and education of their members,

and co-ordinate programmes across workplaces, sectors and whole regions.

To achieve this, the ICFTU has promised to develop worldwide communication networks to:

- Assist and facilitate training and education programmes, particularly in developing and transition countries, through the exchange of information, including for rural workers on the safe use of pesticides and other chemicals.
- Provide information on international standards to the affiliates involved in negotiating collective agreements on environmental protection, health and safety, including provisions for involvement by workers and their representatives.
- Include environmental audits on the agendas of meetings of works councils and company councils.
- Get company agreement on the resources for proper discussion of such issues, including time off for the training of worker representatives.
- Counter the challenge to occupational health and safety and the environment posed by globalization and the international business agenda.
- Co-ordinate trade union representation on issues of concern to affiliates and the ITS in international and regional organizations and agencies dealing with environmental matters.
- Make sure that international protocols and trade agreements reinforce the right of workers to a safe healthy workplace and community.
- Push for the ratification of ILO instruments as a means of implementing sustainable development objectives.
- Co-operate in the work for a trade union strategy in which the demands on a 'sustainable production' are co-ordinated with the efforts to safeguard and create new employment.
- Work for a co-ordinated system of certification for the working environment.

JOINT WORKSITE COMMITTEES AND THE RIGHT TO PARTICIPATE

Historically, unions have set three preconditions for a workplace arrangement that will protect the health and safety of workers:

- Access to knowledge.
- Full participation in decision-making and workplace governance.

- The right of workers to refuse unsafe work, free from fear of job loss or discipline.

Joint worksite health and safety committees have proved to be a workplace mechanism which reinforces the rule-making relationship under collective bargaining as a way of achieving all three preconditions.[14] Every effort should be made to extend their mandate to include broader sustainable development issues.

These committees have functioned effectively only when they were sanctioned by both the employers and employees, were firmly established in legislation, and had the functional authority to pursue their mandates. Their activities must include the implementation of education and training, regular inspections, accident investigation, workers' compensation and light duty programme development, record-keeping, and related health and safety issues. Success depends completely on the unqualified co-operation of both parties, as reflected in an equally balanced structure, including joint chairmanship.

A useful tool for this type of direct, practical trade union involvement has been the 'eco-audit', now recognized by an EU declaration throughout Europe, and many other industrialized countries, as an effective means of assessing and managing environmental performance.

It has been shown repeatedly that the confidence and co-operation of the workforce is a prerequisite to their success, and that this can be achieved when trade unions take part in the audit design, implementation and reporting process. In the same way, trade unions have an important role to play drawing up workplace environmental policy targets and objectives, and helping to communicate them to all involved, including workers and members of the local community.

Participation in programmes directed towards Agenda 21 is crucial if workers are to adopt them personally. They will have faith in partnerships if they see the importance of their involvement in meeting both global and workplace goals. They will be prepared to become more efficient themselves and to take personal responsibility for their workplaces, to keep records and to make positive suggestions and, most importantly, to be prepared to change work and consumption habits themselves and to help change the attitudes of people they work and live with.

At the turn of the next century, will the CSD be in a position to promote joint worksite committees?

THE RIGHT TO KNOW

The consensus which is crucial to changing production and consumption patterns is destroyed wherever decisions are made behind closed doors and where information is either lacking or conflicting. The right-to-know is therefore an essential component in any partnership, and must extend from the workplace to the individual consumer and the community. Workers and their trade union representatives are claiming the right to know the environmental effects of products and processes in which they are involved, as well as the right to independent advice and the right to be consulted on the environmental strategies and planning of their employers.

'Whistle-blower' protection already exists in several jurisdictions which allows workers to report problems to the authorities without jeopardizing their employment. So does the legislated right-to-refuse to do work which is believed to pose a health and safety threat, in itself possibly the single most telling evidence that unions have changed the political regime of the workplace? Similar legal rights must now be won for workplace environmental problems.

The right-to-know underlines the need for education and training. Union efforts at information and education are often not supported by governments or employers; in fact, too often workers are denied time off to attend these programmes. Unions will continue to look for support for green education and training programmes, to reflect the rights already won in several jurisdictions for health and safety training.

OVERCOMING OBSTACLES TO CHANGE

Many examples of good practice are appearing in company management and in collective agreements, but sustainable development requires that so-called 'good practice enterprises' include the majority of workplaces. The trade union movement is committed to dealing with the obstacles that workers and their organizations will understandably pose to a process that is sure to cause massive social, economic and workplace upheaval.

The involvement of the labour movement will be particularly crucial to the success of cleaner production initiatives in Central and Eastern Europe, where unions can play a crucial role to facilitate cleaner production programmes at the national, regional and worksite level.[15] The stakes are high, as failure could stall the transition to the new economies which is taking place in these states.

There is a special challenge in this region for training, education, information sharing and communications – areas in which unions have excelled. Four years of cleaner production programmes have demonstrated that it is possible to design and implement cost-effective programmes that combine training of trainers, company assessments or environmental audits, and certain nil or low-cost measures to produce a 20–40 per cent reduction in wastes.

The trade union movement can play a major role in facilitating cleaner production centres at the national and local level, which have connections with workplaces and communities. With their experience and contacts, unions can take their place at the hub of a nationwide cleaner production (CP) networks, co-ordinating programmes, linking industry, government, NGOs, universities and research centres, and disseminating information.

Financial sources will be encouraged to provide additional funds when they see that the objectives of the Environmental Action Programme are being achieved and that enterprises are capable of making winning investments which yield not just economic benefits, but all-important environmental and political ones as well.

Even representatives of the World Bank have now admitted that the best way of making sure of investment returns is to improve the quality of worker involvement. Making sure that workers participate through trade union involvement will yield higher returns on investment. They understand that, no matter what specific tools and mechanisms are used to bring this about, they will have limited success unless workers adopt the objectives of Agenda 21 as personal objectives.

THE NATIONAL REPORTING PROCESS

The labour movement is particularly heartened by the fact that the CSD has requested all member countries to include information in their annual reports describing how they are:

● Promoting full participation of workers in the implementation and evaluation of Agenda 21.

- Planning by the year 2000 to:
  - Promote ratification of the ILO Convention.
  - Establish bipartite and tripartite mechanisms on safety, health and sustainable development.
  - Increase the number of environmental collective agreements.
  - Reduce occupational accidents and injuries.
  - Increase workers education and training for workers.
- Finding ways for workers to take part in national Agenda 21 discussions and implementation.

The ICFTU and its affiliates are taking this directive seriously, and will develop a monitoring and reporting process in each country to ensure that these are properly documented. By the year 2000, fully integrated reporting mechanisms will establish workplace targets and evaluation procedures which will redefine these national, regional and workplace targets on an annual basis, and encourage joint mechanisms at workplaces to implement plans of action.

RESPONDING TO THE CHALLENGE OF GLOBALIZATION

The ICFTU resolution notes that trade unions approach this new organizing challenge with valuable experience of the effects of globalisation and structural adjustment on health and safety programmes and standards of work generally. As world trade and production increasingly spreads to countries where existing national regulation is weak, it is becoming increasingly urgent to ensure that the pressure of competition does not undermine progress.

Many developing countries, especially in Africa, have become dumping grounds for hazardous waste products from industrialised countries, which is totally unacceptable.[16] Trade and investment liberalization must not be at the price of increases in the rate of workplace deaths and injuries, and a weakening of efforts to prevent environmental damage.

Unions will continue to use every available means to make sure that multinational corporations apply sustainable practices consistently in every jurisdiction in which they are involved, based on our experience that they are not always willing to involve the trade unions to the same extent. We will continue to make sure that the same minimum terms of trade union involvement and the same guidelines apply. European unions have already shown how their European works councils can help to promote the spread of sustainable best practices.

Unions must continue to put pressure on governments to make the intergovernmental process of the CSD work. If it fails, responsibility will rest with the governments which have failed to support it. Unions have also shown that they can work with other major groups to achieve this commitment. This is the type of process that the CSD is best suited to help, and it is a major reason why the ICFTU supports its continuation.

NOTES

1. *See* Castleman, Barry (1986) 2nd edn. *Asbestos: Medical and Legal Aspects, Law and Business Inc.*, Clifton, NJ.
2. Thackrah, CT, 'The effects of the principal arts, trades and professions, and of civic states and habitats of living on health and longevity' in HE Sigerist, *Civilization and Disease*, pp 50–52.
3. *See* Goldoftas, Barbara. 'Hands that hurt: Repetitive motion injuries on the job' in *Technology Review*, vol 94, January 1991, pp 42–50.
4. Parmeggiani, Luiggi (ed) (1983) *Encyclopedia of Occupational Health and Safety*, International Labour Organization, Geneva.
5. For a complete discussion of this approach, *see* Tucker, Eric (1990) *Administering Danger in the Workplace: The Law and Politics of Occupational Health and Safety Regulation in Ontario, 1850–1924.* University of Toronto Press, Toronto, Ontario.
6. A discussion of this reality is provided in the classic book by Kazis, Richard and Richard Grossman (1982) *Fear at Work: Job Blackmail, Labour and the Environment* Pilgrim Press, New York.
7. One of the best-known proponents for this school of thought, economist WKip Viscusi, summarizes the argument against adequate regulation of workplace hazard by saying that exposure to various risks is an intrinsic aspect of many daily activities such as car travel, sports and home repairs, for which workers make similar choices. 'If a worker takes a job he knows to be risky, there must be some other aspect to compensate for this risk'. *See* Viscusi, W Kip (1983). *Risk by Choice: Regulating Health and Safety in the Workplace* Harvard University Press, Cambridge, Massachusetts.
8. One of the most complete and often-quoted studies of an institutional regime was produced in the United States by Ashford, Nicholas (1976). *Crisis in the Workplace: Occupational Disease and Injury: A Report to the Ford Foundation* MIT Press, Cambridge, Massachusetts.

9. Jordan, Bill, address to the DGB Employment and Climate Change, Berlin, Germany May, 1995.
10. Heinz, Bernd (1996). *Social Partnership for Sustainable Development*, IG-Chemie, Germany, the UN Department for Sustainable Development.
11. The text for these presentations is contained in 'The Day of the Workplace', Department for Policy Co–ordination and Sustainable Development, United Nations, 30 April 1996.
12. *See* 'International Labour Conventions and Recommendations, 1919–81', (1985) with supplements, International Labour Organization, Geneva.
13. Gummer, John, speech delivered at a business forum conference in Sofia, Bulgaria, about the CEE Environmental Action Plan, 23–25 October 1995.
14. One of the most authoritative studies of the union approach to health and safety through joint worksite committees is provided by Beaumont, Phil B *Safety at Work and the Unions* (1983). Croom Helm, London.
15. *See* OECD (1995). *Best Practices Guide for Cleaner Production Programmes in Central and Eastern Europe*, Paris.
16. *See,* for example, Ives, Jane H (ed) (1985) *Export of Hazard: Transnational Corporations and Environmental Control Issues.* 'Sustainable development' pp15–16, Routledge & Kegan Paul, New York.

12

Women, Environment and the United Nations

Angela Mawle

At the end of the last century western women were engaged in a fierce and bloody battle to secure the basic right to vote. Viewed as chattels of their husbands, as second class citizens and inferior in every way to men, our maternal forebears carried on the universal struggle of women to care for home and family, supplement meagre incomes and conserve and eke out pitiful resources for the greater good of the community and of the nation.

At the end of the twentieth century women are confronted with no less a task. Seventy per cent of the world's poor are women. Globally, women have less access to education, health care and basic human rights. The world's industrial, economic and political systems are dominated by men and are inexorably drawing the planet to the brink of environmental disaster.

In pre-historic times such inequities did not prevail. The balance of male and female was respected and reflected in humankind's spiritual and temporal life. In societies such as the Minoan which pre-dated ancient Greek civilizations, harmony between nature and humankind was recognised as essential to a happy and healthy community. Men and women participated equally at all levels within this complex but peaceful social structure and the natural environment was revered, respected and replenished as the vital source of all life.

Now, as we reach the end of the twentieth century, with deepening social unease and escalating environmental degradation, women are emerging as a fundamental force to bring about harmonious, holistic and sustainable communities. The urgent need for the next century is for humanity to develop skills of negotiation, consensus-building and mutual understanding.

Aggressive territorial behaviour, the craving for dominion over fellow human beings and the creatures of the Earth, will merely serve to plunge us into oblivion. We must develop and foster those skills which have been traditionally viewed as feminine (and therefore inferior) but which reside, albeit dormant, in us all.

GLOBAL POLITICS AND GRASS-ROOTS ACTIVISM

The twentieth century has seen huge changes in human societies. Two major world wars challenged the validity and integrity of previously cherished precepts and values. Politics moved into a global dimension and the United Nations was born. As the UN Conference on International Organisation opened in San Francisco in 1945, women of the victorious nations were about to be sent back to their traditional householding and child rearing roles after serving as front-line or underground resistance fighters, soldiers, sailors, doctors and nurses, ferrying combat aircraft or as munitions factory workers. However, the cumulative effect of women's demands in the suffragist movement and of their war service made it certain that the new UN Charter must proclaim their equal rights: '... to reaffirm faith in (the) equal rights of men and women and of nations large and small ...' Sadly, however, the talk of equal rights espoused in the 1945 Charter has remained just that – talk. Member States remain at various points along the path of equal opportunity. Even in the 1990s, despite a long list of Conventions and Universal Declarations aimed at promoting gender equality, the UN itself has a dismal record in implementing equal opportunities 'in-house.' In 1994, of 185 Permanent Representatives in the UN diplomatic corps, only 7 were women. At the same time, at the top of the UN Secretariat, Mr Boutros Boutros-Ghali had only 2 women among 19 Under Secretaries General.

Nevertheless, at San Francisco in 1945 a number of women's activists and organizations working under the umbrella of the Inter-American Commission on the Status of Women were successful in having the equal rights of men and women, and non-distinction on the basis of sex, included in the five Articles of the UN Charter. When the consultative system for NGOs was established, 10 women's NGOs were in the first group of 32 NGOs given Category B status in 1947. These NGOs lobbied successfully for the Economic and Social Council of the UN (ECOSOC) to establish a Sub-Commission on the Status of Women, the mandate of which was to act in an advisory capacity to the Commission on Human Rights on issues relating to the status of women. In 1946 the Sub-Commission was transformed into a full Commission of the Economic and Social Council. This was opposed by several Member States including the United States and the United Kingdom who argued that women's rights could be better catered for within the rubric of human rights.

The CSW from its inception was closely linked to the women's NGO community. One commentator has observed that 'in no organ of the United Nations do international non-governmental organisations play a more active and influential role than in the Commission.' During the 1960s the CSW became more involved with economic and social development and in 1970 endorsed a Programme of Concerted Action which set out minimum targets for all Member States to achieve in education, training, health, unemployment and maternity protection for women. As the 1970s developed much of the work of the CSW and the women's NGOs became centred upon International Women's Year, designated by the General Assembly to take place in 1975. The focus of the year was a World Conference which itself would mark the beginning of a Women's Decade.

During this decade women's NGOs grew and flourished. Now, as well as the traditional structured organizations rooted in the suffrage movement, religious or professional groupings, NGOs from very diverse origins became actively involved in representing areas such as peace, domestic violence, female sexual slavery, labour and economic development. This new NGO activity was worldwide, with significant numbers arising from the Southern-based grassroot activity.

Two Decade Conferences took place during 1975–85 at which parallel Forums were held for participating NGOS. The first Conference took place in Mexico in 1975 enabling, for the first time, women from the North and South to come together and share their experience and understand the commonality of their situations. The second Decade Conference was held in Copenhagen attracting far greater numbers of NGOs and offering 150–175 workshops daily at the NGO Forum. The decade concluded with the Nairobi End of Decade Conference in 1985. This was attended by 1,500 official participants and 14,000 women taking part in the NGO Forum.

Thus the staging of UN Conferences became a vital factor in the stimulation of the global networking of women. No longer present by virtue of being the passive partner of the male, they were attending in their own right, expressing their own opinions and concerns and most importantly of all, understanding the global nature of women's experience of oppression and exploitation.

By the mid 1980s therefore the UN had facilitated almost unwittingly what it had failed to do by decree. Women from throughout the globe were uniting to wrest equal rights for themselves and for the daughters of the future.

THE PRE-RIO ERA

The UNCED preparatory process saw a massive escalation of women's involvement in the UN conference system. Throughout the 1980s the growing environmental crisis and the corresponding expansion of the environmental movement led to the involvement of increasing numbers of women both as environmental activists and as advocates of ecofeminism. Ecofeminism refers to a diverse range of women's environmental activity. It also offers a critique of the dominant philosophical and cultural attitudes that underlie Western society's approach to nature and the natural world. Ecofeminists argue that a common belief system, rooted in the principles of patriarchal domination, determines modern attitudes towards both women and nature. Ecofeminism particularly concerns itself with the way in which the degradation of the natural environment impacts upon the daily lives of women, especially in the Third World.

Ecofeminism owes its origins to what had hitherto been two different social movements: the environmental movement and the women's movement. Within the latter, it draws especially upon the women's peace and spirituality movements. The coming together of these movements found natural expression in the groundswell of the global concern centred around the now undisputed planetary environmental degradation, and very naturally focussed upon the then-forthcoming Earth Summit scheduled for June 1992.

THE UNCED PREPARATORY PROCESS

Until 1991 women had not been an explicit concern within the governmental preparations for UNCED. However, through networking, lobbying and organizing, some UNCED delegates were won over, with the result that a women's mandate was adopted at the Third Preparatory Committee Meeting in Geneva in August 1991.

Further momentum was added to women's participation in the UNCED process by two global women's conferences held successively in Miami in 1991. The first was the Global Assembly 'Women and Environment – Partners for Life' organised by UNEP and WorldWIDE, a US based international network of women concerned with the management and protection of the environment. Five hundred invited guests heard women from all over the world present 218 accounts documenting how they were successfully addressing environmental problems in their own communities. The second conference was the 'World Women's Congress for a Healthy Planet' and was convened by the Women's International Policy Action Committee (IPAC) and organized by the Women's Environment and Development Organisation (WEDO).

The five-day Congress drew 1,500 women from 83 countries. These women ranged from full-time activists, agronomists and bankers to nurses, parliamentarians, technicians and zoologists. The women came from United Nations agencies, government, environment, development, women's and religious foundations and the news media. They heard dramatic testimony from women in every region of the world who presented evidence of their battles against ecological and economic devastation before a tribunal of five eminent women judges. From this evidence and their own experience the participants developed recommendations and actions for a healthy planet, the Women's Action Agenda 21 – a blueprint for incorporating the women's dimension into local, national and international environment and development decision making. The Women's Action Agenda 21 was specifically designed to promote women's active and equal participation in preparations for the Rio Conference, and in implementing the resulting plan of action Agenda 21.

In addressing the Congress, Maurice Strong, Secretary General of UNCED, stated: 'One important objective of the UNCED Secretariat is to incorporate gender concerns into all areas of its work and generate global awareness about the important role of women in promoting sustainable development'. He went on: ...'Another issue ... is the need to ensure the widest possible visibility of women in the UNCED process-sand the continuing empowerment of women both at the highest and lowest levels. The role of women in decision making has to be increased as a matter of policy if profound changes are to take place as the outcome of the Earth Summit'.

THE EARTH SUMMIT

From 3–13 June 1992 the Brazilian Women's Coalition together with the Women's Environment and Development Organisation (WEDO) organized and hosted Planeta Femea, the women's conference held within the NGO Global Forum in Rio de Janeiro. Planeta Femea was a concentrated programme of presentations in daily workshops structured around the themes of the Women's Action Agenda 21. A Women's Declaration emerged from the meeting criticizing the UNCED agenda for the exclusion of such crucial factors in global environmental degradation as economic and military systems. The document called for the full implementation of Women's Action Agenda 21 as drafted in Miami.

At the same time a powerful women's caucus at the governmental conference strongly lobbied the official member country delegates. The result of this was the comprehensive incorporation of women in Agenda 21. UNCED acknowledged women's critical economic, social and environmental contributions to environmental management and sustainable development, and endorsed activities promoting the incorporation of women in programme areas contained in the sectoral and cross sectoral chapters of Agenda 21, as well as in the sections on the role of the major groups and on means of implementation.

The conference also endorsed Chapter 24 of Agenda 21: 'Global action for women towards sustainable and equitable development'. This chapter is policy – and management – oriented and contains specific recommendations to strengthen the role of women in sustainable development, particularly focussing on the elimination of obstacles to women's equal and beneficial participation in decision-making activities.

The Influence of the NGOs

Now at last, besides being active within the NGO forums and parallel conferences, women were beginning to influence the sophisticated political processes of the UN system and actually determining the nature of the commitments undertaken. Throughout Agenda 21 the language of the need for women's empowerment speaks through. Chapter 24 speaks of the need to implement previously-adopted conventions to end gender-based discrimination and to ensure women access to land and other resources, education, and safe and equal employment. It states that effective implementation of these programmes will depend on the active involvement of women in economic and political decision making and will be critical to the successful implementation of Agenda 21.

Thus the women at Rio profoundly affected the language and commitments of Agenda 21. They came together in their thousands, united globally in their determination to effect change, empowered by the sheer energy of their common purpose. Women from the South, North, East and West experienced a new profundity in their understanding of global inequities. The environmental and development movements came together and a new understanding developed of the unsustainable economic systems which perpetuated global poverty and environmental degradation.

Of course deep and fundamental questions remained unsolved and undebated. What is the reality of women's claimed 'special' connection with the environment? Bella Abzug, the founder of WEDO, claimed at Rio that women have this special right or connection because they 'care' and are nurturers of the planet. Is this a valid assumption? Are all women content to assume this implicit role? And what of global sisterhood? Does it necessarily imply a cohesive and homogenous worldwide movement of women? At Planeta Femea profound differences did emerge. The Western development model was rejected in its entirety by many Southern women whilst others saw the urgent priority as working within the system, accessing the media and otherwise influencing the conference process to women's advantage.

The Post-Rio period

In the years since Rio these questions and the many others rooted in the frailty of the emergent global women's environment and development movements have remained unresolved. Nevertheless, the UN conference process has continued to offer opportunities to women to become increasingly politicized and to take the world stage.

THE INTERNATIONAL CONFERENCE ON POPULATION AND DEVELOPMENT

From 5 to 13 September 1994 more than 10,000 people from 180 countries gathered in Cairo at the International Conference on Population and Development (ICPD). The Conference agreed on a comprehensive and detailed strategy for population and development for the following 20 years. The resultant programme of action was the culmination of more than three years of intense deliberation and negotiation amongst governments, NGOs, community leaders, technical experts and interested individuals. The Programme of Action established that population issues cannot be addressed in isolation but must be seen in the broader context of sustainable development. Human-centred development is seen as a firm basis for sustained economic growth which can only be achieved by implementing policies based on the fundamental human rights needs and aspirations of individual women and men. Central to the Programme for Action is the recognition that gender equality and equity are essential pre-requisites for sustainable human development and that the empowerment of women must be at the heart of national and international population and development policies.

Inevitably, women were a powerful force behind the International Conference on Population and Development. For three years beforehand efforts were made to organize and integrate women at the community, national and international level to ensure that their voices would be heard. One NGO observer noted that the Conference 'catalysed women and NGOs around the world as they gained access to the international policy making process'.

The ICPD Programme of Action represents thousands of hours of drafting, negotiation and consensus-building by citizens and governments with women playing a key role in the process. The fact that women's empowerment was identified as one of the principal factors essential to sustainable development and to ensuring the success of efforts to improve reproductive health is due in large measure to these women's efforts.

Much of this success stems from the role of women's NGOs acting as 'bridges and buffers' within broad based interdisciplinary groups, many of whom had never worked together before or who were unable to do so directly. NGOs were particularly influential in mobilizing and integrating Southern women into the Cairo process. After Cairo, the President of the International Women's Health Coalition, a global association of NGOs, stated: 'We women, have returned to our home countries to use the language of the document to hold our governments accountable as they restructure budgets and design programmes. We will be equal partners at the policy table and active participants in creating programmes. None of this will happen overnight. None of this will happen easily. But women will write the history of Cairo by translating words into action'.

THE FOURTH INTERNATIONAL CONFERENCE ON WOMEN

After Cairo the efforts of the women of the world were inevitably geared towards the United Nation Fourth International Conference on Women held in Beijing in September 1995. Although the World Social Summit took place in March of 1995 the sheer pace generated by the UN Conference series dictated that most women's NGOs would concentrate their scant resources on the major international women's conference.

Preparatory Committees took place in various regions of the world and became a hotbed of politicization for the women involved. The ECE High-Level Regional PrepCom in Vienna in October 1994 attracted 3,000 NGO representatives from throughout the region, which covers 55 Member States. An NGO Forum preceded the official proceedings and produced a series of recommendations and textual amendments to inform and guide the governmental delegates.

Initially the main interaction between the official proceedings and the NGO caucus took the form of a morning briefing together with the authorization of a very few NGO representatives to attend the drafting committees. It soon became clear that this arrangement was totally unsatisfactory and the NGOs demanded access to the drafting committees as of right. Eventually this right was granted and in the event led to a far more sophisticated level of interaction between the delegatees and the NGO representatives. Textual amendments were drafted which found their way into the final regional platform and a new level of respect was attained between the official delegations and the participating NGOs. This was particularly apparent in Section K 'Women and the Environment' which was significantly influenced by the expert environmentalists and scientists present within the NGO lobbying groups.

By the time of the final PrepCom in New York in April 1995 the international NGOs were fully mobilized and conducting themselves with considerable political astuteness. Despite the fact that the official proceedings had become hopelessly stuck on the issue of women's health and reproductive rights and that 40 per cent of the text of the draft Platform for Action remained in brackets, the NGOs lobbied and manoeuvred and staged high-profile, highly visible protests centred on abuses of women's universal human rights.

The whole lead-up to Beijing had stimulated a high level of international networking and cooperation between women's NGOs. The vexed issue of whether or not to participate in a Conference on women staged in a country where women were subjected to abuses of their reproductive rights led to international controversy and debate within and between the women's movements. Add to this the hugely difficult processes of obtaining accreditation, accommodation and finance to even be present in China and it is a testimony to endurance and dedication that over 30,000 women attended the NGO Forum and UN Conference during August and September 1995.

Despite separating the NGO Forum from the Conference by no less that 53 kilometres and two-hour bus journeys, the organizing committee totally failed to extinguish the spirit of dedication and determination that brought those women to Beijing. Workshops, festivities, celebrations and demonstrations abounded at the NGO Forum whilst at the main Conference NGOs from all over the world gathered to lobby delegates and gain precious amendments to the draft Platform for Action.

Within Section K, for example, it was imperative that the language of Rio was not lost but that it should be reinforced and added to in respect of the commitments made. The degree of sophistication and expertise attained within the environment lobby group could only have come from a combination of political shrewdness, technological expertise, sheer tenacity and vision. The Environment Caucus was formed of women from all parts of the globe, young and old alike, joining together to refine amendments, lie in wait for unsuspecting governmental delegates and to provide persuasive arguments and researched back-up for the textual changes that they were seeking to make.

THE POST-BEIJING PERIOD

Since Beijing, the women's movement has remained galvanized. Inevitably, however, the momentum is with the NGOs and not within the political systems that ordain our daily lives. Equally inevitably the resources available to NGOs are scarce and limiting. The heady sisterhood generated by global networking and coming together in an international conference setting is not likely to be experienced regularly or even occasionally for women working within cash-strapped NGOS. Yet the vigour and vitality of those occasions, the experience of the commonality of the human condition and the eager excitement of the prospect of joining together to overcome the seemingly irresistible forces of global economics is precisely the liberating energy that we need to take us in to a hopeful and harmonious 21st century.

Since its inception, the United Nations has espoused universal human rights. More recently several conventions, including the Convention on the Elimination of all forms of Discrimination against Women and conventions of ILO and UNESCO, have been adopted to end gender-based discrimination and to ensure women access to land and other resources, education, and safe and equal employment.

Yet everywhere women remain disadvantaged and denied access – either overtly or covertly – to positions of decision-making and power. To practically deny full expression to half of humanity must severely limit humankind's ability to renegotiate its complex inter-relationship with the planet and the ecosystems upon which we all ultimately depend.

Although the UN system has certainly facilitated the growth of women's politicization and promoted their participation in global affairs it could be said that it has merely stimulated an appetite and desire for change that cannot and will not be satisfied whilst we remain locked into current inequitable global economic systems.

Major group or not, women are emerging at the end of the twentieth century as more vocal, more liberated and certainly more visible than their sisters of one century ago. The Earth Summit undeniably played its part in promoting that visibility but it will take more than words and conventions to redress the imbalance that has hindered our planet for so long.

BIBLIOGRAPHY

Baker, Susan (1993) *The Principles and Practice of Ecofeminism* RISBO, Rotterdam.

Braidotti, Rose, Ewa Charkiewicz, Sabine Hausler and Saskia Wieringa (1994) *Women, The Environment and Sustainable Development: Towards a Theoretical Synthesis* Zed Books in association with INSTRAW, London.

Connors, Jane (1996) 'NGOs and the Human Rights of Women at the United Nations' in Peter Willets, *The Conscience of the World: The Influence of Non- Governmental Organisations in the UN System.*

Haxton, Eva and Claes Olsson (eds) (1995) *Women in Development Trade: Aspects of Women in the Development Process* United Nations Youth and Student Association of Sweden (UFFN).

International Confederation of Free Trade Unions (ICFTU) (1996) *Worlds Apart: Women and the Global Economy 1996* ICFTU.

United Nations (UN) (1995) *Women in the ECE Region: A Call for Action* UN, New York.

United Nations Population Fund (UNFPA) (1995) *The State of the World's Population* UNFPA, New York.

Women's Environment and Development Organization (WEDO) (1995) *Daughters of the Earth: The Environment and Development Collaborative Web*, proceedings of the Second World Women's Congress for a Healthy Planet, 31 August – 8 September, NGO Forum on Women, Huairou, China. WEDO, New York.

— (1991) *World Women's Congress for a Healthy Planet: 8–12 November 1991*, Miami.

13

Young People and Sustainable Development

Zonny Woods

Young people have been a fundamental force for change throughout history: they speak the truth, they act with passion on the things they believe in and they take risks. It was in this spirit that many youth activists from around the world became involved in the United Nations Conference on Environment and Development (UNCED). They were at the UNCED[1] in unprecedented numbers to demand action on the part of the world community in answering to the world's social, economic and environmental crisis. The process leading up to the Earth Summit was marked with a sense of urgency among youth activists who came together to discuss the environment and development issues throughout the world. Youth felt that, not only did they have something to contribute, but that their failure to contribute would result in the failure of what the Earth Summit had set out to achieve. They came to Rio demanding and exercising their right to participate in determining their future and that of the planet, and they came with a sense of responsibility to act in the search for solutions. Youth left Rio disappointed, and with the bitter taste of having been harassed by UN security, thrown out of Rio Centro, silenced and arrested for speaking out against what they believed were the injustices being perpetrated by the world leaders gathered there. But they also left with a sense of hope, with commitments that they had made to themselves and their communities, and with a renewed sense of the strength of young people to change things when they work together.

In many ways, the impact that young people had in the official UNCED process was marginal. Although Agenda 21 incorporated issues of concern to youth, many were frustrated with its inability to address profoundly issues that they felt were at the core of the current world crisis. Although youth was identified as one of the major groups, officially they were increasingly shut out of the process as the message that they delivered became less palatable and too frank in its criticisms of the Earth Summit process and the performance of countries such as the United States. During the Earth Summit, youth activists often referred to the UNCED as the UNSAID. The UNCED's failure to address issues of militarization, the democratization of international institutions, and inequitable terms of trade was a major weakness of the organization, according to youth activists. Now, five years later, the youth have continued to add their voices in the global conferences which have followed the Earth Summit in 1992, and the messages from youth to the world community remain strong and visionary – and unheard.

All of the youth NGO statements since the Earth Summit have called for social and economic justice, sustainable development that includes the fair distribution of resources, equal participation in decision-making, peace, respect for human rights, access to education, among many other issues. A common theme for all the global conferences has been a call for the inclusion of youth and their perspectives in decision-making. This is reflected in Chapter 25 of Agenda 21 titled 'Strengthening the Role of Children and Youth in Sustainable Development', which states that:

> *It is imperative that youth from all parts of the world participate actively in all relevant levels of decision-making processes because it affects their lives today and has implications for their futures. In addition to their intellectual contribution and their ability to mobilize support, they bring unique perspectives that need to be taken into account.*

The foundation for the inclusion of youth in decision-making has been established and endorsed by nations around the world through different conventions, including the Convention on the Rights of the Child. In addition, the International Conference on Population and Development, the World Summit for Social Development, the Fourth World Conference on Women and the Habitat II Conference, all highlighted the importance of youth participation in the implementation of their plans of action. Even with all of these international agreements and commitments, countries have failed to establish the permanent mechanisms that are necessary for youth participation in national policy-making processes to take place, as established in Agenda 21:

> *Each country should, in consultation with its youth communities, establish a process to promote dialogue between the youth community and government at all levels and to establish mechanisms that permit youth access to information and provide them with the opportunity to present their perspectives on government decisions, including the implementation of Agenda 21.*

In some cases, youth and youth organizations have been consulted in the follow up to these conferences, but consultation is far from what governments committed themselves to in Chapter 25 of Agenda 21, and in subsequent UN plans of action. In April 1997, as the Commission on Sustainable Development meets to evaluate work since the Earth Summit, youth must demand accountability and point to the failure of governments and the international community in meeting its commitments to young people. They have had some level of participation and input to the CSD, but measured against the backdrop of the overall commitment to youth by the international community, it is minimal at best.

One of the obstacles to the participation of youth continues to be the lack of resources allocated to youth organizations by individual governments, international institutions and the United Nations. It is not enough to include youth in policy documents if resources are not allocated for them to be integrated into the process. It is also important to understand that programmes aimed at youth or youth-serving organizations can in no way substitute for youth-run projects and organizations, which lead to greater youth empowerment, allowing them to run their own programmes driven by their own priorities, needs and perspectives. The concept of 'for youth, by youth' has resulted in projects and programmes being more successful, such as peer education in areas of health, environmental issues and youth rights.

The lack of political will to open spaces for youth participation is the norm rather than the exception, even when governments and the international community claim in their documents and statements that youth participation is important. At the international level, countries have adopted 'youth friendly' language, but the evolution of language has not translated into a change in how they deal with youth domestically, and where conditions facing young people are deplorable. China's Agenda 21 states that:

> *Youth organizations should be encouraged to participate actively in social consultative dialogue in regard to environment and development and to voice their opinions and suggestions about policies and principles.*[2]

Without going into recent Chinese history or the human rights situation in China, it is difficult to believe that history would not repeat itself were young Chinese activists to take this statement to heart and attempt to 'voice their opinions about policies and principles' vis a vis the current policies of the Chinese government. This paragraph illustrates perfectly how far removed from reality are the commitments made on paper regarding youth participation.

Even when youth are included, a variety of problems surface, such as dealing with them as a homogenous group without distinctions. Young people cannot be treated as a homogenous group, and although references to them sometimes manage to establish distinctions between male and female, they seldom identify youth in all their diversity. This has been a stumbling-block for youth activists who called for youth participation, while failing to go beyond defining specifically youth diversity in North/South and sometimes male/female terms. This presents the problem of asking which youth and on behalf of whom? Lack of clarity has allowed for the diversity of youth perspectives to be ignored, and in some cases for youth spaces to be filled by young people who do not necessarily challenge the status quo and are content with tokenism. While they, too, may represent an existing youth perspective, the many other diverse realities and concerns in the lives of young people must also be taken into account. Programmes that include young people must meet the needs of all youth, particularly the disadvantaged, and recognize gender differences.

Another obstacle has been little information and a lack of effective ways to monitor the implementation of the commitments made to youth by governments in Agenda 21. Unfortunately, increasing youth unemployment, cuts to basic education, the continuing sexual exploitation of children and young people, all tell us at first glance that we are moving in the wrong direction and that promises remain unfulfilled. We are struggling against deeply embedded attitudes that encourage discrimination against young people, particularly those living in poverty.

There is a need that policies are examined in consultation with young people, ensuring a youth analysis and participation in setting up the direction and the vision for projects and programmes. Youth are not targets of development; they are participants in the process leading to sustainable development.

As the global community examines how far it has moved towards sustainable development, the cost of continued failure to ensure the full participation of young people in the process towards sustainability must be examined. What are the consequences of the injustices and inequities facing young people today for all our futures? The lack of ability in addressing youth in a holistic manner demonstrates our inability to formulate and work towards long-term solutions, because working with young people is about working for long-term solutions. The vision for youth in Agenda 21 is still far from being a reality.

Countries and the United Nations agreed through Agenda 21 to the promotion and creation of mechanisms to involve youth representation in all United Nations processes in order for the young to be able to influence those processes. To date, only a few countries include youth in their delegations to UN conferences and the General Assembly, even though General Assembly resolutions adopted in 1968, 1977, 1985 and 1989 have called for the inclusion of youth representatives in their delegations to international meetings. The true adoption of these resolutions is of extreme importance to young people, because it gives them a voice in an arena that seldom hears the voice of youth and where they are virtually invisible.

Human rights abuses against young people continue in different forms, including sexual exploitation, particularly of young women and girls, persecution of student activists, poor working conditions and child labour, and the lack of legal protection for youth whose human rights are being violated. Although Agenda 21 calls for the protection of the human rights of young people, many of these violations continue while others, such as the commercial sexual exploitation of children, are increasing. The Congress Against the Commercial Sexual Exploitation of Children held in Sweden in 1996 has played an important role in drawing the attention of the world community to gross violations of the human rights of children and youth.

While young people in some parts of the world are the majority of the population, they remain invisible in the design and implementation of development policies. Many countries throughout the world are struggling with how to incorporate youth in national policies, and are unsure of the best way to bring about and help youth development policies that are real and responsive to young people's needs. As countries have gone through Structural Adjustment Programmes, young people have suffered from cutbacks to education, health care and social programmes. Many young people feel alienated and disenfranchised from their communities and institutions, and this alienation, which is sometimes manifested negatively, results in youth being seen as a problem to be controlled rather than as a force for change.

An effective youth policy will have to recognize and adequately analyse the current social, cultural and economic environment that determines the livelihoods of young people. Policies that governments the world over have carried out in the last decade have had an enormous impact on the livelihoods of young people, and these impacts cannot be ameliorated simply by adding a few youth projects to the pot. Young people's basic rights need to be respected – the basic right to a home, clean water, enough to eat, a safe environment, protection from violence, equality of opportunity, a say in their future, an education, a livelihood and health care. The prevailing attitude that their time will come needs to be shed. Youth need to be part of the solution here and now. The absence of youth from policy-making is hindering the much-needed revitalization of countries, the creativity needed in the search for alternatives and the renewal of leadership to take us into the 21st century.

In many cases, it has not been difficult to make an argument for the benefits of involving youth, the incoming generations, those who will inherit the world. What has been difficult is implementing the stated intentions – how and where does intergovernmental equity begin? The first step is a commitment to have youth themselves determine the ways in which they wish to be involved, the types of activities that are appropriate to them and, most importantly, that they are given the space to implement their own initiatives.

RECOMMENDATIONS

- The commitments to youth are there – act on them!
- Develop a clear and integrated plan of action, at the national and international levels, on how to work with youth in sustainable human-centred development planning and implementation.

- Share and learn from what works. There are good examples of youth integration into decision-making and policy-making. These should be shared and used as models by countries that are trying to fulfil their commitments to youth.
- Strengthen UN organizations for meeting the environment and development activities which are of relevance to youth.
- National youth policies and plans for Agenda 21 implementation need to be developed in consultation with diverse young people. Review and evaluation must be incorporated in order to monitor and assess their impact and effectiveness with indicators established by youth themselves.
- Co-ordinate with other international, regional and national organizations which are incorporating youth. Youth initiatives will become stronger and have greater impact if they are part of a co-ordinated strategy.
- Invest in youth. If governments, the UN and NGOs are serious about youth issues, resources need to be allocated for youth work and organizations.
- Work in partnership with youth, truly embracing an inter-generational approach to sustainable and human-centred development.

NOTES

1. UNCED: Earth Summit and Rio will be used to refer to the United Nations Conference on Environment and Development.
2. China, Agenda 21, Paragraph 20.32d.

Part III

MAJOR ISSUES FOR THE FUTURE

14

Trade and Sustainable Development

Caroline LeQuesne and Charles Arden Clarke

The debate about how best to ensure that the rules and practices of international trade do not undermine the goal of sustainable development has been intensifying recently. Two of the most important events to have influenced that debate have been the agreements made at the Earth Summit and the completion in 1994 of the Uruguay Round of the General Agreement on Tariffs and Trade (GATT), which extended multilateral trade rules to almost every area of international commerce, and provided for the establishment of the new World Trade Organization (WTO).

The two agreements claim to have complementary objectives. According to the first: 'An open, multilateral trading system, supported by the adoption of sound environmental policies, would have a positive impact on the environment and contribute to sustainable development'.[1] The WTO's stated objectives include 'allowing for the optimal use of the world's resources in accordance with the objective of sustainable development.'

Moreover, in its report to the 1994 annual meeting of the CSD, the GATT secretariat claimed that there exists a 'widely shared view of the basic compatibility of UNCED guiding principles with the underlying philosophy of the GATT'. And, it asserts, 'the successful conclusion of the Uruguay Round represents the best single contribution GATT could make to sustainable development'.

In reality, however, the relationship between sustainable development and trade liberalization is far more complex than these statements allow. In particular, increasing evidence suggests that international trade rules are themselves preventing or discouraging governments from taking measures to safeguard the environment, and it seems likely that the conflict between them will play a growing part in international politics into the next century. The 1997 UN Special Session therefore offers a critical opportunity to re-examine the issues and to recommend new measures to resolve the tensions between them.

This chapter will examine why current patterns of international trade and efforts towards sustainable development appear to be on a collision course, and will assess the role and progress of existing institutional frameworks, including the CSD and the WTO, in attempting to reconcile them. It will demonstrate that no one institution has both the mandate and the expertise to perform the full range of analysis that will be needed.

It therefore concludes that one of the most effective measures which the UN Special Session could adopt would be to promote the establishment of an intergovernmental panel on trade and sustainable development. Such a panel would provide the WTO Environment Committee and other institutions with the factual and analytic foundation for the urgent reforms that are necessary to integrate the policy objectives of trade, environmental protection and sustainable development.

THE RELATIONSHIP BETWEEN TRADE AND SUSTAINABLE DEVELOPMENT

In theory, the pursuit of international trade liberalization and of environmental protection are quite compatible, since the efficient allocation of resources is the key to them both. According to the theory of comparative advantage, countries will specialize in the production of goods and services in which they are most efficient. This should mean that they are able to maximize their output from a given level of resource input, and therefore to move towards conserving resources.

Trade liberalization can also have significant positive effects on the environment, particularly in addressing policy intervention failures, such as subsidies which encourage environmentally damaging activities, like those of the European Union's Common Agricultural Policy, and in facilitating international access to environmentally friendly technology. Moreover, according to the advocates of free trade, the increased economic growth that results from trade generates the funds needed to invest in environmental protection.

These are the assumptions which inform Chapter 2 of Agenda 21, which examines the relationship between international trade and sustainable development. According to Agenda 21, the links between them are simple: international trade promotes growth, which generates additional resources for cleaning up the environment, which in turn underpins a continuing expansion of trade and growth, and so on, apparently without limit.

What is absent from this analysis is the recognition that, in some cases, when the very process of achieving growth is based on current structures of unsustainable production and consumption patterns, international trade can itself lead to the acceleration of environmental destruction. 'The unison snoring of supine economists in deep dogmatic slumber,' is Herman Daly's withering verdict on this part of the chapter's analysis.

In truth, of course, the relationship between trade and sustainable development is considerably more complex than either the advocates of free trade or Agenda 21 suggest: under certain conditions, a certain amount of some kinds of international trade is beneficial; under others, it is undoubtedly harmful.

The theory of comparative advantage, for example, is based on a number of assumptions, many of which are highly questionable. It assumes that prices reflect the true cost of production. Since this is rarely the case in practice – for instance, the prices of most commodities do not account for the environmental degradation caused by their production or extraction processes – economic inefficiencies will be generated, and countries' real comparative advantages may be mistaken. Under these conditions, trade can act to magnify unsustainable patterns of economic activity and intensify problems of pollution and resource depletion.

The theory of comparative advantage also assumes that the factors of production are not mobile internationally, so that each country's capital and labour stays exclusively within its own borders. In reality, the increasing mobility of capital enables it to follow the logic of absolute advantage and to seek out the location with the lowest production costs. This leads to pressure on those countries without such 'advantage' to reduce labour and environmental standards, as well as investment regulations in a bid to increase their own competitiveness.[2]

Furthermore, while the finance generated by increasing trade *could* be spent on environmental protection, it would require an extraordinary leap of faith to assume that it necessarily would be. And plenty of evidence suggests that higher national income does not *automatically* lead to reduced environmental degradation.[3]

In order to reconcile trade and sustainable development, then, a more sophisticated analysis is needed, together with an international trading system in which the demands of environmental protection are not outweighed by the imperative of trade liberalization.

THE WTO: AN INADEQUATE FRAMEWORK FOR SUSTAINABLE DEVELOPMENT

Unfortunately, the new World Trade Organization which came into force on 1 January 1995 has so far failed to demonstrate such an analysis. A brief examination of some of the most important ways in which existing trade rules undermine efforts towards sustainable development will illustrate the point.

Under current WTO rules, for example, countries are permitted to ban the import of products which will harm their own environments, as long as the standards applied are non-discriminatory between countries, and between domestic and foreign production. But in the absence of a multilateral environment agreement, they are not allowed to protect their own environment, or to safeguard the environments of other countries or the global commons, by discriminating against imports on the basis of the way in which they are produced in other countries.[4]

This makes little sense, since from an environmental point of view, there is no meaningful distinction to be drawn between the environmental harm which is generated by a product, or the harm generated by its process and production methods. Regulations, therefore, should be equally applicable to both sources of environmental damage.

The environmental impact of production methods in other countries also have indirect effects, particularly through differences in the costs of compliance with environmental regulations. When one country's legislation demands a greater degree of cost internalization than another – through environmental taxation or regulation, for example – its firms are likely to fear that their competitiveness will be undermined by competition from other countries with less stringent environmental standards, and hence lower costs.

There are a number of ways in which the loss of the competitiveness argument could in theory be addressed. One of them, border tax adjustment, involves adjusting the price of imports and exports at the border to ensure that products and processes are subject to the same degree of environmental taxation, regardless of origin. But while WTO rules allow adjustment for domestic taxes levied on products, it was presumed prior to the conclusion of the Uruguay Round, that the rules do not allow it for taxes imposed on the basis of processing and production methods. While new provisions included in the Uruguay Agreements, and a 1994 GATT dispute panel ruling, suggest that this latter rule may have been relaxed, this has not yet been confirmed by the WTO.[5]

Nor do WTO rules permit governments to intervene in markets to ensure that prices more accurately reflect hidden costs, by imposing consumption taxes or import levies on unsustainably produced materials.[6]

Reforms to the WTO of the kind outlined above, which would have the effect of setting some minimum environmental standards world-wide, could put an unfair – and in some cases, intolerable – burden on some of the poorest developing countries, unless they are accompanied by significant extra financial resources.

These countries point out, with considerable justification, that poverty is the real cause of low standards. They claim that access to Northern markets is vital to raising these standards. Many developing countries would certainly be unable to afford the clean technologies that are needed to meet higher environmental standards. The Brundtland Commission estimated that in the early 1980s, developing countries exporting to the OECD countries would have incurred costs in excess of $5 billion if they had been required to meet US standards. The sum today would be considerably larger. A forum is therefore urgently needed which would be capable of undertaking the multi-disciplinary analysis to work out how the burden of adjusting to the demands of sustainable development should not fall disproportionately on the South.

Issues to explore would include how to link financial resource transfers, including debt relief, to the adoption of technologies to enable developing countries to introduce higher standards, and how to devise mechanisms to ensure that any revenue generated by 'green tariffs' would be repatriated to developing countries for investment in clean technologies.

The WTO as it is currently constituted, with its narrow focus on trade expansion alone, has neither the competence nor the expertise in this area. Furthermore, many people fear that if the WTO were to be used to formulate and administer trade-related environmental measures, it would fall prey to protectionist abuse. Martin Khor, Third World Network's Director, made the following comment:

> *Any rules developed in this asymmetric forum would most likely serve to legitimise the use of trade weapons which the North and the powerful can use against the South and the weak.*

The secrecy surrounding much of the WTO's work reinforces its reputation as an exclusive club, dominated by the interests of its most powerful members. Decisions are made behind closed doors, and public access to documents is still rare. These restrictions on public access and disclosure contradict the principle that is stressed throughout the Rio Earth Summit: that sustainable development is best achieved with the participation of all concerned citizens, and that governments should therefore ensure that information is made widely available.

At all three of its sessions to date, the Commission on Sustainable Development (CSD) has emphasized the need for improvement in this area. It has identified in particular:

> *The importance of achieving transparency, openness and the active involvement of the public and experts, in relation to work on trade and environment... The Commission recognises that there is considerable need for improvement in these areas, and looks forward to the development of specific recommendations in this regard by governments and the appropriate organisations, in accordance with Chapter 38 of Agenda 21.*[7]

THE WTO COMMITTEE ON TRADE AND ENVIRONMENT

The WTO, like the GATT before it, has had ample opportunity to address these issues but, with a very few exceptions, progress has been disappointing. In 1994 it set up a Committee on Trade and Environment (CTE) to take forward the work of the earlier GATT Working Group on Environmental Measures and International Trade which, although established in 1971, was inactive for 20 years. The CTE's aim is 'to identify the relationship between trade measures and environmental measures, in order to promote sustainable development', and 'to make appropriate recommendations on whether any modification of the provisions of the multilateral trading system are required'.[8]

Among its agenda items have been multilateral environment agreements (MEAs), the export of domestically prohibited goods, charges and taxes for environmental purposes, eco-labelling, and the effects of environmental measures on trade. What it has not considered is the effect of trade policies and agreements on the environment, and in particular, the impact of the Uruguay Round on prospects for sustainable development.

At the time of writing (September 1996) it seems possible that, at the first ministerial meeting of the WTO in Singapore in December 1996, the CTE will present recommendations on two main issues: the relationship between the WTO and MEAs which incorporate trade measures,[9] and on eco-labelling.

In neither case, however, does constructive progress appear to have been made. For example, proposals currently being made by some WTO members would make MEAs subject to 'trade-oriented tests', in order to assess whether the trade measures proposed were 'proportional', 'effective' and 'least-trade restrictive'. Such tests, which would undercut the effectiveness of MEAs, assume that the WTO has the competence to select and evaluate alternative means of achieving environmental objectives, and that it has the power to decide the level of environmental protection a country should regulate to achieve. The WTO, in fact, does not have, and should not have, this competence and power.

Any lasting resolution of the WTO/MEA relationship should instead be based on an amendment which broadens the environmental exception contained in GATT, coupled with an understanding which contains the minimum additional text that is necessary to ensure the environmental effectiveness of this exception.[10] In addition, the jurisdiction of the WTO on trade measures taken 'pursuant' to MEAs should be restricted formally, so that the WTO does not second guess the environmental objectives agreed by MEA negotiators, or the means selected to achieve them. The WTO dispute settlement processes should also be reformed to incorporate the relevant environmental expertise.

Similarly, proposals being made by some members of the CTE to extend WTO disciplines to voluntary eco-labelling schemes – including those run by NGOs – should be put on hold. The WTO rules in question, contained within the Technical Barriers to Trade Agreement, have a heavy bias towards trade objectives and fail to incorporate the precautionary principle.

The mode of operation of the CTE beyond the Singapore

Ministerial Meeting should be changed to incorporate better both environment and *development* concerns, and to enhance public access to the discussions. Oxfam UK and the WWF have seen from first hand experience how unregulated international trade can lead to environmental degradation, which in turn deepens poverty. As these concerns become ever more inter-related, it is becoming essential to see them as one problem. Trade and environment issues cannot be addressed in isolation: they must be tackled in conjunction with development which secures poverty alleviation. .

The final part of this some of the most urgent actions that should be taken by the UN, the WTO and other relevant inter-governmental bodies and governments, to this end, both at Earth Summit II and beyond.

AN ACTION AGENDA

The competence of the WTO on trade and environment is formally limited to 'trade policies and those trade-related aspects of environmental policies which may result in significant trade effects for its members'.[11]

This one-sided WTO remit, ignoring the environmental impacts of trade policy and the need to incorporate development objectives in the policy integration process, means that a range of intergovernmental bodies have to collaborate and new mechanisms have to be set up, to harness trade to sustainable development. Enhancing co-operation between these intergovernmental bodies will be a prerequisite for this, as will greater public participation in the international policy-making process.

The CSD has begun to address this need. At its second meeting in May 1994, the CSD formally recognized the importance of developing analytical and methodological frameworks to assess the environmental impacts of trade policies, taking into account the special needs and conditions of developing countries. And at its third meeting in April 1995, the chairman's report specifically recommended that the relevant UN bodies – UNDP, UNEP, UNCTAD and FAO – undertake such an impact assessment of the agricultural trade liberalisation agreement incorporated in the Uruguay Round Agreement, with the co-operation of the WTO.

Governments and inter-governmental bodies should launch this assessment urgently, and extend it to other sectors of trade liberalised under the Uruguay Round accords. The effects on the environment and sustainable development of the agreements on Trade-Related Aspects of Intellectual Property Rights (TRIPs), Technical Barriers to Trade, Subsidies and Countervailing Measures and the Dispute Settlement Understanding are of particular concern.

The assessment should take account of positive and negative effects of trade liberalisation at local, national and global levels, and should lead to recommendations to the CSD on appropriate responses to observed impacts. Those recommendations should include any modifications of the Uruguay Round agreements necessary to increase their compatibility with sustainable development. NGOs should be actively encouraged to participate in this assessment, which should run together with, and help guide, the implementation of the Uruguay Round agreements.

INTERGOVERNMENTAL PANEL ON TRADE AND SUSTAINABLE DEVELOPMENT

The second session of the CSD in May 1994, and all subsequent ones, have also highlighted the need for a broad international programme of work to integrate trade, environment and development objectives. The official mandates and expertise necessary to do this are widely distributed throughout the UN system, other inter-governmental bodies, academic institutions and NGOs. So the CSD has recognised the need for new institutional arrangements or mechanisms to co-ordinate this work.

An Intergovernmental Panel on Trade and Sustainable Development (IPTSD) could fulfil this need. Such a panel would ensure that trade and non-trade policy mechanisms relevant to sustainable development – such as foreign investment and technology co-operation and transfer – are discussed and analysed in the same forum. The panel would contribute multi-disciplinary analysis and policy formulation on the trade, environment and development interface, and help design cross-sectoral policy instruments to integrate these objectives. It could be mandated to deliver recommendations on policy initiatives and reforms to the CSD, the WTO and other relevant bodies.

The IPTSD would require the involvement of the relevant multilateral institutions – CSD, UNEP, UNCTAD, UNDP, WTO, the World Bank and IMF – national governments, appropriate scientific and legal institutions and NGOs. It would build on and integrate the work of the intergovernmental bodies and institutions, and that of independent expert panels on trade and sustainable development such as that recently established by the World Wide Fund for Nature. Such a forum would be more open and democratic than the WTO, and have an over-riding commitment to sustainable development, rather than pursuing trade expansion alone.[12]

Among its first priorities should be to:

- Explore, and make recommendations on, potential cross-sectoral mechanisms to integrate trade, environment, and sustainable development objectives.
- Develop policy instruments to secure commodity prices which reflect the true environmental and social cost of their production, and recommend the withdrawal of escalating tariffs on primary commmodities exported from developing countries.
- Develop recommendations on meeting the needs of developing countries for technical and financial assistance in the design, utilisation and response to, trade measures and technical regulations.
- Research, and make proposals on, the criteria under which trade measures may be taken, including development of the concept of 'green tariffication', whereby if tariffs are deployed to protect industries meeting higher environmental standards, the revenue generated could be repatriated to developing countries – possibly in the form of an environment fund, administered by a multilateral body, for investment in cleaner technologies.

This chapter has made the case that world trade rules are in urgent need of reform, in order to protect people's livelihoods, and to safeguard the environment. The reforms proposed above outline some of the most important steps that should be taken to integrate trade, environment, and development objectives: only within this broader perspective will it be possible to agree an effective international framework within which all countries would have the capacity and the opportunity to achieve sustainable development.

BANANAS

Current methods of banana cultivation carry high social and environmental costs. Like many crop farmers, banana producers have been struggling for higher yields per acre, partly to meet increased demand, but also in order to lower unit costs of production. Producers are also under pressure to produce more uniform fruit with fewer blemishes.

All of this leads to higher inputs of fertilisers and fungicides. The haphazard practice of aerial spraying has become the norm, while chemical-impregnated polythene sleeves – which are supposed to protect the fruit from disease – litter the fields, and pesticide residues build up in soils, fresh water and on coral reefs along the coast.

A European network of NGOs, supported by Oxfam UK/I, working with banana producers has made proposals for the reform of the European banana importing regime in order to create a quota for banans which have been produced in a fair and environmentally sustainable way. The proposals include a core package of minimum social and environmental standards, and a measurement for certification of sustainable production methods.

They are being blocked, however, by European Commission claims that such reform would be contrary to current WTO rules – which do not allow discrimination on the basis of the way in which products have been produced.

NOTES

1. Agenda 21, Chapter 2, Section B.
2. Paul Ekins, *Harnessing Trade to Sustainable Development*, Green College Centre for Environmental Policy and Understanding, Oxford, March 1995.
3. See Ekins' disucussion of the Kuznets Curve, Ekins, op cit; also Dieneke Ferguson et al, *Dangerous Curves: Does the Environment Improve with Economic Growth?* WWF International Research Report, Gland, Switzerland, February 1996.
4. The notorious 'tuna/dolphin' panel decision ruled that the US ban on Mexican-caught tuna was illegal under GATT rules, not only because it was discriminatory, but also on the more far-reaching grounds that it related to process and production methods, not products, and because the US was seeking to apply its laws outside its own jurisdiction. See Daniel Esty, *Greening the GATT*, Washington 1994.
5. See *Taxes for Environmental Purposes: The Scope for Border Tax Adjustment under WTO rules*, WWF International Discussion Paper, Gland, Switzerland, October 1995.

6. See Caroline LeQuesne, *Reforming World Trade: The Social and Environmental Priorities*, Oxfam, Oxford 1996.
7. Chairman's Text on Trade, Environment, and Sustainable Development, 26 May 1994.
8 WTO Trade and Environment Decision, 14 April 1994.
9. Prominent examples of MEAs which employ trade restrictions to enforce compliance include the Convention on International Trade in Endangered Species (CITES), the Basel Convention on the Control of the Transboundary Movement of Hazardous Wastes and Their Disposal, and the Montreal Protocol on Substances that Deplete the Ozone Layer. However, trade measures within these agreements have raised the prospect on inconsistency with WTO rules, notably the Article XI prohibition on quantitative restrictions on international trade, or the provisions of Articles I and III concerning national treatment and non–discrimination.
10. Sections (b) and (g) of Article XX provides, subject to certain restrictions, for exceptions to trade rules where these are 'necessary to protect human, animal or plant life or health', or where they are 'relating to the conservation of exhaustible natural resources if such measures are made effective in conjunction with restrictions on domestic production or consumption ...'
11. WTO Trade and Environment Decision, 14 April 1994.
12. For further discussion of the panel *see* 'Intergovernmental Panel on Trade and Sustainable Development' in *Making UNCED Work* WWF International, Gland, Switzerland, October 1994, and Caroline Le Quesne, *Reforming World Trade: The Social and Environmental Priorities*, Oxfam, Oxford 1996.

15

Indicators for Sustainable Development

Gary Lawrence

Everybody is a user and provider of information.
Vision and Today's Reality on Information for Sustainable
Decision-making, *Agenda 21,* Chapter 40.1

The creators of Agenda 21 concluded that one barrier to a more sustainable future for our species and our planet is the lack of relevant and accessible information upon which to base our decisions and to measure our progress. In Chapter 40, data, information, experience and knowledge are identified as the types of information needed.

Programmatically, two different information-related problems were called out for specific attention: information we need which does not exist and information we need which exists but which is not accessible. Most of the responses to this call for more and better information have taken the form of activities to develop 'indicators' and 'sustainability indicators'.

Differences between the types of information needed were not defined within the text. For the purposes of this paper, data means those discrete numeric, lingual and written descriptors of the phenomena which make up our life and world.

In the developed world there is an overwhelming amount of data. In many parts of the developing world the basic descriptors of current circumstances do not exist. For data to be useful to us, it must describe things which actually matter to our future. Objective and relevant data needs to be converted into information if it is to be useful in the development of sustainability indicators.

The term information is used to describe the aggregation of data into a form that is both relevant to the issue at hand and accessible to those who are engaged in addressing it. For example, data that is translated into text does not constitute information for those who cannot read, but the same data on a graphically focused compact disk or verbal form in the vernacular of the audience might be. Also data that is available on the Internet does not inform those who don't have access to computers or is not easily accessible without an understanding of Boolean logic.

The most common expression of the need for sharing experience has come through the plethora of 'best practices' initiatives. Both 'worst practices' and 'mediocre practices' produce valuable experience which can and ought to be shared as well, so experience here means a contextual understanding of what we have learned through trial and error. I will assume that knowledge, as differentiated from experience, is not limited to expert conclusions from basic and applied research. What we know in our hearts and what we know from the trial and error of those who have preceded us must also be taken into account.

Agenda 21 recognized not only the need for better, more relevant, and more accessible information, it also recognized some of the barriers which lead to our existing circumstances. Limits to financial and technical capacity, single sector world views, the commercialization of data, and policy and programme implementation without evaluation components have, among other factors, created mismatches between what we need to know and what we have the opportunity to know about our options – not to mention the consequences of those actions for our lives and for the earth.

Putting Chapter 40 into action in the past five years, the United Nations and other international organizations, national governments, local authorities and NGOs have expended significant intellectual and financial capital in attempts to improve the information base for future decisions and for the development of sustainability indicators.

Many of these efforts have provided dramatic increases in the capacity of communities to understand the causes and effects of the change in relationship to sustainability goals. Others have been more successful collecting data than they have increased their understanding.

This paper is not an evaluation of any of these particular efforts.

Instead, it draws some conclusions from efforts to date and suggests ways in which one might approach a goal of making 'everyone a user and provider of information'. Sustainability indicators can be an important tool for helping individuals, institutions, communities and societies make different and better choices about their futures.

It is important to remember, however, that they are not by themselves 'the answer'. If done well, they can lead us to better answers, but only if they provide trustworthy information about the things in life that we value.

Sustainability indicators are supposed to help people to understand what is happening to those attributes of the earth which make existence possible and pleasurable. More and better information is critical to the development of reliable indicators. But unless the knowledge compels people to examine their lives and to change their own individual and collective unsustainable behaviour, more information will not be particularly helpful. The wisdom to use the information in the interests of society seems to be the key.

INFORMATION AND INDICATORS

The concept behind sustainability indicators is very simple. They are intended to answer the question: 'How might I know objectively whether things are getting better or getting worse?'

Each of us has an intuitive sense that we rely on to answer the 'better or worse' question for ourselves, our families and our communities. Through this subjective process we develop a set of beliefs which guide our behaviour. Since most of us are not omniscient individuals, institutions and societies occasionally develop beliefs which are inconsistent with what might be concluded from more complete information. Many of those concerned about the ability of our planet to sustain our species, including the authors of Agenda 21, believe that one of the principal causes of our self- and planet-destructive behaviour is the reliance upon errant beliefs as guides to action.

Indicators built upon better information are supposed to help us to reduce our reliance upon errant beliefs. Proponents of indicators also assume that sources of more objective information which we can understand and which we are willing to trust either exist or can be developed. Indicators are intended to provide the quantitative or qualitative measures from which we can deduce the current state, direction and rate of change for the attributes of our existence. Once this information is easily accessible to societies, communities and individuals, it is reasoned, that we will reduce our reliance on intuition and increase our reliance on more objective information, and therefore make better, more sustainable decisions.

There are a number of different types of indicators, some of which will be discussed in the following section of this chapter. But first, we will examine some of the factors that should be considered when developing or using indicators.

Indicators will only be as good as the data that supports them. Yet even the most objective indicators based in solid science have subjective aspects. The decisions about what to measure, how to measure it, where the measurements will take place and how to describe the results, all have subjective components. Even more subjective is the choice one makes about what data to include as the basis for developing indicators.

Does the lack of perfect objectivity mean that we should not rely on data or experts? Of course not. Without the gathering of good data we would be lost. But it does suggest that those developing indicators need to be deliberate in their choice of sources, and they must accept that reasonable people can disagree and acknowledge the limits to certainty.

Once you have good data, who decides what the data means? Often we rely upon our institutions and experts for their interpretation. The experts, who have usually decided what data to collect, organize it into information, tell us what the data should mean to us and then tell us how we should change our behaviour in response.

The only difficulty with this method is that it does not seem to change people's behaviour very much. For example, public health and air quality experts have been very good at collecting data on the public health consequences of automobile emissions. They regularly issue reports that describe the situation, present alarming statistics, and tell us that we need to use single occupant automobiles less and lower-polluting forms of transport more. They have translated their data into information that identifies causes and recommends alternative behaviour. In many cases they also develop indicators to measure our progress toward better air quality and reduced congestion.

In the meantime, the vehicles per household, vehicle miles travelled and trips per household continue to increase in the developed world and are often among the first consequences of increased economic prosperity in the developing world. Why does our understanding of the consequences not lead to behavioural change?

In large part it is because few of us are willing to change our behaviour which is based upon someone else's determination of meaning. Successful indicator projects have to involve the community in deciding how to translate the data into information that is accessible to those whose behaviour needs to change. Too often the data gets translated into information that is accessible only to the people who collected it in the first place. This results in information that is poorly suited to communication with those who are not experts.

Once you have data in a form that the community can access, successful indicator projects will invite the community to decide what the information means to them and how they ought to act in response. People are very good at working out solutions when they believe that the problem is theirs to solve. Giving them the opportunity to translate the information into meaning for their own lives will give them 'ownership' of the problem. When the community 'owns' the problem, they are much more likely to act than if they believe that it is someone else's problem to solve.

People should be encouraged to let their emotions be engaged in deciding what the data mean to them. We are seeing too many indicators projects that are exercises in accounting. Few people get passionate about spreadsheets. For indicators to lead to change, there needs to be emotional content: people need to care in their hearts as well as in their minds.

This is not to suggest that we abandon rationality as the basis for indicators. There are many things that we can understand that ought to inform our choices. But if the understanding of this information is to be widespread, an interface is needed between the science and the individual – something that helps to make the information meaningful to them.

Communities can develop indicators that symbolize what the data means in terms of community values. Sustainable Seattle is a long-term voluntary initiative which has brought different stakeholders in the community together. Following extensive community involvement, they came forward with a set of relevant indicators. In Sustainable Seattle's work, for instance, the indicator for water quality is the number of wild salmon that return to the rivers and streams each year. They could have measured turbidity, temperature, percentages of oxygen, chemical composition, or any number of scientific measures, but people don't get emotional about facts such as 'parts per billion'.

In the Pacific Northwest, people do get emotional when their major cultural and economic resource – salmon – are in decline. Since the number of wild salmon is related to the quality of the surface waters, any solution to the salmon problem will necessarily involve improvements to water quality.

As we evaluate the success of the global response to Agenda 21's call for more and better information, we should consider whether the information gathered actually leads to better, more sustainable decisions. If the development of information from the data collected does not relate to the things which people value, then they probably do not matter very much. If indicators which link people's hearts and minds are developed, it is likely that they will be a much more effective tool.

TYPES OF INDICATORS

There are a number of different types of indicators. Each has its own strengths and each can be very useful if one knows, during the project design, the purpose towards which they will be used. Indicators can generally be categorized into three types: distinct, comparative, and directional.

DISTINCT INDICATORS

The tables in the United Nations Development Programme's Human Development Report, the Oregon Benchmarks and the governmental statistical reports on population or employment, are all examples of distinct indicators. They measure one thing, such as unemployment among white males aged 14 to 16 in Yorkshire. They have no normative content; there is no determination whether the number is good or bad, it just is.

Selecting at random from the 1996 Human Development Report, we find that 30.7 per cent of the total land area of Costa Rica was forest and woodland in 1993, and deforestation in Costa Rica in 1993 equalled an annual rate of 3.1 per cent, and so on.

Distinct indicators are beloved by many governmental institutions, economists, scientists and others who are interested in making sure that we have good data which allows for comparison across time. The best of this kind of data allows an understanding of what the conditions and forces were behind the change. Often, however, the reader just has the number with which to work.

A favourite example of a distinct indicator comes from Douglas Adams' *Hitchhiker's Guide to the Galaxy*. In a part of the book, the largest computer in the universe replies to the question: 'What is the meaning of life, the universe and everything?' – the ultimate sustainability index – with the answer '42'. Because the meaning was not in the least bit obvious, it became necessary to build an even larger computer to answer the question 'What does 42 mean?' Many people look at distinct indicators with the same comprehension as those in the *Hitchhiker's Guide* had for the answer 42.

Most distinct indicators are numerical representations of a condition that do not arouse the lay person to act: they lack the mechanisms which allow individuals to conclude 'intuitively and, therefore, I should do something about this'.

Many sustainability indicators projects statistics count without knowing what maatters for the future of a given nation or community. In the developed world, we often have more data than we can ever use. In most cases, what is lacking is not data but an understanding of what is important and the resolve to act.

In many parts of the developing world, there is a legitimate need to develop distinct indicators projects as the basis for change. But here again, knowing something and deciding to do something about it are two different steps. Collecting data is not a legitimate end in itself with regard to achieving the goals of Agenda 21. We must be willing to do something about what we learn.

COMPARATIVE INDICATORS

One way to start supplying meaning to distinct indicators is to compare them to similar indicators in other places. In the Human Development Report tables, there is some grouping of countries into categories for their rates of urbanization, social conditions, economic status, health status, and so on.

A better example is the European Sustainability Index Project's report which set out to 'develop indicators which can be measured in cities throughout Europe, thus enabling a comparison of sustainability levels between cities'. The comparison, it is suggested, is a 'valuable *leit-motiv* for development, analysis, adjustment and improvement of local policies'. This project looked at 12 European cities and compared statistics such as the percentage of registered companies which are involved in recycling, the average usage of water in litres per capita and the average number of trips per annum by means of public transport per inhabitant.

There are at least two advantages of comparing governmental bodies' responses to an important problem. One advantage is that the leaders in any category validate that making progress is plausible. Most public institutions are unwilling to take the political or financial risk. Knowing that it is achievable increases the likelihood that others will try to achieve the same ends, plus a little more.

The other advantage is that being last in quality of life measures carries significant political risks as well. No elected official or bureaucrat has made a successful career out of being the worst. If it can be demonstrated that your community has the worst air quality or the worst water quality or the lowest educational attainment, it is very likely that constituents will hold local politicians accountable for remedying the situation. The rebirth of Chattanooga, Tennessee, in the USA, is directly related to being named 'the most polluted city in America' in the recent past.

The problem with comparisons is that those in the middle often conclude that being in the middle is good enough. It is often politically safest to be average. If your nation or city was the 'best' and someone does better, then you are getting worse, and in a very public way. This is true even if you are maintaining the status quo: you were the best, now you aren't and you have some explaining to do. And, if you aren't the worst, then all you need to do is to avoid becoming the worst. Most of your constituents will probably think that you are doing well enough. Those communities which find themselves being successful will need something more than comparisons to spur them on.

DIRECTIONAL INDICATORS

Directional indicators are less focused upon numerical representations and are more focused upon action. Some people measure progress in relationship to specific standards or benchmarks. Others measure change in relationship to the state of nature which existed when the indicators were first developed. Each group is more concerned with direction than with absolutes.

Some good examples of directional indicators are Rescue Mission Planet Earth's Indicators for Action, which were developed as part of Habitat II, and Sustainable Seattle's Indicators of Community Sustainability. In many cases, it may be more important to know whether you are making progress towards the goal than it is to know the gap between the current situation and the goal you have set.

To understand whether the efforts undertaken over time are having an effect, you would focus more on the direction. To illustrate this point, imagine that a society or community has developed a reading comprehension test and that a score of 80 per cent or higher equals 'adult literacy'. Further, this hypothetical society has a goal that 100 per cent of their members should be able to meet this adult literacy standard by their 16th birthday.

Through testing, it is possible to determine, for any given period of time, the actual achievements compared to the goal. This information tells you what the situation is, but provides few clues about what to do. If you measured over time and understood whether the rates were improving or getting worse, you would know whether the efforts you are undertaking to increase adult literacy were working or not. Knowing the relative change over time, in this case, represents more effective information for evaluation and intervention.

In some cases it will not be possible to agree on an acceptable standard. In our example, some may think that a 70 per cent score equals literacy, while others may believe that it should be 90 per cent. A tremendous amount of energy is spent in battles over opinions about what is acceptable. In these circumstances, one may be better off forgetting the standard and just concentrating on the direction. You may not be able to agree on what score equals adult literacy, but you can probably agree that if scores are improving you are making progress, and that if scores are falling, then you have a problem which must be addressed. In many cases, the distinct indicators are used eventually as standards or benchmarks in directional indicators projects.

Using the Costa Rican examples above, let us say that the people of Costa Rica decide that acceptable standards for the percentage of land area in forest and woodland is 40 per cent, rather than the 30.7 per cent they had in 1993. Further, they have decided that there should be a

1 per cent increase each year. Their indicators would measure change towards the annual benchmark as well as change against the standard.

Questions can certainly be raised about the value of indicators without standards and benchmarks. Most revolve around concern that, unless we determine in advance what we are trying to achieve, it will not be possible to know when we are finished. Advocates for indicators which measure direction without benchmarks take the view that the most important attribute of sustainability indicators is agreement on what direction the community should be going, and that arguments over standards are barriers to achieving agreement upon direction.

CONCLUSION

In assessing progress toward the goals in Chapter 40 of Agenda 21, it will be much easier to measure activity than to evaluate results. Many important and well-conducted international, national and local initiatives have been dedicated to producing better and more relevant data. Often this work has been accomplished against tremendous odds. Best practice projects are proliferating and exchange networks are growing. Indicators projects are under way in most parts of the world. Everyone involved in these efforts to increase our body of knowledge and to make it more broadly available deserves both recognition and praise because all of this work is important. If activity is to be the measure of success during the five years since Rio, we have certainly been successful.

If by success we mean that this activity has resulted in information that is relevant to our lives being generally available in an accessible form – and opportunities exist to make choices based upon that information – then we probably have some work ahead of us.

In developing information and indicators there is no one right way for a community to proceed. There are a variety of models from which one might choose, and there are more models all the time. Communities all over the world in vastly different economic, political, social and environmental circumstances are experimenting with ways and means to develop information and indicators for neighbourhoods, communities or nations. Through the process they are also building consensus on what actually matters to the future of the groups involved.

While the processes and projects are different, there are some attributes which increase the chance that the outcomes are perceived to be legitimate and effective, no matter the particular form. They are:

- The data must be as objective as possible.
- The people whose behaviour needs to change for the community to have a more sustainable future must have a role in translating the data into information that is accessible to the diverse elements of the community.
- The people whose behaviour needs to change for the community to have a more sustainable future must be allowed to decide what the information means to them.

Information that is measured should evoke happiness when the situation improves and unhappiness when it gets worse. If the change doesn't matter to the community, you are not monitoring the right data. If the process of developing the shared knowledge, shared understanding and shared vision for the future of your community isn't enjoyable, you should discover a different way to do it.

Chapter 40 of Agenda 21 addresses a critical element in achieving a more sustainable future. Without better information it will be mere chance that produces better decisions. Institutions have an obligation to make data available in a form which is accessible to those who need it. Institutions also have an obligation to listen to what the information means to those whose quality of life is in the balance.

It is true that everyone must be both a consumer and a provider of information if we are to get the future envisioned in Agenda 21, but only if everyone listens to the information provided and feels empowered to use it.

16

Financial Resources for the Transition to Sustainable Development

Barbara Bramble

INTRODUCTION

Among the unfinished business of the 1992 Earth Summit in Rio, the one issue that has poisoned co-operation on the transition to sustainable development ever since has undoubtedly been the lack of follow through on 'new and additional financial resources' to assist that transition in developing countries.

Instead of an increment in official development assistance (ODA) specifically to finance sustainable development, which many Southern governments expected, overall ODA levels have stagnated with several traditional sources actually declining since 1992. Even the funding for the conservation of biological diversity, which was highlighted in both Agenda 21 and the Biodiversity Convention, has not increased. The industrial nations, led by the United States, have pointed to private investment flows and a reliance on market forces, as more promising alternatives to finance the transition to sustainability. But private capital is disproportionately available to only a very few countries and can depart without warning.

This chapter outlines the recent history of ODA and other financial flows to developing countries, and the current state of the debate over where the financial resources can be found for the transition to sustainable development. It points out the NGO view that how funding is made available, what it is used for and who decides, is often more important than levels of funding.

In order to advance beyond stalemate, a group of NGOs proposes that the Commission on Sustainable Development (CSD) should establish an InterGovernmental Panel on Financing for Sustainable Development. Modelled on the Inter-Governmental Panel on Forests, it would be charged to review evidence of the need, sources and methods for providing the finance needed by those developing countries and countries in transition which are embarked on a process to achieve sustainability. It would also make recommendations concerning the need for intergovernmental agreements to advance this goal. It should report back to the CSD in 2000.

THE EVOLUTION OF THE RIO COMMITMENT

During the preparatory negotiations for the UN Conference on Environment and Development (UNCED), the gulf between the positions of the G77 representing the developing nations and that of most of the industrial countries, was stark. The UNCED Secretariat had prepared preliminary rough estimates of the costs to the developing countries of the transition to sustainability – $625 billion per year in total, with $125 billion seeming a fair share to be provided from external sources. Since external aid then averaged about $60 billion per year depending on the method of calculation,[1] the implication was that more than a doubling of financial assistance would be required.[2]

The G77 leadership frequently and ardently pressed their case for continuing the existing aid pipelines and priorities, with the new demands of Agenda 21 being financed from 'new and additional resources.' During the negotiations leading up to the Earth Summit in June 1992, the industrial countries were of mixed views, with several European nations accepting the need for substantial new and additional resources, and the United States in the lead of those who felt that 'sustainable development' should be funded by shifting existing aid flows to more sustainable uses. Most European negotiators made considerable efforts to sound accommodating to the G77, whether or not they agreed with the United States' position, while the latter refused to make any new commitment to meet a development assistance target.[3]

In return for this elusive commitment for financial assistance, the bulk of Agenda 21 forms the broad outline for mutual commitments and understandings for national action and policy change to achieve sustainable development.[4]

In the end, a sort of subterfuge was adopted, in Principles 6,7 and 9 of the Rio Declaration, and Sections 13 and 14 of Chapter 33 of Agenda 21. This language allowed all parties to read into the agreement what they wanted to see.[5] With this history of the negotiations, it was almost inevitable that expectations among the participants would be sharply divergent for future aid allocations from donor countries.

A Snapshot of Financial Flows

Official Development Assistance

Ironically, 1991–92, the years of the UNCED negotiations, saw the high-water mark of development assistance, measured in constant dollars. Overall aid levels began to recede thereafter, and have dropped sharply since. Only four countries – Denmark, Sweden, Norway and the Netherlands – have met their 0.7 per cent of GNP target. Japan has greatly increased its aid allocations, becoming the world's largest donor at $14.5 billion in 1995. But because of larger GNP growth, it has fallen to 15th ranking in terms of its percentage of GNP. Almost all the other donor countries have decreased their ODA allocations: France by 12 per cent in 1995, Germany by 5 per cent, the United Kingdom by 6 per cent. The starkest case is the United States, which dropped by 28 per cent in 1995, and further reductions are on the horizon. The US is now fourth in absolute terms, and last among donor nations in terms of percentage of GNP. Collectively, the OECD countries have reduced their ODA to well under 0.30 per cent of GNP.[6]

The fall of total development assistance is not even slowed by the significant rise in allocations by the European Union, from $4.8 billion in 1994 to $7.5 billion in 1995.[7] Disbursements from the Multilateral Development Banks have held their own, but the future is clouded by US reluctance to negotiate its continuing share in these institutions. At the same time, there are many new claimants to this shrinking pie. The countries of Eastern Europe and the former Soviet Union were not significant borrowers or donees in 1992. Nor was South Africa. Furthermore, increased priorities in the Middle East can be envisioned if the peace process resumes progress.[8]

As a result, there is a pervasive sense of betrayal among all parties.

The G77 nations feel that a promise for financial help was made and broken. Leading spokesmen for nations of the South have warned against 'backtracking' and 'lack of political will.' The countries of Eastern Europe and the former Soviet Union (countries in transition) feel that they were left out of the Rio process altogether. The industrial countries feel there was a commitment by all participants to adopt certain policy changes to promote sustainable development and to improve the use of existing financial resources, which is not being kept.[9]

The spill-over effect from this loss of trust was exhibited in the negotiations for the subsequent UN summits and conventions on Population and Development (Cairo, 1994), Social Development (Copenhagen, 1995), Women (Beijing, 1995) and Human Settlements (Istanbul, 1996). With each negotiation, it became increasingly difficult to agree on the appropriate language to describe the goals of that conference and its resulting action plan. Consensus began to fall apart even on the meaning of the phrase 'sustainable development' and how it would apply to each of the 1990s conferences. Many government negotiators and non-governmental observers had hoped that the series of 1990s conferences would produce a clear picture of the road to sustainable development, comprising the action plans of all the related conferences. But this vision has been muddied because of the lack of agreement on responsibility, including financial responsibility, for what must be done.

Wholly apart from the question of the overall levels of ODA is the issue of how much of the current ODA flows is being used for sustainable development. It is difficult to track ODA to the commitments of Agenda 21, because statistics are not collected in many of the necessary categories.[10] While the OECD is working to correct this, at present their statistics assume that *all* ODA is devoted to sustainable development. Moreover, the majority of technical co-operation is excluded from the key compilation.[11] And although the OECD Working Party on Statistical Problems claims that support for environmental projects has risen, a study of trends in funding for biological diversity conservation found no evidence of an increase, despite the formation and replenishment of the Global Environment Facility.[12] Finally, the all-important question of the quality of aid also bears on how to measure the ODA shortfall; but this issue is far beyond the scope of this paper.

PRIVATE / COMMERCIAL FINANCIAL FLOWS

Rather than official financing, what has grown is direct foreign investment, commercial bank lending and bond lending. Over the last ten
years, net flows from private/commercial sources of funding increased
from approximately $25 billion to over $170 billion. This includes
direct corporate investment from DAC countries, which grew from
$10.7 billion in 1986 to $60 billion in 1995; international bank lending, which rose from $7 billion in 1986 to $75 billion in 1995; and bond
lending, which rose from $1 billion in 1986 (and actually $1 billion in
1987) to $19.3 billion in 1995. [13]

Although there has been an overall trend of growth since in late
1980s, the increase in private sector flows has been marked by surges
and slow-downs – for example, from $11 billion to $31 billion in 1992,
and back to only $9 billion in 1993. In addition, this growth was
unevenly distributed among the developing and transitional countries.
Almost three-quarters of the direct corporate investments were made in
only 12 countries,[14] and there is no reason to suppose that this investment would have been made to promote the objectives of Agenda 21.

DEBT AND STRUCTURAL ADJUSTMENT

Although space precludes a thorough analysis of the role of external
debt and structural adjustment in the financing of Agenda 21, it must
be pointed out that, for some countries, these factors loom larger than
the prospects of either ODA or private investments. Far from being
under control, as many have assumed from the lack of headlines, the
total debt of all developing countries rose by 8 per cent in 1995 and
now stands at over $2 trillion.[15] For the severely indebted low income
countries, the debt situation has not improved, despite the recent
agreement of bilateral lenders to enhanced relief through the 'Naples
Terms,' and the September 1996 World Bank/IMF first step toward
debt reduction.[16]

The statistics on debt and debt service by themselves do not determine the severity of the problem; the real question is whether an economy faces insolvency. But further analysis shows that the progress
recently touted for developing countries applies by and large only to the
middle income countries. [17] The majority of low-income countries still

face year after year of debt overhang, which combines with the pressures from interest groups to crowd out public expenditures for 'new'-looking priorities such as sustainable development. Many NGOs have called for further action to reduce debt, particularly for the poorest nations. Birdlife International, among many others, recalls that Agenda 21 includes debt relief within its definition of 'new and additional resources' and recommends linking relief with environmental and sustainable development programmes agreed with the countries concerned. [18]

Similarly, many observers blame structural adjustment programmes for promoting anti-sustainable economic trends, such as reductions in key government expenditures for social needs, increases in poverty and consequent over-reliance on fragile natural resources. At the very least, adjustment programmes could be designed specifically to enhance and safeguard domestic funds to promote sustainable development, but they rarely are. While the impacts of the typical adjustment package (including deficit reduction, currency devaluation and trade liberalization) depend entirely on how they are administered and in what time frame, care is needed to design a programme that does not result in increased poverty and reductions in key budget areas such as health care, education and natural resources management. A nine-country study commissioned by the World Wide Fund for Nature found that attention to such a design was the exception rather than the rule, and negative impacts on the environment and natural resources occurred in almost every case. [19]

FUTURE PROSPECTS TO IMPROVE THIS PICTURE

Most commentators do not see prospects improving for a significant increase in the amount of traditional official development assistance, for either concessional loans or grants, in the near future. Those countries which have maintained their commitments or even increased them (the Nordic countries and Japan) are now likely to wait for others to catch up. Even if the United States is able to arrest the decline in its aid funds, a major increase is unlikely. And until the downward trend is reversed in the United States, there is little incentive for major European donors to halt their own declines. Thus, even the most optimistic forecasts look for more or less steady ODA commitments, or perhaps small increases. And the increases in future are likely to be targeted – for example, to child survival and girls' education, not to general development assistance.

Direct foreign investment, while drastically increasing at the present time, will likely continue to be characterized by rapid fluctuations, not a steady upward trend. The area that may well increase significantly is public/private financing, arrangements by which public sector financial institutions such as the World Bank boosts private investor confidence – for example, through co-financing, loan guarantees and political risk insurance for private sector activities in developing countries. Serious consideration is being given in the US, for example, to increasing participation in the private sector windows [20] of the MDBs. In addition, the US might agree to increase its contributions to the public sector windows of the MDBs in return for changes in their charters to permit funding directly to, and to support the growth of, the private sector. [21] Several bilateral export credit agencies are also expected to increase their activities.

Although this kind of funding might assist the growth of private investments in activities that feature sustainable development, there is little indication that it will be the purpose or the result. Policies are still needed in most developing countries that would steer these investments in sustainable directions, through either regulations or incentives. The US Export Import Bank, the World Bank's Multilateral Investment Guarantee Agency and International Finance Corporation, and the Japanese Export Import Bank have all recently announced new policies and procedures to integrate social and environmental concerns into their financing decisions. But officials of these private sector windows stress that they depend on 'customers' coming to them; they claim to have little possibility of promoting businesses that would further sustainability, such as those that feature high employment and low resource use, energy efficiency, clean industrial process technology or non-timber forest products, etc.

Moreover, in a pattern established over recent years, as mentioned above, only a few countries are likely to benefit from the expected increases in these private sector investments in the foreseeable future.

Finally, prognostications of future refinements in the international politics of debt forgiveness and adjustment conditionality are far beyond the role of this paper.

INNOVATIVE SOURCES OF DONOR FUNDS

A number of proposals have been made over the last few years for ways to raise funds among the industrialized nations and wealthy publics to support increased assistance to countries that implement their own sustainable development action plans. At the last count, there were at least 20 different kinds of fees and taxes mentioned as possible candidates. [22] Most of the proposals break down along the following lines:

- The dedication of a share of national taxes on pollution emissions or related activity. This category could include an international agreement to split the revenues from, for example, a carbon tax, with a portion going to assist developing countries.
- Allow a sustainable development purpose to be carried by a tax or fee imposed for an unrelated purpose – many of the investigators of the feasibility of a Tobin-type fee, which is intended primarily to reduce dangerous volatility in the currency speculation markets, have proposed to dedicate at least part of the revenues to support the UN sustainable development agenda, particularly in developing countries.
- A fee for the exploitation of resources over which no existing nation has sovereignty (the global commons). This could include deep sea minerals, civil aviation, and satellite parking fees.

The more promising among these options have recently begun to be the subject of serious study. [23] All of these proposals raise a host of questions, including: Does the tax or fee promote sustainable development itself? Does it further distort appropriate market incentives or does it correct for market imperfections? Are its distributive effects neutral, or could it be deliberately slanted to benefit a particular group? Could it be easy and cheap to collect, and hard to evade? Who would benefit, who would lose out, who would oppose it and how could agreement be reached? Are there any legal barriers in existing treaties, or new instruments needed? What might be the yield from imposing the fee and what objectives or organizations might lay claim to the revenue? [24]

Among these, the biggest stumbling block at present is that any such solution would require the agreement of all the members of the UN. With the conservative Congress of the United States challenging that nation's participation in the UN on many fronts, the prospects for agreement on an international tax at this time seem slim indeed.

A Perspective on Financial Resources for the Transition to Sustainable Development

There are two different perspectives from which to view the subject of this chapter – financial resources for the transition to sustainable development. One is that because the developing countries have specific financial limitations, and because sustainable development imposes additional financial burdens at least in the short and medium term, the primary necessity is to provide donor assistance to developing countries to help cover these additional costs.

From this point of view, the key information to judge progress on financing Agenda 21 includes the current status of traditional sources and the amounts of donor assistance; forecasts of the potential for increases in these flows; and innovative sources and mechanisms for increased ODA flows in future. See *A Snapshot of Financial Flows*, a brief distillation of this data.

But another perspective is that *all* nations are far from the path of sustainability, and all face an essentially similar task: to rearrange economic and financial incentives and other market signals as part of the process of conversion to sustainability. In this view, the goal is to ensure that these incentives and signals all pull in a sustainable direction. This latter view posits that most financial resources for sustainable development can be found as a result of the policy changes demanded by sustainability itself. This implies that the question is not limited to, or even principally about, mobilizing donor funds, but instead *redefining what are considered financial resources*. The main problem in this view, in both North and South, is to surmount the short-term political hump which the new approach to economics presents, when interest groups object to changes in the current order. Financial resources may be needed to cushion the distributional costs which some interest groups face during the conversion. For all countries, there are significant start-up costs in the form of improved regulatory and enforcement systems, and providing adequate information and investment vehicles to overcome investor reluctance. This analysis would indicate clear and limited priorities for the highest value use of donor assistance in the short term: to lever significantly larger private investments for sustainable development.

In the limited space here, the author regrets that she is not able to do justice to either of these two perspectives, but hopes that this brief summary will spur the reader to more detailed treatments.[25]

As part of their contribution to the deliberations of the CSD, Japan and Malaysia have for the last three years hosted an experts group which has assessed the various alternative methods of attaining the domestic and external financing requirements of Agenda 21. The report of the latest meeting of this group in Manila earlier this year catalogues several key categories of improved policies which can yield both sustainable development and sources of funding.

MEASURES WHICH ALL COUNTRIES CAN IMPLEMENT UNILATERALLY

Without a large increase in public expenditures, most countries could go a long way toward sustainable development through promoting favourable private sector behaviour and investment. In fact, with proper encouragement, including the implementation of the 'polluter pays' principle, the great majority of funds needed for investment in clean industrial technologies; energy, water and sanitation services; housing and improved mass transit; and sustainable agriculture, soil conservation and wetlands rehabilitation, can come from private landowners and investors. This can be accomplished either through requirements imposed by regulation, such as pollution emission limits, through tar-geted financial incentives, such as favourable interest rates, tax credits, speedy permit procedures, or tradable permit systems, or through a mixture of the two approaches.

The magnitude of the incentive that is necessary depends on the risks and costs of the venture as it is perceived by the investor.

Therefore, the incentive-based mechanisms would be more economically viable to the extent that the investor perceives the extra costs as relatively small (so the government can reimburse them at a manageable cost). Several prerequisites can ensure this, which are within the domestic policy control of governments:

- Sound and predictable macro-economic and environmental policies: These are necessary to convince businesses, farmers and others that they can depend on predictions of future inflation, tax, interest and exchange rates, and the certainty of regulatory requirements to make their investments worthwhile.
- Credible and stable regulations based on broad public consensus and effectively enforced: Businesses can afford to increase expenditures

for sustainability, such as new technology for pollution reduction at source, as long as their competitors face the same costs.

- Specific measures to reduce the market risks and transaction costs of investments in new technologies: These could include modest revolving funds for pre-investment studies (costs to be recovered from successful deals).
- Information, training, clearing-house services and marketing assistance: Investors need introductions to promising opportunities.[26]

The Expert Group also examined the use of environmental funds, such as pollution abatement funds (PAFs) and conservation trust funds (CTFs). These instruments are dedicated lines of credit for environmental or other sustainability investments. Both kinds of funds can generate needed investments, especially where capital may be scarce or regulation weak. But they 'can potentially lead to a mismatch between investment needs and financial allocations' because preferential credit terms will attract investments away from other purposes.[27] On the other hand, the fact that PAFs and CTFs are dedicated to environmental purposes has been shown to increase public support for the fees or taxes necessary to generate the funds.

MEASURES WHICH WOULD BETTER BE IMPLEMENTED BY MANY COUNTRIES IN CONCERT

Other methods of promoting sustainability through economic instruments have cross-border implications. For these, much like the analogous experience with phased tariff reductions through the General Agreement on Tariffs and Trade, international agreement for concerted action is indicated. For example, reducing agricultural, energy or other subsidies, or raising depletion charges on the extraction of natural resources, would be candidates for concerted action, since all nations would fear a competitive disadvantage from unilateral action. Imposition of eco-taxes, such as for pollution-emissions, would seem to have a similar disincentive, although several countries have gone ahead with sulphur and carbon/energy fees already.[28]

PROPOSAL FOR INTERGOVERNMENTAL PANEL ON FINANCING FOR SUSTAINABLE DEVELOPMENT

As noted above, the political repercussions of the failure to come to an agreement about financial resources for sustainable development have been serious. Despite the five years of post-Rio debate among governments, little progress has been made to develop a consensus on what financial resources are actually needed to implement Agenda 21, much less how to bring them to bear. The Japan/Malaysia Expert Group meetings have produced increased understanding about the many options available for financing sustainability, but they have not been able to move into a detailed examination of the methods for their implementation. This group does not have a mandate either to make recommendations or to explore the areas where concerted governmental action is needed. The report of the Secretary General to the last meeting of the CSD concerning financial resources and mechanisms recommended that:

> *The Commission may wish to advance the policy dialogue on economic and fiscal instruments through an active exchange of information and review of experiments with a view to removing obstacles to their effective use.*[29]

In response to this suggestion, the NGO Working Group on New Financial Mechanisms[30] proposes the establishment of an Intergovernmental Panel on Financing for Sustainable Development to address this gap. The panel would be composed of government delegations authorized by the CSD to examine in detail:

- The actual costs of the transition to sustainable development, including analysis of those costs which are best financed by external assistance; those costs that are more appropriately covered in the process of domestic policy change; and the special needs of low-income countries for concentrated use of scarce development assistance funds.
- The sustainable development impact of development assistance resources made available to date, including both the purposes to which funds were dedicated and the quality of aid.
- Experience (both successes and failures) with use of all relevant financial mechanisms to promote sustainable development, including economic instruments which both encourage behaviour change and raise revenue.

- Identification of those economic instruments, such as fees and taxes, which would be implemented more effectively through international agreement to maintain fair competition.

The panel should draw upon existing work, such as that of the Japan/Malaysia Expert Group. It would be charged to bring together a larger and more diverse body of experts to aid in its investigations, and to make available detailed information on its findings on the above matters. It should include, and perhaps be chaired by, representatives of finance ministries as well as by environmental and/or social development ministries. It should make recommendations on the question of whether intergovernmental agreements are necessary or useful to implement appropriate actions to finance Agenda 21 and the related action plans.

We recommend that the panel be established by the CSD during its 1997 session to review the implementation of Agenda 21. The panel should meet a minimum of four times, submitting its first report to the CSD in 1999. The final recommendations would be completed in 2000.

NOTES

1. *Development Cooperation – 1995 Report*, 'Total Net Resource Flows to Developing Countries,' Table 1, Organization for Economic Co-operation and Development, Paris, 1996.
2. In providing its estimate of financing needs for Agenda 21, the UNCED Secretariat assigned costs to the long list of major sector– and resource–specific environment and development problems under discussion for the UN conference. *See* A Markandya, 'Financing Sustainable Development: Agenda 21,' (1994) Harvard Institute for International Development, Harvard University. This was a different approach from that taken at the Cairo International Conference on Population and Development, where costs were assigned to a specific agreed action plan with limited objectives. Some participants in the negotiations observed that the international share of Agenda 21 costs came close to the total that would result from multiplying the GNP of the 24 member countries of the OECD by 0.7 per cent, which since 1970 had been an agreed, but largely unmet, target for official development assistance.
3. During and after this debate among the governments, a number of non-governmental organizations took a different tack. After several years of following the lending practices of multilateral development banks (MDBs) and some bilateral agencies, they knew that simply making

additional resources available was not necessarily a solution. In fact they had found that much MDB financing had adverse impacts on both poor people and the environment. They had been pushing for MDB reforms to emphasize the basic elements of sustainable development, even before that term was well understood – social equity and public participation in decision-making; broad-based economic improvement, with an emphasis on reducing poverty; and environmental health, for both people and eco-systems.

Throughout the UNCED negotiations and the later CSD sessions, the NGOs pressed for public participation and transparency, and monitoring of all development assistance, with open accountability to the supposed beneficiaries. They also recognized that debt relief, reduction of Northern trade barriers against products from the South, and innovative funding sources would prove more important than aid flows. *See*, for example, 'Informal NGO Paper on Financial Resources and Mechanisms,' presented to the First Session of the Commission on Sustainable Development, 16 June 1993.

NGOs were also seeking funding mechanisms that would make financial resources preferentially available to those official and non-governmental actors who were undertaking projects which embodied all the characteristics of sustainability and were democratically organized and managed. National environmental funds have since come into being in over a score of countries in response to this call.

4. Many of these general commitments would require specific arrangements and action plans to bring them to implementation. Some areas that were only sketched in Agenda 21 were filled in, in depth and detail, in the Conventions on Biological Diversity, Climate Change and Desertification, and in the subsequent UN conferences of the 1990s, on Population and Development (Cairo, 1994), Social Development (Copenhagen, 1995), Women and Development (Beijing, 1995) and Human Settlements (Istanbul, 1996).

5. In Section 33.13, nations agreed that 'Developed countries reaffirm their commitments to reach the accepted United Nations target of 0.7 per cent of GNP for ODA and, to the extent that they have not yet achieved that target, agree to augment their aid programmes in order to reach that target as soon as possible ...' The point to remember here is that the United States had never made *any* commitment to reach that target, so they had no commitment to reaffirm. Beyond that, they had only agreed to try to reach that target as soon as possible, which is no more than business as usual. European countries, many of whom *had* made the commitment to reach the 0.7 per cent target over the years, faced a more difficult ethical dilemma.

6. *Development Cooperation – 1995 Report* (1996) OECD, Paris.

7. 'Total aid by all EU Members combined, including that channelled through the EU and other multilateral bodies, amounted to $31.5 billion, a fall of

over 8 per cent in real terms' from 1994 levels. 'Financial Flows to Developing Countries in 1995,' OECD News Release SG/COM/NEWS(96)63, 12 June 1996, p.7.

8. Nineteen nations reached agreement in 1996 to establish a new Middle East and North Africa Development Bank. Although the majority of the capital for lending will come from the private bond markets, there is no reason to expect that the 25 per cent of paid in capital agreed by the members will be 'new and additional resources.' This institution will increase the competition for the already stressed foreign affairs budgets of the donor countries.

9. See, for example, proceedings of 'Financing Sustainable Development into the 21st Century', a series of NGO–government panel discussions at the UN Commission on Sustainable Development, sponsored by the UN Environment and Development UK Committee and National Wildlife Federation of the US under the auspices of the CSD NGO Steering Committee (1996–97, in manuscript); and 'CSD Expert Finance Meeting Produces Menu of Financial Options,' Third World Network, 16 February 1994.

10. 'Financial Resources and Mechanisms, Addendum, Report of the Secretary-General,' Commission on Sustainable Development, Fourth Session, E/CN.17/1996/4/Add.l, 22 February 1996.

11. OECD 'Official Development Assistance Data,' Review of DAC Statistics, Reporting on the Purpose of Aid, OECD DAC Working Party on Statistical Problems, 1996.

12. 'New and Additional? Financial Resources for Biodiversity Conservation in Developing Countries 1987–1994,' Royal Society for the Protection of Birds, UK, 1996, pp. 8, 13–16.

13. Development Cooperation – 1995 Report 'Total Net Resource Flows to Developing Countries,' (1996) OECD, Paris.

14. Those 12 countries are: Argentina, Brazil, Chile, China, Greece, Hungary, Indonesia, Malaysia, Mexico, Nigeria, Poland, Thailand. World Debt Tables 1996, The World Bank, Washington, DC, USA.

15. World Debt Tables 1996, The World Bank, Washington, DC, USA.

16. The principal remaining stumbling blocks are the refusal of bilateral creditors to deal with the full stock of debt, and the World Bank/IMF delay of six years before relief becomes effective, combined with tough conditionalities that in most cases do not take sustainability goals into account.

17. World Debt Tables 1996, The World Bank, Washington, DC, USA.

18. Op.cit note 12, p 24.

19. David Reed (ed) Structural Adjustment, the Environment and Sustainable Development, (1996) Earthscan, London.

20. The 'private sector windows' of the MDBs are established to lend or provide investment guarantees directly to private corporations. This includes the International Finance Corporation and Multilateral Investment Guarantee

Agency of the World Bank and their counterparts at the regional MDBs. This is in contrast to the 'public sector windows,' such as the International Bank for Reconstruction and Development, and the International Development Association and their regional counterparts, which can only make loans to government entities.

21. 'U.S. and the Multilateral Development Banks,' Task Force Report, prepared by the Center for Strategic and International Studies, Washington, DC, USA, 1996.
22. 'New Sources of Finance for Development,' Briefing Paper, Overseas Development Institute, London, February 1996.
23. 'Implementation Strategies for Environmental Taxes,' Eco-taxes OECD, (1996); Gunnar S. Eskeland and Shantayanan Devaranjan, 'Taxing Bads by Taxing Goods: Pollution Control with Presumptive Charges,' (1996) The World Bank, Washington DC; *Wuppertal Bulletin on Ecological Tax Reform*, (1996) Wuppertal Institute, Spring. Tobin fees: *The Tobin Tax: Coping with Financial Volatility*, Mahbub ul Haq, Inge Kaul and Isabelle Grundberg (eds) (1996) Oxford University Press; *Futures: The Journal of Forecasting, Planning and Policy, Special Issue: The United Nations at Fifty–Policy and Financing Alternatives*, vol 27, no 2, March 1995; David Felix, 'The Tobin Tax Proposal: Background, Issues and Prospects,' UNDP Policy Paper, 1995. Global commons: Rolf Selrod (ed) 'A Painless Solution? An Analysis of Two Alternatives for Global Taxation for Financing Climate Activities under the United Nations Umbrella' (1995) 'Center for International Climate and Environmental Research, Oslo.
24. Overseas Development Institute, *op cit*, note 22, p2.
25. *See* Theodore Panayotou, 'Financing Mechanisms for Environmental Investments and Sustainable Development,' UNEP Environmental Economic Series paper no 15, Nairobi, August 1994; and 'Financial Issues of Agenda 21,' Report of Third Expert Group Meeting, sponsored by the governments of Japan and the Philippines, the Asian Development Bank and the UN Department for Policy Co-ordination and Sustainable Development, Manila, 6–8 February1996.
26. *See* 'Financing Issues of Agenda 21' *op cit*, note 25, p3.
27. *Id* at p 4.
28. *Environmental Taxes in OECD Countries*, OECD, Paris, July 1995.
29. Report of the Secretary-General, 'Financial Resources and Mechanisms for Sustainable Development: Overview of Current Issues and Developments,' Commission on Sustainable Development, E/CN.17/1996/4, February 22, 1996, para 33.
30. The Working Group on New Financial Mechanisms for Sustainable Development is one of several working groups of the CSD NGO Steering Committee.

17

Building Sustainable Production and Consumption Patterns

Elizabeth Dowdeswell

As this century and millennium draw to a close, as we mark the 50th anniversary of the founding of the United Nations and enter into a new – although still undefined – world order, there is ample cause for reflection.

There is a desire, a need, to make sense of what we are doing, to make sure that we are not repeating past mistakes and that we are cleaning up the unfinished business of the 20th century. Will society, through the state, the entrepreneurial sector and other social sectors, be able to forge a new culture that is more altruistic and equitable to replace our society of superfluous consumption and inequitable holding of land and resources, in which the short-term earnings of the few prevail over the integrity of nature and the well-being of present and future generations?

In Stockholm in 1972, the international community assembled to consider another threat to peace – the destruction of the environment. Two decades later, environmental conditions on the planet have deteriorated even further. Three Mile Island, Bhopal, Chernobyl, holes in the ozone layer, climate change, desertification, habitat destruction, species extinction, marine and freshwater pollution, overfishing – the list goes on and on.

It is clear that there are structural reasons for this continuing destruction of the planet's natural resources. But the point is that, in the face of ample evidence that we are destroying the earth's capacity to support life, we continue to do it. Conventional wisdom continues to be overwhelmed by other forces.

In the last four decades, the population of the world has more than doubled and by 2030, it is expected to stabilize at between 8 and 12 billion. From 1950 to 1985, manufacturing output increased by a factor of 7 and electricity output increased by a factor of 8. The impact on the global environment has been dramatic: in 150 years, human activity has increased the atmospheric concentration of carbon dioxide by 25 per cent and doubled the concentration of methane. Both are potent greenhouse gases. The global deforestation rate for the tropics is 0.8 per cent per year. As a result, we are observing an alarming loss of biodiversity.

Human-generated emissions of lead, cadmium and zinc – all toxic metals – exceed the natural flux by 18 times. Currently, an average person in North America consumes almost 20 times as much energy and resources as a person in India or China, and 60 to 70 times more than a person in Bangladesh. In fact, if 7 billion people were to consume as much as they do in the West today, we would need 10 worlds, not one, to satisfy these needs.

These figures are well known and have been reported and quoted in many reports and publications. They put in a nutshell the challenge addressed at the Rio Earth Summit. Unless we come to grips with the structural forces that seem to constrain our ability to establish a healthy relationship with the environment, that relationship will, ultimately lead to our downfall. The question is, can we now change course?

I tend to be an optimist. I like to think that problems can be solved, and I believe that human beings are capable of averting the looming environmental crises. But I must admit that my deep concern and worry is that, given current trends, I do not see this happening. There is an environmental reality with which we are failing to come to grips. And I believe that it is time to be honest and to deal with what we know to be the trends on this planet that constrain our ability to respond.

In our world, the agenda is set by economics. This is reality. There is almost no room any longer for qualitative assessment of the world we are creating. Everything is quantitative. We constantly find ourselves trying to draw the links between the environment and economics. No matter what we feel, no matter what our intuition tells us about the needs of the environment, we must prove its worth in dollar terms.

We are engaged in cost-benefit analyses, in putting monetary values on aspects of the environment, we argue for the internalization of the true costs to the environment into pricing. We are dreaming. We are at best a minor ripple on the great tide of liberalized trade, and we are making no appreciable progress in this struggle.

The concept of sustainable development, elaborated by the Brundtland Commission and then entrenched in policy by the Earth Summit, was viewed by many as a great step forward for both the environment and the development agendas. Among other things, it represented an attempt by the environmental community to engage the economists with language they could use. Here was a term that everybody could buy into. The question is, who captured whom?

The environmental movement has had some moments of glory, some significant successes, but, compared to the scope of the change that is needed, we are tinkering largely in the margins. We are unwilling to deal with the real causes and confront the forces of our own making that are destroying the planet. We are deluding ourselves.

But we must also look more deeply than this. We must look at ourselves as a species and understand what it is about us that has made it possible to engage in so damaging a relationship with our environment. It is our view of ourselves as being separate from nature that is at the heart of the matter. We put ourselves in a management role outside of nature.

We study nature as we might study the mechanics of an automobile engine, imagining that we are capable of knowing enough to take full responsibility for its operation. We make ourselves gods in our dealings with nature. We are denying our humanity, our mortality, our fallibility. Because in reality, we cannot hope to manage all the complex dynamics of nature, we inevitably make mistakes. But because we have put ourselves in essentially a god's role, we have no means of acknowledging our mistakes. Instead we deny them. We rationalize them away as not being so important in the scheme of things.

If we could reconnect with ourselves as mere mortals, as fallible human beings, we could acknowledge and learn from these mistakes. If we could, with humility, return to our position within nature in an interdependent relationship with all its living organisms, we could take responsibility for our action and their impacts on all life forms.

Hope lies in whatever ability we have to reconnect with our own humanity, to see that our aspirations for peace and security are closely bound up with the health of the environment in which we live. We must see that we are part of nature, and that our relationships with it are essential for our survival. We must recognize that as important as the economy is, it must be viewed and used as a tool in the service of the people, in the fulfilment of human needs. We must recognize that the market has distinctly limited abilities in attributing value to many aspects of life that contribute to our well-being.

The answers do not lie in an 'end-to-development' philosophy, or in restricting the legitimate aspirations of developing nations, or through coercive policies or limiting individual choice, or in deepening ideological divisions. What is required is:

- A global commitment to action.
- The assumption of individual responsibility.
- A return to the original meaning of the word development.

Embracing the concept of 'sustainable development' is not simply an acceptance of a semantic shift from the words 'environmental protection'. It is a fundamental rethinking of how our world works. It strikes at the heart of our economic and political systems and decision-making.

Making the environment a forethought, not an afterthought, is a radical concept. Our fundamental definition of development must change. It can no longer be regarded as merely a problem of modernizing traditional societies. It should not be a mere duplication of the energy- and resource-intensive development path pursued by the developed countries. It has to recognize local circumstances, the potential for internally generated growth, the contribution of traditional institutions and knowledge. It has to be inherently geared towards sustainability.

The new paradigm of development must have a human face. It has to focus on human needs and poverty alleviation as well as on economic growth. It must concern itself with equity and should enlarge people's choices, increase opportunities and develop human capabilities.

Secondly, we have to realize that natural capital is a scarce and limiting factor rather than a free good, and that new socially and ecologically based methods of economic analyses are needed to account for the depreciation of natural and human capital.

Until recently, the language of mainstream economics has defined the economy in market terms, without giving much attention to non-market elements such as subsidies provided by eco-system services, subsistence activities, household labour or cultural aspects of human social systems. This must change.

Building sustainable production and consumption patterns globally is a task of immense complexity. It means changing the underlying economic principles, including the relationship between the North and the South, in a co-operative long-term endeavour. It means examining our societal goals and life-styles, injecting an ethical perspective to our action. It means living within the ecological limits of our planet and the social limits of society. It means reducing our 'footprint' on earth.

The UN Environment Programme (UNEP) is aiming to create awareness of the need to change production and consumption patterns, and to build consensus on the policies and tools which will achieve the necessary corresponding increase in resource productivity, as well as related pollution prevention at source.

As we define the ecological ground rules of sustainability, let us think like people of action and act like people of thought. After all, there are only two choices in life – to accept things as they are or to take responsibility for changing them. I am counting on the latter.

BOX 5: SUSTAINABLE PRODUCTION AND CONSUMPTION

Current trends in population, industrialization and consumption growth release wastes and pollutants faster than the earth can absorb them. Natural resources are consumed faster than they can be restored. So the need to reorient production processes, products and services, as well as the demands expressed by consumers, is a key issue on the sustainable development agenda. Recognized at the United Nations Conference on Environment and Development (UNCED), sustainable production and consumption has been identified as one of the five UNEP work programme areas. UNEP's Cleaner Production Programme is one of the other initiatives under way.

Cleaner production is the continuous application of an integrated preventive environmental strategy applied to processes, products and services. It aims to increase eco-efficiency and reduce risks to humans and the environment:

- Production processes: Conserving raw materials and energy, eliminating toxic raw materials, and reducing the quantity and toxicity of all emissions and wastes.
- Products: Reducing negative impacts along the life-cycle of a product, from raw materials extraction to its ultimate disposal.
- Services: Incorporating environmental concerns into designing and delivering services.

Cleaner production requires changing attitudes, responsible environmental management and evaluating technology options.

Other preventive approaches, such as eco-efficiency and pollution prevention, serve similar goals.

Much of the current thinking on environmental protection focuses on what to do with waste and emissions after they have been created. The goal of cleaner production is to avoid generating pollution in the first place. But it can also be the most efficient way to operate processes, produce products and to provide services. Costs of waste, emissions and environmental and health impacts, can be reduced and benefits from these reductions and new markets can be found.

The Cleaner Production Programme aims to:

- Increase worldwide consensus on a 'cleaner production' vision.
- Catalyse the implementation of: policies and strategies, environmental management systems, environmentally sound technologies and products, and set up national cleaner production centres.
- Support the growing network of organizations dedicated to promoting cleaner production and eco-efficiency activities.
- Help to enhance capabilities through training and education.
- Support demonstration projects and provide technical assistance.

The programme brings together international organizations, governments, industry, non-governmental organizations and academics.

Part IV

PERSPECTIVES ON
THE FUTURE

18

Perspectives on the Future from the UN: The First Steps from Promise to Performance

Nitin Desai

The Earth Summit in Rio was seen by many as a decisive acceptance of sustainable development as the basis for policy, both in the framework of development co-operation and in the work of the United Nations in development. Five years later, in June 1997, the nations of the world will meet to assess the extent to which these hopes have been realized, and what needs to be done to revive them and to ensure a more effective move from promise to performance.

WHAT HAS BEEN ACHIEVED

The Commission on Sustainable Development (CSD) is the body which is charged with the responsibility for the follow-up of the Earth Summit. A mere reading of the mass of resolutions and decisions which have emerged from the CSD does not make the main achievements very clear. Their major successes, in fact, include the Global Water Assessment, the establishment of the Inter-Governmental Panel on Forests, the work programmes on sustainable development indicators, on environmentally sound technology, and on consumption and production patterns – all of which go much beyond what existed earlier.

In a different way, the presentation and discussions of national experiences and the use of expert panels to inject informed advice into the work of the Commission during its annual sessions, also constitute a significant advance.

There have been major achievements outside the Commission on sustainable development, some of which are reflected, for example, in the reorientation of the work programmes of the FAO and the UNEP, and the evolution of the convention's related processes. Among these, one can point to the finalization of the Convention on Desertification, the further developments in the Climate Change and Biodiversity Conventions, the establishment of the Intergovernmental Forum on Chemical Safety and the initiative to give a legislative basis to the prior informed consent procedure for chemicals, the agreement on land-based sources of marine pollution.

Balanced against these important achievements are areas where the expectations have not been fulfilled. These include the issues of finance and technology.

Much of the ground already covered during the UNCED has repeated itself in the CSD. This is an area where real progress has been made in the restructuring and replenishment of the GEF and in the reorientation of existing aid flows. But it is also true that the absolute flow of development assistance has declined from around $60 billion at the time of the UNCED, to around $55 billion in 1995. The decline is even greater if we take account of inflation and the growing share of emergency relief assistance.

When it comes to technolgy transfer, the sense of disappointment is just as great. Innovative approaches have been proposed both for finance and for technology transfer as part of the deliberations of the CSD, but they have not been pushed to the point of implementation.

With regard to process, the CSD has been a success, with several achievements:

- The relationship between the national–international dimensions has been elucidated through the CSD. They have high-level involvement of the people from headquarters and capitals who are responsible for the implementation at the national level.
- There is an increasing realization that sustainability needs a broad-based consensus involving not just governments, but also civil society, activists groups and NGOs. This idea is well accepted in the CSD and continues to permeate the post-Rio processes.
- Recognition that discussion of sustainability in a two-week session of the CSD is not enough is reflected in the frequent formal and informal discussions at national and international level, including

intersessional working groups of the Commission, and in the pro-
grammes and agendas of other bodies.
- In the United Nations, it is clear that the entire system services the
CSD.

The first phase of the Commission's work has been innovative and,
because of this, has retained the interest of senior policy-makers and civil
society. But a second phase that simply repeats the thematic structure of
the first stage may become repetitive and too caught up in detail, thus
running the risk of losing this interest.

The CSD does not oversee directly the specific programmes for
implementation, but its influence comes from its co-ordinating role, its
openness to ideas and its credibility as a mechanism for setting strategy
and policy. It must continue to innovate in terms of process and, in its
next phase, needs a structured approach that keeps the basics of sustainability in sight.

THE TASKS AHEAD

Sustainable development is a complex concept. It permeates Agenda 21
and the flow chart may help to understand this concept and the underlying structure of Agenda 21. The flow chart is simplified and is a
graphical way of presenting a long sentence. In terms of chapter headings, the driving forces and the resource categories are readily identified
in Agenda 21 – as are some of the sectoral categories such as agriculture,
fisheries and forestry.

A crucial element of Agenda 21 which is missing from the flow
chart is the role of the different actors. This additional dimension is relevant for each of the elements of the chart, and could be illustrated with
the addition of an axis protruding from the chart. The chart shows the
driving forces which determine the level and pattern of economic sectoral development. This in turn drives the pattern of resource use by
which goods as well as 'dis-services' are produced, with the overall
resulting impact on the welfare of current and future generations. Our
objectives, both for environmental and development policy, must be
defined in terms of these ultimate impacts.

Working back from these impacts, which are at the bottom of the
chart, it is clear that sustainable development requires actions which are
oriented around resources, economic sectors and driving forces.

MANAGING RESOURCES

A great deal of our work has focused on the right-hand side of the chart – on the management regimes for resources, and the negative economic and environmental impacts.

The earth's resources are being depleted or degraded already at a rapid rate and it is essential that we find more efficient ways of using them. Many useful measures can be taken with resource categories, such as land, water, oceans, atmosphere, and so on, to provide the organizing principle for action. Broadly speaking, these would include:

- Resource monitoring and assessment – for example, setting up or strengthening national resource surveys or arrangements for the international exchange of information.
- Setting standards – for example, for air and water quality.
- Regulatory arrangements and policies to ensure responsible resource use, as with land-use controls and fishing quotas.
- Global or regional agreements for the sharing of resources; agreements for the management of interstate rivers or regional seas.
- Eco-system research for understanding better the linkages between resources, like the SCOPE project of the International Council of Scientific Unions (ICSU), the Man and Biosphere project and the World Climate Programme.

The task of establishing appropriate regimes for the responsible management of resources at the local, national and global level is by no means easy. But for most natural resource categories, the required processes are under way and, in some cases, global conventions are in place. For resources such as land, fresh water, forests and oceans, Agenda 21 provides a unified framework that places the diverse uses of these resources in an integrated context. The CSD has maintained this unified approach in the co-ordination arrangements that support its work in relation to fresh water and oceans, and in the initiative it has taken for the Global Water Assessment and the Inter-Governmental Panel on Forests.

Yet the available evidence on land degradation, air and water quality, the depletion of fisheries, the loss of forest cover and biodiversity remains disturbing. The improvements in process have not yet led to results. One part of the task now is to move forward in a co-ordinated way at the national and international level, to ensure that the unified approach to resource management is reflected in specific programmes and, most importantly, to ensure adequate funding for all types of resource management activities. But more than this, resource management has to be embedded in development policy and in the policies that influence the pattern of resource use.

Integrating the Environment and Development

To integrate the environment with development, we must look for solutions not just through environmental action, but also through developmental measures.

In the case of forests, for example, there are many instances where, despite strong legislation, they continue to be depleted. In such cases, the real solutions may lie in enhancing land productivity in areas near forests, or in providing alternative energy sources for villages and small towns. Such development measures are seldom the subject of forestry policy.

More generally, it is clear that the way in which people use resources is determined as much by the pressures and incentives generated by prices, taxes, subsidies and the general framework of development policy, as by regulatory measures and other environmental programme initiatives. So our approach on environmental matters has to be broadened to ensure that environmental concerns are incorporated into all areas of development policy.

The reverse is equally true, and when environmental standards are set, they must take account of developmental imperatives.

The left-hand side of the flow chart is the subject of development policy in its broadest sense. What is needed is real integration of both the left- and the right-hand sides – for example, we must look at land, forests and fresh water in the context of agriculture and agricultural policy.

This is the importance of sectoral approaches. The chart shows an organizing principle which will help us to look at Agenda 21 sectorally. Thus one can ask what Agenda 21 requires us to do in economic sectors such as agriculture, industry, transport or energy. This is important because economic policies are generally organized by economic sector and are by far the dominant influence on the way in which resources are used.

Sustainability needs to be injected into the agendas of the entities that determine sectoral policies for agriculture, industry, transport, tourism, energy, and so on. The CSD can help to do this by bringing together, in a coherent way, the implications of Agenda 21 and the Rio principles for such sectoral policies.

The contributions of the Commission could be considered in the forums where the primary responsibility for the sector rests. But there are some sectors for which appropriate international forums are not available and the Commission itself can fill the gap.

In this sectoral work the Commission must remember that it is not an environmental forum but a body committed to sustainable development. In terms of the flow chart, the focus must be as much on maximizing the services provided as minimizing the 'dis-services', or negative impacts generated.

The crucial importance of the sectoral approach is illustrated in the chart. Sectoral development provides the link between the driving forces and the resource and environmental impact. Unless sectoral issues are addressed, any discussion of the impacts of consumption or population growth, for instance, will remain incomplete or overly general.

ADDRESSING THE DRIVING FORCES

Sectoral development and resource impacts are interlinked and driven by more basic factors, such as growth in demand, technological developments, value systems that shape consumption preferences, population growth and persistent poverty.

The international economy can be thought of as a driving force because of the way in which trade, resource flow and technology transfer affect the national capacity for sustainable development.

The CSD has attempted to address these driving forces. At least two – population growth and poverty – are being addressed very directly in the follow-up processes of other UN conferences – in particular, the UN Conference on Population and Development, the World Summit on Social Development and Habitat II. The role of the follow-up process to Rio must be seen in the light of these later developments.

The CSD needs to take the lead in calling for appropriate actions to alter the pace and pattern of resource-intensity in consumption growth. Some of such action, such as tourism in coastal areas or energy efficiency, will inevitably be sectoral and more logically considered as part of what is described above as the sectoral approach. But others, such as the monitoring of overall trends, guidelines for consumer information, recycling, waste minimization, raising awareness and promoting responsible consumption, are generic and would have an impact across the sectors. The Commission has to continue to assume the prime responsibility for pursuing these goals.

When it comes to technology diffusion, the focus for defining actions is probably more clearly sectoral. A discussion about the orientation of research, technology transfer and diffusion at the sectoral level can lead to conclusions that are specific and operational in three key areas:

- Building up national capacities.
- Providing for concessional transfer in areas of global importance.
- Developing multinational co-operative programmes of technology development between public authorities, research institutions and industry.

Much of this discussion has to be technical and the real responsibility of the Commission must be to work towards a consensus that such a discussion does take place in an appropriate forum – such as the Consultative Group on International Agricultural Research (CGIAR) for issues relating to agricultural technology and the governing bodies of UN entities that are involved in field-level implementation.

Within the Commission itself, the focus would be on general issues about how public policies can stimulate innovation and diffusion of technologies that are more conducive to sustainability.

The issue of financial resources can be considered at different levels. At one level, it is an issue about the level and distribution of global savings, a matter that is linked in some ways with the level and distribution of global consumption. Addressing this brings us into some core issues of international economic relations, including the phenomenon of globalization which is under discussion and negotiation in a variety of forums.

The real challenge is injecting the principles of sustainability into the formulation of macro-economic policies to make sure they are effective tools of sound development.

To illustrate this, we can look at the subject of trade. Earlier discussions on trade and the environment were peripheral to discussions on trade policy, but the CSD has raised the profile of the subject.

Parameters set out in Agenda 21 and developed in the Commission have resulted in a situation where the discussions in the World Trade Organization (WTO) start with the basic premises of Rio and the CSD. Thus, we have been able to inject sustainability into the mainstream of trade policy discussions.

A similar approach is needed in finance to ensure that the ideas of sustainability influence the mainstream discussions on development assistance and private investment flows.

Apart from the macro issues there is another level – the flow of finance for Agenda 21 activities. The hope was that the work of the Commission would lead to concrete commitments, probably in other forums, and give specific recommendations to multilateral financial institutions about needs, adequacy and related policy matters. This hope has yet to be fulfilled, and developing the relationship between the Commission and multilateral financial institutions is an important task ahead.

RECOGNIZING THE HUMAN DIMENSION

Agenda 21 is clearly focused on changing the way in which resources are used to meet needs. In doing so, however, it addresses the human dimension of sustainable development in several ways – in its discussion of poverty, demographic dynamics, education and health, and the role of major groups.

In this area there is a large overlap between Agenda 21 and the programmes of action resulting from other global conferences. In the interests of a coherent response at the intergovernmental and national levels, this dimension of Agenda 21 must be seen as part of a co-ordinated response to UN conferences, through the ECOSOC and the interagency task forces that have been established to follow up the recommendations of Cairo, Copenhagen and Beijing.

There are, however, more specific matters like the links between the environment and resources on the one hand, and health, education and empowerment on the other. These have to be discussed as a part of the core agenda of sustainable development.

In many ways the issue of values is linked to the human dimension. There are broad questions with regard to the relations of humans to nature, to each other and to future generations. More specific questions relate to rights and obligations, responsibility and liability, reflected, for instance, in the Rio Declaration on Environment and Development.

But what could be the nature of a follow-up on the issue of values? One possibility is to keep under review the extent to which the Rio principles are reflected adequately in the other follow-up actions. Another would be to discuss the issue regularly in the Commission, simply to remind ourselves that value systems matter.

THE CRITERION FOR ACHIEVEMENT

With reference to the flow chart, the effectiveness of the post-Rio process will have to be measured ultimately in terms of its impact on the welfare of current and future generations:

- Are we closer to meeting human needs?
- Is the quality of life improving for the world's population?
- Are we reducing risks to the quality of life and our capacity to meet needs?
- Are we broadening options for the future?

It is easy to lose sight of these ultimate objectives, and the whole exercise of developing and agreeing to sustainable development indicators is meant to address this. It is an area where some progess has been made both in securing political agreement and in the technical work. But much more remains to be done.

The measures of achievement are not yet available, but whatever evidence we have suggests that the results are still modest – increased awareness, some changes in the stance of policies and improvements in process. We must remember, however, that our present condition is the result of at least two centuries of unsustainable development which can hardly be corrected in five years. At best, we have taken the first steps and the road ahead remains long and arduous.

SUSTAINABLE DEVELOPMENT CHART

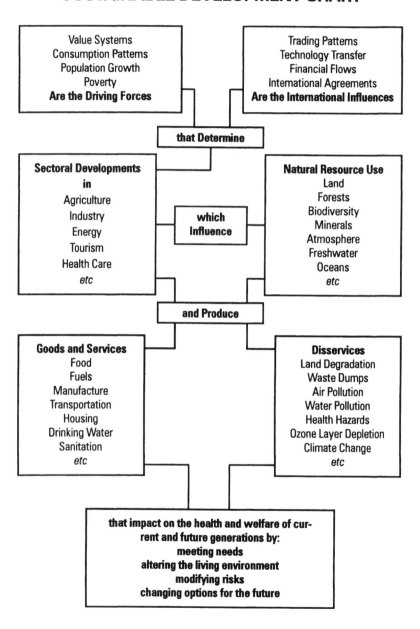

Value Systems
Consumption Patterns
Population Growth
Poverty
Are the Driving Forces

Trading Patterns
Technology Transfer
Financial Flows
International Agreements
Are the International Influences

that Determine

**Sectoral Developments
in**
Agriculture
Industry
Energy
Tourism
Health Care
etc

**which
Influence**

Natural Resource Use
Land
Forests
Biodiversity
Minerals
Atmosphere
Freshwater
Oceans
etc

and Produce

Goods and Services
Food
Fuels
Manufacture
Transportation
Housing
Drinking Water
Sanitation
etc

Disservices
Land Degradation
Waste Dumps
Air Pollution
Water Pollution
Health Hazards
Ozone Layer Depletion
Climate Change
etc

**that impact on the health and welfare of current and future generations by:
meeting needs
altering the living environment
modifying risks
changing options for the future**

19

The NGO View of the Next Ten Years: Thoughts on Moving from thé Basement of the UN to Global Implementation

Peter Padbury

LEARNING FROM THE PAST

During my first few years in the meeting rooms in the basement of the UN, I was very optimistic. We seemed to be breaking new ground in both the process and content. NGOs seemed to play a significant role in the policy dialogue. There were breakthroughs in the process which allowed NGOs to participate more fully in both formal and informal meetings.

NGOs also devoted considerable financial and human resources to research, policy development and advocacy for UN processes. We were rewarded, in a way, when a significant amount of NGO text was incorporated in the declarations and action plans for the conferences on the environment and development, climate change, biodiversity, desertification, social development, women, population, human settlements and food security. But something just did not seem right.

Between 1992 and 1996, UN intergovernmental meetings created at least nine action plans and attempts at an agenda for peace and one for development. The NGOs who worked on these negotiations began to understand some of the structural or systemic problems, of which the weak and vague action plans are only a symptom.

There are many ways to account for the slow pace of change in the transition to sustainability. Large parts of the global accords failed to move to implementation because they were too abstract and the transition strategy to make them real was not clear yet.

Some threatened the established order of sovereign states with inordinate demands. There was an unwillingness to set goals – to reduce CO_2 to 1990 levels, for example – which would have forced us to focus our efforts. There was little or inadequate funding as traditional sources of development funds shrank and even disappeared.

There was also a new agenda and new priorities with the political swing to the right, and we were unable to demonstrate the economic, social and environmental significance of sustainability in the debate over the last few years.

The fact that the role of the state, the market and civil society are undergoing profound change all over our planet, does not make our task easier. Indeed, politicians who are frantically trying to stabilize the situation by reducing budgets and promoting growth in the economy probably don't see sustainability as their salvation.

The core of the problem is that we, the readers of this book, are the 'early adopters' at the beginning of a long change process, perhaps a century-long process. If we are going to succeed, we must be far more effective and strategic than we have been in the immediate past. This chapter outlines some of the key challenges that we face over the next ten years and then explores the actions we could take to address these challenges in the context of governance, the market and civil society.

Many of these ideas have been shaped by years of conversations with colleagues who are active in UN processes, at The Canadian Council for International Co-operation (CCIC), at the International NGO Forum and especially with Junie Kalaw of the Earth Council.

THE KEY CHALLENGES AHEAD

SHIFT FROM POLICY DIALOGUE TO IMPLEMENTATION

On many key sustainability issues, the international policy dialogue has probably gone as far as it can at this time. The next step in the learning process is to press for greater implementation. In the next few years one of the major tasks is to move from the abstract to the specific, to operationalize the term sustainability at each level from local to global.

OPERATIONALIZE SUSTAINABILITY

There is much confusion and growing cynicism about the term sustainable development. It is a conceptual fog for many people. We need to be clearer about our strategy to promote it.

One of the important challenges is to define what it means in concrete terms. Many NGOs have suggested a very precise meaning – we should focus on developing sustainability. This process involves developing the indicators, plans, data, tools, operational policies, business practices, public commitment and institutional arrangements at every level from local to global to ensure that humanity lives within the carrying capacity of the global, life-support system.

FINDING NEW RESOURCES

The transition to sustainability will require resources. At a time when government budgets are shrinking, we need to think about the problem in new ways. Some people point out that there is no shortage of financial or human resources on this planet – we just have to find ways to mobilize those resources so they help to develop sustainability.

LEARNING TO MANAGE A GLOBAL SYSTEM

Global issues are emerging which can only be solved through international co-operation. Environmental problems are the clearest examples of global issues: without significant international co-operation, little progress can be made.

The behaviour of sovereign governments is blocking significant progress. We need to reinvent the system of governance so that it includes all citizens, because each day they all shape the future through their hopes and fears, actions and choices.

BUILDING PUBLIC AND POLITICAL SUPPORT

It is often forgotten, but this may be the limiting factor and thus the most important point. Many of the people who are on the inside of the policy dialogue assume that a few simple, essentially technical, changes can solve most of the problem. But there is considerable resistance to many technical fixes because they trigger more fundamental issues for many people. Given the progress in the last few years, public and political understanding and support has to be put near the top of our list.

LAYING THE FOUNDATIONS FOR IMPLEMENTATION

All of these challenges are different faces of the same problem: we are trying to change a system that is becoming increasingly unsustainable. The common element in each one of the challenges is the need to work together. The structure and culture of most organizations discourages co-operation across organizational boundaries. Sustainability will require an unprecedented level of co-operation and co-ordination so that long-term objectives can be achieved and problems dealt with, rather than be dumped on someone else who is uninformed or poorer or far away.

The following focuses on what we have to do to lay the foundation for co-operation to ensure that these challenges are addressed and implementation occurs.

BUILDING A GLOBAL SYSTEM FOR GOVERNANCE

We need to build a system that works with and empowers actors at each level from local to global – it is not a global government, therefore. If we take the challenge of sustainability seriously, we will have to build new mechanisms of co-operation between governments, businesses and civil society that are more like a network of relationships than independent islands.

Below is a brief analysis of some of the problems with the current system and then some proposals for changes that would move us from rhetoric to action.

THE PROBLEMS OF THE CURRENT SYSTEM

- There is little synergy between the levels of governance from local to global. The strategies and agendas do not reinforce each other – sometimes they even undermine each other. Each level is a system on to itself. At the global level, no one is minding the shop. In most intergovernmental processes at the UN – the board of directors for Planet Earth – the member states act in their own short-term self interest. States seldom speak from the perspective of our long-term collective interest.

- The UN process of consensus-building is very impressive. But on major issues, the products are frequently of little consequence. Often the initial negotiating text prepared by the secretariat after consultation is very good, but with each round of negotiations it becomes more general, abstract and rhetorical.

  The diplomats who are uncertain whether anyone in their country cares about the issue will act to ensure that the document does not bind or embarrass their governments – in other words, they make sure that nothing happens. The people who 'own' the problems seldom have the opportunity to use the international mechanisms to resolve global issues.

  It is not a simple matter, however, there are many reasons, including major North–South differences, which help to explain but not to overcome the stalemate.

- It is striking that much of the decision-making and financial infra-structure to support the transition to sustainability is focused on the international level, but much of the actual work is on the local and national level, where there is very little infrastructure to support that transition.

- The whole 'international system' was built during the age when the nation state was powerful, when there were resources to control, and when the state had a large role to play in building and managing the economy.

- Despite the emergence of a global economy with global problems, much of the debate at the UN is still from the perspective and needs of the nation state. Nation states are competing to preserve their fleeting advantages rather than co-operating to create a world that is equitable, just and sustainable for all.

RETHINKING THE SYSTEM OF GOVERNANCE

- **The UN as a network** The key change is to recognize that gov-ernments at each level, from local to global, have international responsibilities. For instance, most cities do not see that they have a responsibility to limit or reduce carbon emissions.

A network is a vehicle for sharing information, resources, decision-making and implementation. The objective is to promote greater co-ordination and synergy. The people who own the problem and are willing to act are involved. The principle task is to build the infrastructure that allows all of the players to play their part. Some of the following proposals will help to turn the UN into more of a network.

- **The role of the global citizen**   Our role as citizen is our most encompassing role. It needs to be reinvented in the context of a global system. We are simultaneously citizens of a city, a province, a nation and a planet and we have responsibilities at each level. As each level of government accepts its responsibilities in managing a global system, our responsibilities as global citizens will become clearer to people.

  Tools like sustainability indicators will help people to see the global system, but politicians, educators and NGOs will have a special role to play.

- **Politicians as facilitators**   In the 1990s, the accepted role of national governments is to provide a supportive policy environment which encourages and supports market forces to promote growth. The real challenge over the next ten years is to reinvent a public sector that we can afford.

  With fewer resources in the foreseeable future, it is very likely that the state and politicians will become more like a facilitator, a consensus-builder, a catalyst and a mobilizer, bringing together elements of civil society and business to address social goals and responsibilities.

  This facilitator role is also consistent with what is required to promote sustainability at the local, national and international levels. It will help to create a culture of co-operation.

- **Create a system of forums for sustainability**   The CSD should move beyond monitoring Agenda 21 to a forum for policy dialogue and co-ordination on specific sustainability issues where there was a will to act. The unique niche for the CSD is to identify and address the problems that countries encounter in the transition to sustainability, and that require international co-operation to solve.

  At the local and national levels, parallel multi-stakeholder forums have to be created or recruited, such as like the national commissions on sustainable development and local Agenda 21 exercises. This network of forums should:

– Provide factual overview reports on the progress and coming problems.

– Manage an agenda-setting process to identify the strategic issues where there is a collective will to act.

– Experiment with innovative processes for policy dialogue and collaboration among actors at different levels.

– Build consensus on the indicators, instruments, policies and institutional arrangements that are necessary for developing sustainability.

– Promote risk assessment of threats to global environmental services and develop risk-reducing policies and risk management strategies, if appropriate.

– Model and encourage co-ordination and collaboration with all major groups.

● **A new agenda-setting process** The key to a relevant, effective and strategic CSD is an agenda-setting process that identifies issues and problems where there is a will to act. As we start the implementation phase, we need to allow the people who are doing the implementing – and thus who own the problem – to influence the agenda-setting process so that it is facilitating implementation.

The 'national report process' should identify the problems the country has encountered in implementing sustainability that require international co-operation to solve. In formal session, the CSD would identify those problems where there was a collective will to act. Discussing real problems and catalysing strategies to solve these problems would make the CSD a useful and more strategic forum.

● **Expand participation in the consensus-building process:** The people who own the problem must have more opportunity to influence the decision-making process at the CSD. The CSD has to give the diplomats the tools to facilitate quickly and effectively a more direct relationship with the people in capitals who own the problems.

The secretariat should take full advantage of electronic communications to expand participation in the document drafting process and allow all interested government departments and others to use the opportunity in more concrete and constructive ways. In particular, it should allow governments and major groups who cannot afford to come to the meetings to contribute.

- **Improve governmental accountability**   The UN, like many similar institutions, is suffering a crisis of public confidence. Much of the responsibility for the failure of the UN must lie collectively with the governments who run it. One of the standard ways of dealing with such a crisis is to make the system more transparent and accountable for its results.

    The problem with the UN is: who are they accountable to? The UN is a servant of the member states. A case can be made to democratically elected governments that mechanisms to increase their accountability are in their interest. Increasingly, national policy cannot be made in isolation from international policy. A citizenry that understands global issues will be an asset.

    An effective and accountable system of global governance will take decades to build. There are now several ways to increase accountability:

    - Make the process more accessible and visible. Open all the doors and processes to NGOs – the witnesses for the general public. This will help to rebuild public credibility.
    - Use the CSD national report process and sustainability plan reports as an opportunity to work with major group networks to assess progress, to identify the lessons learned and to promote accountability.
    - Bring the CSD agenda home to the local and national sustainability forums.
    - Work at the national level with major group networks to develop national positions for the CSD.
    - Include NGOs on delegations.
    - Report the positions taken at the CSD and the results achieved to the media and major group networks.

THE ROLE OF CIVIL SOCIETY

Civil society is an important player in promoting sustainability. There is much debate about what civil society is. Simply, it is formal and informal groups, usually non-profit making, that are working to promote the public interest as they define it. Civil society usually includes groups for the environment, development, church, women, youth, labour, consumerism, and so on. Civil society plays a number of important roles to promote sustainability that government and business cannot or will not play:

- It builds public understanding and political will for change.
- It challenges unacceptable behaviour in the media and courts.
- It sets targets and standards about appropriate behaviour.
- It stands witness for the general public in the eyes of the media and thus can legitimize and bring credibility to an event or process.
- It has helped to shape the way we think, by means of research and concept development.
- It has tested and demonstrated many practical changes.

Civil society has evolved rapidly. In the beginning, its organizations were formed by citizens who were concerned about one aspect of the public interest, but, as time passed, they often recognized that their issue was part of a system and they had to work with other groups to promote change systematically. So, over the last 20 years, we have seen the development of issue, national and international networks, and finally networks of networks.

Generally, international networks are formed to address global issues. If the world was working properly, global issues would be resolved by an effective system of global governance; that system would be able to articulate the global public interest and develop effective global policies to preserve global public goods. So these networks work together to attempt to articulate the global public interest and to build a national political constituency to change national positions in international forums.

Several networks have started to define the norms and processes for working together. They want to be more effective and more accountable in working for change in UN intergovernmental processes. In doing so, they are starting to lay the foundations for a global civil society.

It will be 20 years before the mechanisms are in place that allow the development of co-ordinated and shared strategies involving hundreds of millions of people in many countries, who are concerned about the same global public interest question. But it is coming.

The Philippine NGOs are a good example of what an organized civil society can accomplish. Over the last five years they have:

- Set up the Philippine Commission on Sustainable Development – the PCSD has 14 appointed cabinet ministers and 7 elected NGO network representatives – with a counterpart NGO secretariat to serve the civil society processes.

- Run a training programme on sustainable development for many bureaucrats, politicians, NGOs and people's organizations.
- Developed a set of community indicators and accounts to facilitate local and regional planning and decision-making for sustainable development.
- Begun to experiment with endowment funds to finance consensus-building processes and new ways to finance sustainable development projects.
- Conducted a national consultation – two rounds of three months each – to prepare a draft national sustainability plan (Philippine Agenda 21) which the NGOs will use in the coming debate on the national five-year plan.
- Persuaded the President of the Philippines to put sustainability as the top concern in Asia Pacific Economic Cooperation (APEC) discussion.
- Strengthened the co-operation between their own networks with a formal treaty.

Clearly, civil society can be a very significant ally in the effort to move from UN documents to implementation in the real world. The following actions would help them be more effective:

- Create an enabling environment for civil society organizations; this would include the protection of human rights, access to information, preferential tax status to encourage donations, ideally some government support for core costs, and so on.
- Open the decision-making process. Much time has been spent on the question of resources at the UN – the problem is not a shortage of money. There is plenty of money in the world – the real task is to engage civil society in the planning process so that when the plan is finished, civil society wants to invest in and implement the plan because it is *their* agenda.
- Treat civil society organizations like partners: NGOs bring analysis, expertise and solutions to the policy dialogue and implementation process. They are catalysts which can help to mobilize significant public will and resources. More than many others, they can link local action with global dialogue. They want their role and contribution to be recognized and understood by governments. They want to be treated with respect.

In the next ten years it is likely that we will see continued rapid growth in national and international networks, working on different aspects of the transition to sustainability. They will be co-ordinating their efforts locally, nationally and internationally. Civil society organizations are ready to be partners or to be critics. They would like to be partners.

THE BUSINESS COMMUNITY

We have witnessed some significant shifts in the business community in the last ten years. Phrases like 'responsible care', 'life-cycle planning' and 'eco-efficiency' are now in the business literature. Insurance companies are forcing businesses to avoid environmental liabilities. Businesses have seen the damage that bad environmental practice can do to shareholder earnings and are attempting to be more open, transparent and responsive to public and environmental criticism; many are even moving quickly to adopt various voluntary codes and standards.

Many NGOs are now accepting that business is a key player in the transition to sustainability. In laying the foundations for the implementation of sustainability and co-operation with business, it is likely that the following concerns will be on the minds of NGOs:

- **Corporate volunteerism** Although NGOs are happy that terms like eco-efficiency are now included in business literature, many are very unhappy with the collapse of government capacity to monitor and enforce regulations. The move towards voluntary compliance could become a new battleground. Independent environmental audits by trustworthy firms, paid for by the corporation and reporting to the public, could help to give credibility and accountability to corporate 'volunteerism'.
- **Market-based instruments** Environmental cost accounting has been recommended by economists for some time as the most promising policy instrument to promote sustainability. It allows producers to incorporate the cost of behaving sustainably in the price of the product or commodity. It could result in a very significant resource transfer from North to South.

  If it is really one of the most promising tools to promote sustainability, then we need to advance the debate to the next stage, and to test it. We need to set up a demonstration or experiment. We should choose one commodity as a test case. This is not a complex economic question: the right price is the one that changes production and consumption patterns so that they are sustainable, although it may be a complex scientific and political question to decide what we mean by sustainable.

If it is not feasible to define sustainability, there are very significant implications for any strategy to promote it.

- **The importance of monitoring** For many NGOs, the current strategy is to get the facts on the table. Environmental indicators will pay a key role in educating the public and monitoring progress. A situation that is improving will confirm current policies; a situation that is deteriorating will raise two questions. The first concerns the needs for targets to ensure progress and the second concerns the issue of carrying capacity. What are the limits to the load that we can put on environmental services and sinks?

- **Public discussion of risk assessment** There is scientific uncertainty about the carrying capacity of local and global eco-systems. Many variables are involved, including the economic notion that the market will find or invent substitutes for scarce goods. There has been reasonable doubt about the need to act.

But there is growing evidence that we have crossed three global eco-system thresholds – CO_2, ozone and declining marine bio-mass. Given the potential high cost of misjudgement, we need to bring the process of risk assessment and risk management into the public policy dialogue.

Politicians often speak of the need to anticipate and prevent – it is one of the principles of the Rio Declaration. But we have not assembled the data and tools to help us to assess and manage the risks of approaching a global eco-system threshold, nor have we taken the time to develop the strategies for sharing global environmental services at below threshold levels before a crisis occurs. In ten years' time, risk analysis could shape energy policy or even trade strategies.

Each one of the above issues is an important element in laying the foundation for business participation in the transition to sustainability. Businesses that are committed to sustainability will address these concerns in their political advocacy and commercial practice. Of course, NGOs will be happy when business starts to live the spirit of the sustainability paradigm and sees the earth as a living system to be cared for rather than exploited.

SUMMARY

It is a long way from the drafting process in the basement of the UN to global implementation. We are at an early stage in the change process, and we are attempting to change a system that is unsustainable. It will take considerable co-ordinated effort over a long period of time, involving many people all over the planet. Governments, businesses and civil society all have essential roles to play. At this stage, we would be wise to develop the organizational and management tools that we need to work together.

20

Perspectives on the Future – From a Northern Government

Klaus Töpfer

SUSTAINABLE DEVELOPMENT IN AN URBANIZING WORLD

The struggles for the access to scarce resources threaten to increase in the future if we do not succeed in reducing underdevelopment in the world. Mass poverty in many countries in the southern hemisphere, coupled with a steadily increasing world population, means unbridled exploitation of natural resources, rapidly progressing environmental destruction, worldwide streams of refugees and a threat to global peace.

But it is not poverty and underdevelopment in the developing countries alone which is threatening natural resources and the stability of the global eco-system. The life-styles and economic patterns in the industrialized countries are extremely resource-depleting and are causing global risks.

The global threats – mainly, resource depletion, environmental degradation and climate change – require global partnership. This global partnership has become a central issue for world peace. Global environmental and development policy is the peace policy of the future. Just as the Helsinki process prepared the end of the Cold War between East and West, so the Rio process must encourage partnership in the field of the environment and development, and thus help to prevent a new Cold War between the North and the South. Agenda 21, the final act of the Rio Conference, must be given the same significance as was given to the final act of Helsinki.

The principle of sustainable development is the central model for global environmental and development policy. It involves 'development that meets the needs of the present without compromising the ability of future generations to meet their own needs'. Sustainable development requires the integration of three different development components: the economic, the social and the ecological. The poor parts of the world especially need development. There we must succeed in breaking the vicious circle of poverty, underdevelopment, population growth and environmental destruction.

But a different kind of 'underdevelopment' can be seen in industrialized countries – the general application of 'old' techniques whose development can be explained by the historical structures in the North. Technical progress was based on the shortages found here. This is why technical progress, up to now, has been mainly labour-saving, but at the same time involved an extravagant use of energy and raw materials, and produced high levels of waste and emissions.

Technical progress and its impact is gaining increasingly a global dimension, but unfortunately this is not to everyone's advantage. There is a growing suspicion that the advantages of this progress are being used in the North, and the burdens and risks are being passed on to other regions and future generations. The Rio Conference made it clear that we can no longer maintain a division of labour in this one world which gives the advantages of the use of natural resources and technical progress for the most part to the countries of the industrialized North, while at the same time placing the burden of a large proportion of the direct and indirect consequences of this increased prosperity on the countries of the South.

The situation must not be allowed to continue whereby the advantages of increasing prosperity are isolated pockets, while the disadvantages are globalized. The globalization of the disadvantages must give way to a globalization of responsibility. In a 'common home' we are all members of a global risk-bearing community in which an international 'liability' for risks and dangers is necessary.

In order to respond adequately to these global problems, we need – taking the industrialized countries as a starting-point – a radical ecological structural change in the economy and society, and the extension of our economic and social systems to include the ecological dimension. We must alter our technologies and our behaviour. Our guideline to this is sustainable development. In a nutshell, this means: preserving our natural capital and preserving the branch we are sitting on. We can no longer afford to go on living 'beyond our natural means'.

This new definition of the term 'capital' makes clear that a global environmental and development strategy of this kind must be integrated into economic policy processes. It must be borne in mind that we have up to now been paying far too low a price for the benefits provided by 'environmental capital', there is a tendency for people to make excessive demands on it and slowly to use it up. Hence, we say that the prosperity of the industrialized countries is subsidized to a large extent. We are living with an 'illusion of prosperity' because we are not facing the full costs which are caused directly or indirectly by this prosperity.

Since it is possible to live very well for a time off one's reserves, the failure to reinvest in 'environmental capital' only becomes noticeable at a comparatively late stage, with the result that subsequent generations will have to foot the bill. But our prosperity is provided not only at the 'expense' of our own environment but at the 'expense' of the environment of the countries in the southern hemisphere – for example, the undesirable development in the countries of the South in agriculture, in the over-use of soils and the exploitation of mineral resources on the part of the countries in the northern hemisphere.

Just as we globalize the risks of (misguided) technological developments, so we also pass on a large share of our environmental emissions to others. In the light of this subsidization, the international debate about debts is given a new focus. If we extend the term 'capital' to include the environmental dimension, then we must also extend the term 'debt'. If we consider environmental assets as capital, then – still using the language of economics – loans may also be taken from this capital (which would not be serious in itself, as long as a corresponding reinvestment is made). But then the ordinary capital debts that the countries of the South have with us have to be matched by the 'environmental debts' we have with these countries. Therefore, in the frequent discussions about debt relief, it is not really a question of 'debt-for-nature swaps' but of 'debt-for-debt swaps'.

These ideas provide the basis for a fairer discussion, not only on the conditions for debt relief but also on the provision of 'new and additional financial resources' to which the industrialized countries committed themselves in Rio in order to financially promote the efforts of the developing countries to achieve sustainable development.

If we take seriously our ecological debts *vis-à-vis* the developing countries, then these financial resources are not a form of charity, which unfortunately they are often regarded as, but the price for measures designed to remedy ecological problems which we are constantly calling upon the countries of the South to take.

Ecological subsidization, like any other form of economic subsidization, has various negative consequences. False prices give not only false signals for individual behaviour, but also false signals for research and technology development. Where premiums that take proper account of scarcities are not paid for the development of an environmentally sound technical progress, this type of necessary progress will not take place. A change of production and consumption patterns can be brought about in a market economy system, in particular through prices – that is, through the integration of ecological soils and scarce raw materials, which must have ecologically correct price-tags attached.

Ecologically honest prices stimulate not only environmentally acceptable behaviour, but also promote a form of technical progress that corrects and overcomes the negative side-effects of previous technical developments – for example, the extravagant use of energy and raw materials, and the production of high levels of waste and emissions. Innovations only occur where bottlenecks have to be overcome. Present technological structures and patterns of behaviour are a reflection of price structures that were valid in the past. In exactly the same way, present prices will determine the level of technology and the pattern of behaviour in the future.

In the search for ways to realize sustainable development, we must not rely on single isolated fields of policy. According to Agenda 21, we must broaden our view and try to integrate many different aspects of human life. For example, Agenda 21 recognized very clearly the crucial issues of urban development as priority areas for global, national and local action.

The future of humankind and its natural basis for survival will depend in large measure on the degree to which we are able to steer the dramatic process of urbanization in the direction of sustainability. As we approach the turn of the millennium, half the earth's population already lives in cities. By the year 2025, there will be nearly 100 mega-cities with more than 5 million inhabitants.

The Second UN Conference on Human Settlements – Habitat II – in Istanbul has reinforced awareness that the world of the 21st century will be urban in nature. We will not be living in a global village, but in a global agglomeration. This should not be a cause of pessimism or even of resignation. For all the problems we face, the city is – or even better must be – the best form of organizing human life. The reasons are clear. First, there are the so-called urbanization economies: the city is the best way to tap economic potential. Secondly, the city was from the very beginning, and must be in the future, the optimum setting for social integration and personal freedom and development. Thirdly, since the city is able to support large numbers of people within a limited space, it can offer the highest possible degree of ecological efficiency. Fourthly, the city has always been the theatre of cultural diversity and the engine behind cultural development, tolerance and solidarity. The city therefore offers a future – economically, socially and ecologically. This is what we really mean by sustainability. The task of the future will be to utilize this potential without subsidizing the city at the expense of rural areas.

Urbanization is now a major part of the problem; it is up to us to make it a part of the solution. What we have to do is to channel the urbanization process in a sustainable direction. In other words, this means not pitching environmental, economic and social aspects against each other, but rather seeing them as integral parts of a single whole. Urban economic growth is necessary to meet the urgent needs of a growing population, in particular in developing countries. But urban development in the future must be different from development in the past.

The yardstick for the success of Habitat II will be the extent to which the political momentum at all levels – local, national and international, public and private – can be triggered here and how the decisions we have taken can lead to a change in the political agenda across the world. We cannot afford for the Habitat agenda to be just another piece of paper. It must be transformed into real political action.

We are not only moving towards an urbanized world; we are also moving towards the globalization of markets, products and information. This makes closer international co-operation absolutely essential. This is true in particular of global urban development which, it must be admitted, has been somewhat neglected up to now by the international community.

The developing countries in particular are faced with the pressing task of creating healthy living conditions and a basis for social and economic development in their cities. Undoubtedly, they will need, more than has been the case in the past, the comprehensive backing of us all.

The same is no less true of countries with economies in transition, given the very urgent urbanization and shelter problems they face. We need a renewed culture of solidarity.

However, important steps towards future-oriented urban development must be taken in the industrialized countries themselves, since both their patterns of production and consumption, and also their urban structures and architecture are more or less unsustainable.

Urban problems in developing countries will be insoluble without changes in industrialized countries. It is there that innovations must be developed to give the decisive push to realizing the precautionary principle in practice. It is there that technologies and patterns of behaviour must be conceived or discovered anew, in order to take account of the scarcity of energy, fresh water and clean air. It is there that the throw-away society has to give way to the life-cycle economy. New labour-intensive and energy-saving technologies must take their place alongside traditional capital, and energy-intensive ones, in particular in the light of the carrying-capacity of rural areas.

Our urban planning and architecture are also coming under the microscope. Urban development must return to the concept of the 'short-distance city' where home, work, education, services and leisure facilities are once again grouped together within the same neighbourhood. This is important, not only to solve the ever more pressing traffic problems in cities and urban agglomerations. Shorter travel distances, combined with a better mix of urban functions, are an important prerequisite to ensure social integration and social stability in our cities.

In the past, attention has not focused adequately on the importance of cities' social function. We have to address the impact of modern technologies on urban development as we move towards the 'telematic city'. Seen in this light, cities have an important role to play in giving the people who live there a local identity and a sense of belonging.

In the urban world, a stop must be made not only to the degradation of the natural environment, but also to emotional and social degradation. Spatial, social and psychological barriers in our cities must be broken down. Cities must redefine their traditional role and become places where people communicate and exchange ideas and experiences, and where diversity and tolerance can flourish. Above all, they must be places where people can move around without fear, and where men and women can develop their personal lives in freedom. Preventing individual isolation in our cities is a bulwark against radicalism.

To find the characteristic attributes and forward-looking momentum generated by Habitat II, we need look no further than the special role played by non-governmental organizations and local authorities. For the first time, these groups had the opportunity of taking an active part in advising a UN conference. Their far-reaching involvement has decisively inspired and influenced the discussions and results of Habitat II.

Local authorities must also be involved in the international implementation of the Habitat agenda. This includes having a greater say at an institutional level – for example, in shaping the UN Commission for Human Settlements and indeed in the review of the UN system as a whole. This will be an important indicator of the success of Habitat II.

The decentralization of decision-making processes, the realization of the principle of subsidiarity, the enhancement of local democracy and municipal self-government, and the widespread participation of all groups within society are essential prerequisites for future-oriented urban development.

The dialogue successfully embarked upon in Istanbul on global settlements issues must continue at a high political level. The next opportunity to do so will come at the 1997 special session of the UN General Assembly which will cast a critical eye over the entire Rio follow-up process. Then we shall have to ask ourselves the question: have we kept the promises we made in Istanbul?

One very important result of Habitat II is a renewed and strengthened mandate, backed up by a strong political will, for sustainable urban development. This must now be implemented at local and national level, through public–private partnerships and through the commitment of NGOs and civil society; last, but not least, it must also be implemented by the international community. This is the challenge facing the UN Centre for Human Settlements in Nairobi. It is our important task to use this momentum as a driving force behind the development and ongoing work of the Centre.

One thing is clear. The state in which we leave our world to our children and grandchildren will be decided mainly in human settlements. It is the cities of tomorrow that will decide over war and peace. Therefore, the UN blue-bereted peacekeepers should be joined by the green berets, whose job it will be to care for the cities. Worldwide co-operation on the environment and development, in particular in settlement issues, is thus the peace and disarmament policy of the future.

21

The UNCED Process: In Search of Sustainability for the South

Henrique Cavalcanti

The view from the South regarding sustainability must always be taken as one of hope and confidence, regardless of the obstacles to be faced in the process. After all, much of what is at stake, in terms of population, natural resources and biological diversity, is in the South, along with the oldest civilizations, the longest records of religious beliefs and much of the world's cultural heritage.

The South represents about two-thirds of all nations, an extremely diversified set of economic and social circumstances, but also most of the poor people and the unstable institutions on Earth. Practically all human conflicts – with few exceptions – take place in those countries, whether in Africa, Asia, the Middle East or Latin America. On the other hand, rapid development and brighter prospects for their future in the past few years have given many areas in the South a new reason for trusting in their own prospects. It is not, therefore, a static situation, and the practice of multilateralism may well have made a difference towards those changes.

For the developing nations, the UN should not be just a forum of equals, nor should the Bretton Woods entities be just houses of finance. For they represent, in spite of their natural limitations, an answer to the less flexible and compulsive aspects of a competitive world.

Treaties, conventions and other forms of agreement are the basis on which the foundations of a mature and responsible international relationship can be built, where sovereign nations that subscribe to a set of principles and action plans are submitted to the judgement of their peers and are expected to comply with their commitments.

For those reasons, few occasions in history will carry the image of universal consensus and the exercise of political will as did the Rio Summit. Never before had the majority of heads of state and government come together to express their concerns about patterns of development, and to recognize the need for changes in their approaches to social, economic and environmental issues, whether national, regional or global.

It would be fair to say that most developing nations look at the UNCED process as a new opportunity for themselves and their people, based on a mature and holistic vision of the world's and mankind's strengths and weaknesses. They wish to share this experience with the more developed countries in an equitable fashion, by reviewing the premises, analysing the issues and defining the roles of the various players.

THE PREMISES

The UNCED provided member states with instruments aimed at fulfilling the expectations raised in Rio. Towards that purpose, the Rio Declaration firmly associates, in cause and effect, the concepts of the environment and development, while Agenda 21 maps out a general strategy that is applicable to all levels of political organization, from global to local. A number of international agreements tackle critical aspects of the environmental agenda.

Whatever assessment there is to be made in 1997 of the progress achieved so far, it must stem from a closer look at basic concepts, such as 'common but differentiated responsibilities', 'access to sustainable technologies and financial resources', and 'enhanced international co-operation'. It also requires a critical view of the main features and prospects of Agenda 21, and an objective evaluation of national responses to the Climate and Biodiversity conventions and to the Declaration on Forests, among other agreements.

Those three basic concepts attempt to determine what an equitable relationship between nations should be in our uneven present-day world. They suggest, first of all, that the initiative for change lies primarily in the hands of the more advanced and capable societies – namely, the OECD countries. It would be up to those, in a concerted effort with the recipient counterparts, to work out the appropriate institutional mechanisms, to develop innovative technologies and to set good examples of sustainable performance.

Agenda 21, a broad, all-encompassing proposal for action towards sustainability, addresses two key issues:

- How to make sure that the participation of society in the decision-making process is equitable.
- How to manage environmental resources rationally.

In both cases, these make use of social and economic instruments, and the assistance of international co-operation.

There are up to now about 180 international agreements and their amendments which relate to the environment, each with its own roster of signatories. Environmental integrity of the oceans and seas has been, so far, the predominant cause of concern among those texts. Those signed at Rio, and the forthcoming Convention on Desertification are perhaps the most significant at the present time, together with the Basel Convention and the Montreal Protocol.

The Issues

The wide variety of subjects addressed in Agenda 21 could be clustered in many ways, under the headings of environmental, economic, social and institutional issues. Social issues would include cultural aspects, whereas legal, political and organizational aspects would be considered as institutional, and spatial or physical aspects would be taken as environmental issues. Certain topics related to those issues, and relevant to sustainability, are reviewed below.

Environmental Issues

In spite of methodical advances in the understanding and the management of major environmental issues, there are still critical aspects for developing nations which have yet to be dealt with in a decisive and consequential manner. For example, the continuing threat to living species and eco-systems in terms of forest resources, marine fish stocks and freshwater supplies.

The driving forces behind these threats may originate from basic needs, such as food supplies, trade opportunities or just the unsustainable way of life of specific human groups. Their persistence can be attributed to a variety of causes, such as inadequate or insufficient institutional capability because there is no effective legal framework or the limited access of the population to basic social services. In certain cases, the responsibility lies both with the supply and the demand ends of the trade flows.

With regard to biodiversity, there must be a clear recognition of the existence of territorial limits which divide fully protected areas from those where natural resources are to be managed rationally for productive purposes. Even the protected areas may require careful wildlife management. But this objective can only be achieved if human and financial resources are made available through the country's own efforts, backed by outside assistance where needed.

Biodiversity and trade in forest products are features of the work programme established for the Inter-Governmental Panel on Forests, due to be completed in 1997. One of the recommendations of the panel may be the drafting of a Forest Convention where the certification of forests and their products – as well as a concerted effort to develop reliable and sustainable forest management technologies – could become central issues.

The conservation of ocean resources seems to be more pressing every day in anticipation of the International Year scheduled for 1998. Implementation of the Law of the Sea, including its judicial instrument, is a fundamental tool in this respect, in order to safeguard the rights and expectations of member states and especially those that are more vulnerable to unsuitable practices.

Energy and transportation are still key elements in any development strategy. This is an area where the contribution of the industrialized nations towards effective technologies, that would have a positive impact on air quality and climatic conditions, is most decisive. Research on the harnessing of competitive alternative sources of energy would allow less developed countries to bypass inefficient systems that are now in use, and dispel some of the concerns regarding the impact of their economic development patterns and rising standards of living on global environmental conditions.

ECONOMIC ISSUES

Economic development is clearly an essential factor in sustainability for most countries. Few other features in the sustainable development agenda have shown, however, such visible changes since UNCED, as a result of the rapid globalisation of economic structures and trends. Those changes have affected individual countries and places in different ways, and have made short term perspectives either unclear or even unfavourable for some of them.

Market-driven capital flows have emphasised the importance of direct private investment, compared to the traditional overseas development assistance (ODA) programmes. This is one area where perhaps quantity is just as relevant as quality, because – in most developing nations – capital is frequently a scarce resource.

A logical but imperfect conclusion for this state of affairs is that ODA should favour those countries where, in spite of their strenuous afforts to attract capital flows, the investment climate is not yet enabling. On the other hand, faster rates of growth induced in part by those capital flows will increase the pressure on the institutional and infrastructural capability of the respective countries. This is where multilateral and other international financial institutions will continue to play a significant role, especially in view of their increased interest and competence in incorporating social and environmental concerns into the scope of their operations.

Globalisation has also brought about rising unemployment figures that may affect the political and economic stability in certain countries – where urbanisation is particularly acute and the informal sector of the economy already significant. Social deprivation may be ameliorated by recycling jobs and supporting small, medium-sizes and self-owned companies, and other measures.

SOCIAL ISSUES

Four major international conferences since 1992 have given a high profile to those issues with a predominantly social ingredient. They have all addressed subjects of prime importance in Agenda 21 such as poverty, demography, the status of major groups, basic social services and the quality of life in urban and rural communities.

This is of course a very sensitive area for many of the developing countries, and one where tact and full awareness are required on the part of other nations, especially when it comes to the cultural implications of proposed measures for sustainability at the personal, community and national levels, and in terms of their respective identities.

The role of each of the major groups and the deadlines for implementing programmes are necessarily flexible and adapted to every circumstance, so as to allow for a constructive approach to their increased participation in the decision-making process. Some of these objectives, including the access to adequate basic social services can and have been reached, regardless of the specific political framework or the relative degree of economic achievement of the individual country.

Special attention should naturally be given to the evolution and expansion of educational systems, with due regard to their cultural and scientific content and to their capacity for the development of appropriate technologies.

INSTITUTIONAL ISSUES

Perhaps the most relevant topics under this heading for developing countries would include the new roles of the private sector and organised society, as well as decentralisation of government activities with greater emphasis on decisions taken at the local level. The legal and administrative implications of this trend on public finance and the balance of power have not been fully evaluated in every country, but there is generally a feeling of beneficial change in terms of institutional strengthening. Once again the formation of regional blocs introduces new variables in this equation and may well magnify the end result of these trends.

On the negative side, developing countries have not been exempt from the worldwide spread of illegal or downright criminal practices with distinct impacts on governance and social behavior. The institutional response to these serious elements of instability has not been effective enough and may eventually jeopardise the efforts of individual countries, since it requires the competent exercise of social control as well as meaningful educational initiatives, where the teaching of ethical values would represent a basic factor.

The rich experience of participatory decision-making structures, where responsible citizens – whether appointed or elected and with varying degrees of accountability – would sit on equal footing, has not been fully assessed. For that reason, further ground should be covered in its analysis in order to make its strengths and weaknesses more apparent to those forums where the system has not been adopted.

THE PLAYERS

When looking at the possible ways of rating developing nations, two approaches may be taken as parameters. One is simply to take their figures for economic performance, and the other to use sets of cross-disciplinary indicators, as proposed for example by the UNDP or the World Bank.

The first option has proved to be very limited and so the second alternative should be adopted as a basis for this particular exercise, taking also into account other variables like scale and geographical location of the individual countries. Another assumption is not to include the economies in transition in this category, even though the less developed ones are sometimes inadequately classified as industrialised nations.

The developing world obviously does not present either a uniform situation or even the same trends. As such, it would not provide a single view on the respective achievements and expectations. But four groups of countries could perhaps be identified, bearing in mind their economic and human development performance and the relative complexity of their natural environment and institutional arrangements. Notwithstanding the need for those countries to have their cases taken individually, there are common patterns which may be applicable to each of the four groups in approaching their national and international policies.

The first group encompasses the nearly 50 least-developed countries, mostly in Africa. Often heavily indebted, their situation needs special attention and the goodwill of both North and South.

At the opposite end, included in a group of 50 developing and industrialised nations displaying high indexes of human development, there are at least 11 countries in Latin America and the Caribbean, as well as five in Asia and the Pacific, and three in the Near and Middle East which display above average rates of economic growth and per capita income levels.

The third group includes those developing countries that cover extensive land and sea territories, and similarly large populations, where intra-regional imbalances, the institutional complexities introduced by intermediate levels of government, and the environmental effects of their development strategies may represent significant challenges for themselves – and potentially major impacts on the whole world. China, India, Brazil, Pakistan, Indonesia and Nigeria are examples.

Finally, the fourth group covers a broad range of almost 70 countries in the medium and medium to high or low categories of human development, 20 in Latin America and the Caribbean, 13 in Asia and the Pacific, 10 in the Near and the Middle East and the remaining ones in Africa and the Indian Ocean.

The upsurge of common markets and free trade areas has of course introduced new variables in this subjective partition of the South. Such is the case for Mexico, a partner in the North American Free Trade Agreement (NAFTA) and of Brazil, listed above under the third group, a member of the South American Common Market (Mercosul). Similar associations are under way in other continents, providing for specific synergies to be tapped in promoting sustainability.

These remarks may point to a desireable review of the present arrangement of the so-called Group of 77 and China, and therefore to a more effective UN dialogue with the OECD countries on the question of international co-operation.

It is perhaps obvious that the assistance to the first group of countries should go beyond the timely and generous debt redemption process now under way by their multilateral and bilateral creditors. It should encompass a sizeable rescue operation that would improve their chances of viability as sovereign nations.

Lessons can also be learned from the success stories in the second group of countries and, bearing in mind cultural and other differences, these sometimes provide novel examples of South–South co-operation.

The performance of the third group, along with those of the larger and often populous industrialized nations like the United States, Russia, Germany, Canada and Australia, is bound to influence the fulfilment of the objectives set out in the Climate and Biodiversity conventions, the Declaration on Forests and many of the targets in Agenda 21. Their leading role, along with those countries in the second group, may provide new approaches to sustainability at the regional level which may benefit both the first and the fourth group of countries.

An indication of the extent to which major groups have increased their participation in the decision-making process of developing nations is the number of National Sustainable Development Councils which were organized or restructured since 1992, with the invaluable assistance of the Earth Council. Another relevant pattern is the formulation of national and local versions of Agenda 21 and national development strategies, as promoted principally by the Commission on Sustainable Development (CSD). This is a valid instrument, not only because of its cross-disciplinary approach to the management of complex human communities, but it has also been a way of implementing a potentially participatory process, where responsibility and commitment are necessary elements and where priorities based on the realistic evaluation of ends and means can be established.

An auspicious novelty of the UNCED process is the role of NGOs, a generic acronym that encompasses a great variety of spontaneous associations focusing on environmental, human rights, major group representation and other issues. Their contribution to the cause is not always evenly regarded by governments and the public, partly by virtue of their own diversified profile. The net result of their action has an obvious impact, through specific proposals, criticism and material initiatives, or their ability to mobilize public opinion, the media and volunteer participation.

Restructuring the UN system, as a major player in the context of sustainability, would have to aim at improving co-ordination among its many bodies and agencies, not only at the policy level but also in the field, as partners of individual member states and their societies. Co-ordination like this can be enhanced by the establishment of strategic interdisciplinary programmes with objectives, task managers and timetables. Recent examples of this trend are the decisions made by ECOSOC, the United Nations Economic and Social Council, and by the United Nations Development Programme (UNDP).

ECOSOC, for instance, has set up three interagency task forces and their subgroups, to address a range of key issues, as well as interagency committees on sustainable development, and on women and gender equality.

The UNDP, on the other hand, has decentralized at country level to interagency committees to follow up on conference decisions. In certain countries, these initiatives involve national and local authority and NGO participation.

PROSPECTS FOR 1997 AND UP TO 2000

International events planned for 1997 seem to follow a logical sequence. The Rio5 meeting will provide an open forum where NGOs and other major representative groups and personalities will discuss progress since 1992, in their own terms and with no visible constraints.

Then the CSD will take stock of the developments in each chapter in Agenda 21 and their respective linkages, identify the gaps or omissions that can still be found in the overall picture, and come up with conclusions about new strategies for sustainability until the year 2000 and beyond. The recommendations from the CSD will then be reviewed by ECOSOC at a special session of the UN General Assembly so that final decisions can be made on the main topics.

What is at stake is not just the ability of member states to comply with their international commitments and to respond to the legitimate aspirations of their peoples, but also, in the context of the UNCED process, to usefulness of the multilateral approach through the UN system. Should the latter fail to perform in a dependable fashion, the world would inevitably return to old and seldom sustainable practices.

It is everyone's responsibility to do their utmost to reach the 21st century with the feeling that the necessary efforts were made and that some progress has been achieved. For the developing nations, in particular, it is important not only to expect an equitable treatment among nations but also to implement similar attitudes and behaviour internally. Fair and consistent attitudes on the part of industrialized nations, and a more effective and well co-ordinated international development co-operation should also be matched with an equivalent degree of understanding and generosity.

But it would be over-optimistic to bring the horizon closer than we can. Only a medium-term perspective, no less than a generation span of 30 years, would be required to consolidate the advances in the various continents, minimize conflict and build the foundations for peaceful co-existence, and generally improve the practice of environmental stewardship, which is essential to global sustainability.

The basic premises agreed in Rio should thus remain valid for years to come. They underline the main features of a style of international co-operation which aims to increase the competitiveness of developing nations as a means of achieving the major social, economic and environmental objectives. These objectives are required as a condition of global sustainability that would allow individual rights to be assured and legitimate aspirations to be realized.

The Way Forward Beyond Agenda 21: Perspectives on the Future from Europe

Derek Osborn

The European countries, both individually and collectively, played a key part in the preparatory work for the Rio Summit, and in forging the final agreements made there. Countries of the European Union made a particular contribution as the largest grouping of developed countries in the world. The countries of Central and Eastern Europe also made a distinctive contribution, particularly since the political transformation which began at the beginning of the 1990s in those countries had as one of its objectives the establishment of a more sustainable pattern of development for the future.

Europe has played an equally vigorous part in the follow-up to Rio. Immediately after Rio, the heads of government of the countries of the Union pledged at the Council Meeting of June 1992[1] to take early action to ratify the climate change and biodiversity plans, and to follow this up with action in their own countries. They also agreed to prepare sustainable development plans or strategies to follow through the proposals in Agenda 21.

Meanwhile, in the wider Europe, the East–West process which had been launched at Dobris Castle in 1991 was developed and extended through subsequent meetings and supporting work into the Environment for Europe programme.[2]

Within the European Union, the main systematic machinery for following through the Agenda 21 programme lies in the Fifth Action Programme for the Environment adopted by the Union at the end of

1992.[3] The implementation of this programme and its review during 1995–96, have been the main strategic machinery for driving forward the overall programme.

At international level all the countries of the wider Europe have played an active part individually in the Commission for Sustainable Development (CSD), in the conferences of parties of the climate change and biodiversity conventions, and in the resumed negotiations on forestry. European Union countries have also taken successful steps together with the European Commission to concert their positions on these issues, and this has enabled them to play together a key shaping role as the voice of Europe.

Within many individual European countries, sustainable development strategies and plans have been developed since 1992, and new alliances have been made at national and local level to promote the new ways of thinking and the new styles of policy that are needed to make a reality of sustainable development.

The European Environment Agency's 1995 Report on Europe's Environment ('The Dobris Assessment')[4] provides a base-line picture of the state of Europe's environment and the pressures on it. It highlighted 12 key issues as particularly important for the establishment of sustainability:

- Climate change.
- Stratospheric ozone depletion.
- Loss of biodiversity.
- Major accidents.
- Acidification.
- Tropospheric ozone and other photo-chemical oxidants.
- The management of fresh water.
- Forest degradation.
- Coastal zone threats and management.
- Waste reduction and management.
- Urban stress.
- Chemical risks.

This list is similar to those identified as high priorities in other OECD countries and gives a good general picture of the environmental issues on which most attention needs to be concentrated in the next few years.

For the countries of the Union, the Agency Report for the Review of the Fifth Environmental Action Programme[5] gives a more specific assessment. That report is based on detailed information from all the countries of the Union and shows that good progress is being made in some areas. Fifth Action Programme targets for the year 2000 should be met for sulphur dioxide emissions and for the production of ozone-depleting substances, and possibly for CO_2 emissions, although this is still uncertain and risks being reversed in the years beyond 2000 unless further measures are taken promptly.

In a number of other areas, the Union is heading in the right direction, but meeting targets is uncertain, including:

- Acidification, where limits are widely broken, although not so much as in earlier decades.
- Volatile organic compounds (VOCs), where emissions are clearly beginning to be reduced, but where meeting the 2000 targets is not yet assured.
- Nitrates in ground water.
- Waste management and promotion of recycling.
- Urban environment where environmental pressures, particularly those related to traffic, continue to worsen in most cities.
- Conservation and protection of biodiversity, largely because of the impact of transport and tourism.

Current policies are not sufficient to tackle some key issues, including:

- CO_2 emissions after 2000.
- Traffic-related issues such as NO_x emissions, noise, water abstraction and the quality of marine water and ground water.
- Chemicals in the environment.
- Coastal zone management.
- Erosion and desertification.

The general picture for economics is that good progress is being made to improve the environmental performance of industry, particularly the larger firms, through systematic efforts to reduce their emissions, and to improve the efficiency with which they use energy and other raw materials and minimize waste or recycle it. But some of the smaller and medium-sized enterprises, and the diffuse sources of environmental problems represented by agriculture, tourism and transport, are more intractable.

The thrust of sustainable development policy in Europe, both at the level of individual member states and in the Union as a whole, is to try to overcome this by integrating the environment more closely into the development of policy on agriculture, tourism, transport, energy, and so on. But progress on this is comparatively slow. Measures that can be taken by environment ministers and departments acting on their own are easier to push forward than those that depend on creating alliances with departments of transport, agriculture, energy, and so on, which have other objectives as well as the promotion of the protection of the environment.

Of course, if properly expressed, it is difficult for anyone to oppose the objectives of sustainable development, but it is difficult in practice for other departments and policy communities to broaden their objectives away from promoting their particular subject concerns, towards a more holisic concept that gives proper weight to the protection or enhancement of the environment and natural resources as a goal alongside their specific sectoral objectives.

What is gradually becoming clearer in Europe, as elsewhere, is that successful synthesis on these issues will not be achieved simply by accommodations reached by bureaucratic processes behind closed doors. These are fundamental political issues which touch the lives of individuals in the community at all levels.

Transport is perhaps the most conspicuous example at the moment. There is slowly and reluctantly a growing recognition in many European countries that unlimited growth of road traffic, particularly private cars, is a collective disaster. This is so even though it has so far provided a major benefit to individuals in terms of greater range and speed of movement.

It is only when this message is fully appreciated and accepted widely that it will be possible to move forward, so what we will begin to see dimly the necessary solutions – for example, designing communities so that there is less need for traffic and transport, and providing more reliable and user-friendly public transport for more of the journeys that are necessary.

Similarly, it is only as there comes to be widespread understanding and support for the proposition that agriculture is not simply about maximizing agricultural output, but also about preserving and enhancing patterns of rural life and development, and protecting the countryside and wildlife, that we shall move more decisively to a more environmentally friendly and sustainable agriculture.

The agri-environment measures adopted by the Agriculture Council[6] are beginning to provide incentives for moving farming practices in the right direction, but there is a long way to go yet in this area.

At the heart of the problem is the conduct of the economy itself. So long as we assess progress purely on the basis of GDP growth, we shall be pointing ourselves in the wrong direction. Of course, prosperous economies are a necessary condition of positive action on the environment, as on many other issues. But it is quite wrong to see the environment as another add-on extra of vaguely worthwhile objects of spending which can be pursued in prosperous times, but must be deferred when times are hard. On the contrary, a satisfactory environment is part of the overall goal we need to aim at.

If our environment is improved, we all have a better quality of life, which is the only form of growth that ultimately is worth aiming at, even if there is no parallel growth in the GDP as conventionally measured. Conversely, if GDP grows but quality of life declines substantially, it is not obvious that society is the gainer.

Europe has been gradually working its way towards some more sophisticated thinking on these issues. The European Commission's White Paper on Growth, Competitiveness and Employment[7] was a seminal document in this respect. Its Chapter 10 pointed out that the key to decoupling future economic prosperity from environmental pollution will lie ultimately in the creation of a new green technology. Particular objectives identified were to reduce the material resource input into the production process, to improve process technology, to reduce emissions further, to work towards longer product life times for manufactured products, to promote more reuse and recycling, and to develop safer products.

A number of countries in Europe and the Commission are now developing indicators of sustainability as a means of monitoring progress on these wider issues about the sustainability of the environment and the economy. And attempts are gradually moving forward to improve the measures of the economy itself through the development of green accounts and green GDP measures. All of these will be crucial, both as instruments in themselves and as a means of changing the focus of public and media attention to more worthwhile longer-term goals.

The European Union does not act alone in the world, and is currently engaged in two sets of challenging interactions with other parts of the world in dialogues about sustainability. First, there is the dialogue with Central and Eastern Europe through the Dobríš process and other channels. They are now undergoing very rapid economic and social changes. When the changes first began at the beginning of 1990, the desire to make development more sustainable and to protect the environment better was a strong motive force. But the pace of change and the economic problems of the transition, have subsequently made it hard to give the environment as much priority as desired in some of the countries. The vigorous pursuit of the Environment Programme for Europe, and its support by the major financial institutions of the World Bank, the European Bank for Reconstruction and Development, and the European Commission, are therefore of crucial importance in the years ahead.

Some air pollution problems have improved through restructuring of the economy, but there is much still to be done to introduce cleaner technology more widely, especially given the difficult fuels such as brown coal – which are common in some of the countries involved – and the legacy of unsatisfactory nuclear power stations with which others have been left. Water supply and quality issues are a major issue in many of the countries. So, too, are measures to protect wildlife and habitats.

The other crucial international dialogue in which Europe plays a key part is with the developing countries, in the CSD itself, in the UNEP, and in the Conferences of Parties of all the environmental agreements. The key challenges proposed by the countries of the South to those of the North as preconditions for developing the necessary political will to action in the South, have been first, to establish that the North should show itself to be ready and willing to undertake measures to make its own economies more sustainable, and secondly that it should be willing to provide appropriate assistance to the South in conducting its own development in a more sustainable way from the outset.

Aid flows are one part of this progress, together with debt relief. Europe has played its part in some aspects of this dialogue, such as the creation of the Global Environment Facility and the Paris Club moves on debt relief. Equally important is the way in which trade and capital flows are conducted, and the transfer of technology. Some useful measures have been taken on these issues since Rio. But it is hard to say yet that the dialogue has advanced sufficiently on either front, either in terms of a major move by the North towards a more sustainable economy, or in terms of sufficiently significant change in patterns of aid, trade and debt relief to alter the pattern of development in the developing world in a substantially more sustainable way.

The world will need to take stock of these major dialogues in the international review meetings five years after Rio. New efforts will be needed by both North and South if a new momentum towards sustainability is to be achieved.

Europe will undoubtedly have a key part to play in the debate. Its own progress within its boundaries is patchy, as is its own record on aid, debt and trade, and its relationships on sustainablity issues with the rest of the world. But it has probably made as much progress since 1992 as any other region of the world, and is fully entitled to enter the next round of negotiations as a region that has made respectable efforts since Rio. And it can put these on the table as it seeks to engage other parts of the world in a new dialogue to broaden and speed up the rate of progress in the years ahead.

NOTES

1. The Lisbon Council of Heads of Government from the European Union, 1992.
2. The Lausanne Conference conclusion, held at Dobris Castle for East and West Europe, 1991.
3. The European Union Fifth Action Programme for the Environment, 1992
4. European Environment Agency (1995) *Europe's Environment: The Dobris Assessment* Earthscan, London.
5. European Environment Agency (1995) *Environment in the European Union 1995: Report for the Review of the Fifth Environmental Action Plan* European Environment Agency, Copenhagen.
6. European Union's Agriculture Council Agreement.
7. European Commission's White Paper on Growth, Competitiveness and Employment.

Appendix A

PROGRAMME OF WORK FOR THE COMMISSION ON
SUSTAINABLE DEVELOPMENT

**Agenda 21 clusters as recommended at the organizational session
of the Commission**
Critical elements of sustainability
International co-operation to accelerate sustainable development in
developing countries and related domestic policies: Chapter 2.
Combating poverty: Chapter 3.
Changing consumption patterns: Chapter 4.
Demographic dynamics and sustainability: Chapter 5.

Financial resources and mechanisms
Financial resources and mechanisms: Chapter 33.

*Education, science, transfer of environmentally sound technologies, co-operation
and capacity-building*
Environmentally sound management of biotechnology: Chapter 16.
Transfer of environmentally sound technology, co-operation and
capacity-building: Chapter 34.
Science for sustainable development: Chapter 35.
Promoting education, public awareness and training: Chapter 36.
National mechanisms and international co-operation for capacity-
building in developing countries: Chapter 37.

Decision-making structures
Integrating the environment and development in decision-making: Chapter 8.
International institutional arrangements: Chapter 38.
International legal instruments and mechanisms: Chapter 39.
Information for decision-making: Chapter 40.

Roles of major groups
Preamble to Section III on strengthening the role of major groups: Chapter 23.
Global action for women towards sustainable and equitable development: Chapter 24.
Children and youth in sustainable development: Chapter 25.
Recognizing and strengthening the role of indigenous people and their communities: Chapter 26.
Strengthening the role of non-governmental organizations; partners for sustainable development: Chapter 27.
Local authorities' initiatives in support of Agenda 21: Chapter 28.
Strengthening the role of workers and their trade unions: Chapter 29.
Strengthening the role of business and industry: Chapter 30.
Scientific and technological community: Chapter 31.
Strengthening the role of farmers: Chapter 32.

Health, human settlements and fresh water
Protecting and promoting human health: Chapter 6.
Promoting sustainable human settlement development: Chapter 7.
Protection of the quality and supply of freshwater resources, application of integrated approaches to the development, management and use of water resources: Chapter 18.
Environmentally sound management of solid wastes and sewage-related issues: Chapter 21.

Land, desertification, forests and biodiversity
Integrated approach to the planning and management of land resources: Chapter 10.
Combating deforestation: Chapter 11.
Managing fragile eco-systems: combating desertification and drought: Chapter 12.
Managing fragile eco-systems: sustainable mountain development: Chapter 13.

Promoting sustainable agriculture and rural development: Chapter 14.
Conservation of biological diversity: Chapter 15.

Atmosphere, oceans and all kinds of seas
Protection of the atmosphere: Chapter 9.
Protection of the oceans, all kinds of seas, including enclosed and semi-
enclosed seas, and coastal areas and their protection, rational use and
development of their living resources: Chapter 17.

Toxic chemicals and hazardous wastes
Environmentally sound management of toxic chemicals, including
prevention of illegal international traffic in toxic and dangerous prod-
ucts: Chapter 19.
Environmentally sound management of hazardous wastes, including pre-
vention of illegal international traffic in hazardous wastes: Chapter 20.
Safe and environmentally sound management of radioactive wastes:
Chapter 22.

Proposed programme of work
1993 session Adoption of multi-year thematic programme of work (item
2 of the provisional agenda).

1994 session Review of cross-sectoral clusters:

- Critical elements of sustainability, with particular reference to
  Chapters 2 and 4.
- Financial resources and mechanisms, Chapter 33.
- Education, science, transfer of environmentally sound technologies,
  co-operation and capacity-building, with particular reference to
  Chapters 34 and 37.
- Decision-making structures, with particular reference to Chapters 38
  and 39.
- Roles of major groups, Chapters 23, 24, 25, 26, 27, 28, 29, 30, 31,
  32.

Review of sectoral clusters, first phase:

- Health, human settlements and fresh water Chapters 6, 7, 18, 21.
- Toxic chemicals and hazardous wastes Chapters 19, 20, 22.

1995 session Review of cross-sectoral clusters:
- Critical elements of sustainability, with particular reference to Chapters 3 and 5.
- Financial resources and mechanisms: Chapter 33.
- Education, science, transfer of environmentally sound technologies, co-operation and capacity-building, with particular reference to Chapters 16, 34, 35.
- Decision-making structures, with particular reference to Chapters 8 and 40.
- Roles of major groups: Chapters 23, 24, 25, 26, 27, 28, 29, 30, 31, 32.

Review of sectoral clusters, second phase:
- Land, desertification, forests and biodiversity: Chapters 10, 11, 12, 13, 14, 15.

1996 session Review of cross-sectoral clusters:

- Critical elements of sustainability: Chapters 2, 3, 4, 5.
- Financial resources and mechanisms: Chapter 33.
- Education, science, transfer of environmentally sound technologies, co-operation and capacity-building, with particular reference to Chapters 34, 36, 37.
- Decision-making structures: Chapters 8, 38, 39, 40.
- Roles of major groups: Chapters 23, 24, 25, 26, 27, 28, 29, 30, 31, 32.

Review of sectoral clusters, third phase:
- Atmosphere, oceans and all kinds of seas: Chapters 9 and 17.

1997 session Overall review and appraisal of Agenda 21 in preparation for the 1997 Special Session of General Assembly envisaged in General Assembly resolution 47/190.

Appendix B

ADDRESSES OF CONTRIBUTORS

Chapter 1
Chip Lindner
Senior Advisor to the Chairman &
Executive Secretary
Geneva Secretariat
12th World Aids Conference
c/o Division of Infectious Diseases
Geneva University Hospital
CH 1211 Geneva 14
Switzerland
Tel 41 22 372 9806
Fax 41 22 372 9820

Chapter 2
Tom Bigg
UNED-UK
c/o UNA
3 Whitehall Court
London
SW1A 2EL
Tel 0171 930 2931
Fax 0171 930 5893

Felix Dodds
UNED-UK as above

Chapter 3
Peter Newell
Politics and International Studies
University of Warwick
Warwick

Chapter 4
Fiona McConnell
c/o UNED-UK

Chapter 5
Camilla Toulmin
39 Regent Street
Portobello
Edinburgh
EH15 2AY
Tel 0131 624 7040
Fax 0131 624 7050

Chapter 6
Carole Saint-Laurent
WWF International
c/o 70 Mayfield Avenue
Toronto,
Ontario
M6S 1K6
Canada
Tel/fax 00 1 416 763 3437

Chapter 7
Philippe Sands
FIELD, 46 Russell Square
London WC1
Tel: 44 171 637 7950
Fax: 44 171 637 7951

Chapter 8
Peter Mucke
Ruppenkampstrabe 11A
Osnabruck
Germany
4500
Tel 00 49 541 71 010
Fax 49 541 70 7 233

Chapter 9
Jeb Brugman
International Council for Local
Environmental Initiatives (ICLEI)
8th Floor, Toronto, Ontario,
M5H 242 Canada
Tel: 1 416 392 1462
Fax: 1 416 392 1478

Chapter 10
Bjorn Stigson
WBCSD
160, route de Florissant,

CH-1231 Conches,
Geneva
Switzerland
Tel 00 41 22 839 3100
Fax 41 22 839 31 31

Chapter 11
Lucien Royer and Winston
Gereluk
c/o 10712-123 Street,
Edmonton,
Alberta
Canada
T5M 0C5
Tel: 00 1 403 483 3021
Fax: 00 1 403 484 5928

Chapter 12
Zonny Woods
204 Daly Avenue
Ottawa
Ontario
KIN 2G6
Canada
Tel/fax 00 1 613 562 1363

Chapter 13
Angela Mawle
c/o UNED-UK
Tel 0117 9224 488

Chapter 14
Caroline LeQuesne
Oxfam
274 Banbury Road
Oxford OX1 7DZ
Tel: 44 1865 312 389
Fax: 44 1865 312 417

Charles Arden Clarke
WWF International
Avenue Du Mont Blanc
CH-1196
Gland
Switzerland

Tel 41 22 364 91 11
Fax 41 22 364 53 58

Chapter 15
Gary Lawrence
Centre for Sustainable
Communities
University of Washington
Seattle
Washington
USA

Tel 00 1 206 616 2035
Fax 00 1 206 543 2463

Chapter 16
Barbara Bramble
National Wildlife Federation
(US),
1499 16th Street NW
Washington DC, USA

Tel: 1 202 797 6800
Fax: 1 202 797 5486

Chapter 17
Elizabeth Dowdeswell
United Nations Environment
Programme
PO Box 30552, Nairobi, Kenya

Tel: 254 2 623292
Fax: 254 2 623927/3692

Chapter 18
Nitin Desai
UN Department for Policy

Co-ordination and Sustainable
Development (DPCSD), United
Nations,
New York NY 10017 USA
Major Groups Focal Point
Zehra Aydin

Tel: 1 212 963 8811
Fax: 1 212 963 1267

Chapter 19
Peter Padbury
Earth Council
Apdo 2323
1002 San Jose
Costa Rica

Tel: 506 223-3418/256-1611
Fax: 506 225-2197

Chapter 20
Klaus Topfer
Bunderminister
fur Raumordnung, Bauwesen and
Stadtebau
53179 Bonn
Deichmanns Aue

Tel 00 49 228 337 3000
Fax 00 49 228 337 3013

Chapter 21
Ambassador Cavalcanti
Caixa Postal 7068,
71619-970 Brasilla, DF
Brazil

Tel: 00 55 61 37 1228
Fax: 00 55 61 224 7340

Chapter 22
Derek Osborn
c/o UNED-UK

Appendix C

ADDRESSES OF KEY ORGANISATIONS

Basel Convention Secretariat,
Geneva Executive Center, 15
Chemin des Anemones, Building
D, 1219 Chatelaine Geneva,
Switzerland
Tel: 41 22 979 9111
Fax: 41 22 797 3454

Centre for Sustainable Communities
University of Washington
Seattle
Washington
USA
Tel: 1 206 616 2035
Fax: 1 206 543 2463
Email: lawrejg.washington.edu

Climate Change Secretariat
Geneva Executive Centre
11–13 Chemin des Anemones
1219 Chatelaine
Geneva Switzerland
Tel: 41 22 979 9111
Fax: 41 22 979 9034
Email: secretariat, unfccc@unep.ch

Web site: http://www.unep.ch/unfc-
cc/html

Consumers International
24 Highbury Crescent
London N5 1RX
Tel: 44 171 226 6663
Fax: 44 171 354 0607
Email: prodec@consint.dircon.co.uk

Convention on Biological Diversity,
Secretariat
World Trade Centre
413 St. Jacques Street, Office 630
Montreal, Quebec H2Y 1N9
Canada
Tel: 1 514 288 2220
Fax: 1 514 228 6588
Web site: http://www.unep.ch/biodiv

Convention to Combat
Desertification 11/13 Chemin des
Anemones,
BP 76,1219 Chatelaine, Geneva
Switzerland

Tel: 41 22 9799411
Fax: 41 22 9799030
Email: secretariat.incd@unep.ch

CSD NGO/MAJOR GROUPS
STEERING COMMITTEE:
Southern Co-Chair:
Esmeralda Brown
Southern Diaspora Research
Centre, 391 Eastern Parkway
New York NY 11216 USA
Tel: 1 212 6823633 (work)
Fax: 1 212 6825354
Email: umcgbgm@undp.org

Northern Co-Chair:
Michael McCoy, Citizens Network
   for Sustainable Development
73 Spring Street, Suite 206
New York NY 10012 USA
Tel: 1 212 431 3922
Fax: 1 212 431 4427
Email:cca@igc.apc.org
Web Site:
   http://www.igc.apc.org/habitat/cs
   d-97

Development Alternatives
B-32 Tara Crescent, Qutab
   Institutional Area, New Delhi
   110016
India
Tel: 91 11 66 5370
Fax: 91 11 68 66 031

Earth Council
Apdo 2323
1002 San Jose
Costa Rica
Tel: 506 223-3418/256-1611
Fax: 506 225-2197
Email: eci@terra.ecouncil.ac.cr

Earth Negotiations Bulletin
c/o IISD, 161 Portage Ave East
6th Floor, Winnipeg, Manitoba
R3B 0Y4 Canada
Tel: 1 204 958 7710
Fax: 1 204 958 7710
Email: enb@econet.apc.org
Web site: http://www.iisd.ca/linkages

Earthscan Publications Limited
120 Pentonville Road
London N1 9JN
Tel: 44 171 278 0433
Fax: 44 171 278 1142

Environmental Development Action
   in the Third World
ENDA Maghreb
196, Quartier O.L.M.
Rabat-Souissi
Morocco
Tel: 212 7 756414
Fax: 212 7 756413
Email: magdi@endamag.gn.apc.org

Environmental Liaison Centre
   International (ELCI), PO Box
   72461,
Nairobi, Kenya
Tel: 254 2 562 015
Fax: 254 2 562 175
Email: elci@elci.sasa.unep.no

Food and Agriculture Organization
   of the UN, Via delle Terme di
   Caracalla 00100
Rome Italy
Tel: 39 6 579 71
Fax: 39 6 578 2610

FIELD, 46 Russell Square
London WC1
Tel: 44 171 637 7950
Fax: 44 171 637 7951

Friends of the Earth
26–28 Underwood Street
London N1 7JQ
Tel: 44 171 490 1555
Fax: 44 171 490 0881

German NGO-Forum on
    Environment & Development
Projekstelle
Am Michaelshof 8-10
53177 Bonn
Germany
Tel: 49 228 359704
Fax: 49 228 359096

Global Environmental Facility
1818 H Street NW, Washington
DC 20433 USA
Tel: 1 202 473 5102
Fax: 1 202 522 3240
Email: anpraag@worldbank.org
Web site: http://www.oneworld.org/
    panos/

Greenpeace International
Keizersgracht 176, 1016DW
    Amsterdam, The Netherlands,
Tel: 31 20 523 6222
Fax: 31 20 523 6200
Email: information.unit@green2.
    greenpeaceorg

HABITAT
UN Centre for Human Settlements,
    United Nations Office at Nairobi
PO Box 30030, Nairobi, Kenya
Tel: 254 2 624 260
Fax: 254 2 621 234
Web site: http://www.igc.apc.org/
    habitat

International Confederation of Free
    Trade Unions (ICFTU),
Boulevard Emile Jaqmain 155 B1,
1210 Bruxlles, Belgium
Tel: 32 2224 0211
Fax: 32 2201 5815
Email: ICFTU@GEO2.poptel.org.
    utc

International Council for Local
    Environmental Initiatives (ICLEI)
8th Floor, Toronto, Ontario, M5H
    242 Canada
Tel: 1 416 392 1462
Fax: 1 416 392 1478

International Institute for
    Environment and Development,
3 Endsleigh Street
London, WC1H 0DD
Tel: 44 171 388 2412
Fax: 44 171 388 2826

International Labour Organization
    (ILO), 4, route des Morillons,
CH-1211 Geneva 22, Switzerland
Tel: 41 22 799 61 11
Fax: 41 22 798 86 85

Intergovernmental Panel on Forests
    Secretariat
Tel: 1 212 963 6208
Fax: 1 212 963 3463
Web site: http://www.un.org/dpcsd/
    dsd/ipf.html

International Chamber of
    Commerce,
38 Cours Albert 1er
75008, Paris France
Tel: 331 4953 2926
Fax: 331 4953 2859

International Monetary Fund
700 19th Street NW Washington
  DC, 20431 USA

Tel: 1 202 623 7000
Fax: 1 202 623 4661

National Wildlife Federation (US),
1499 16th Street NW
Washington DC, USA
Tel: 1 202 797 6800
Fax: 1 202 797 5486

New Economics Foundation (NEF)
  1st Floor,
Vine Court
112–116 Whitechapel Road
London E1 1JE
Tel: 44 171 377 5696
Fax: 44 171 377 5720

OECD, 2 rue Andr Pascal
75775 Paris Cedex 16, France
Tel: 33 1 45 248200
Fax: 33 1 49 104276
Web site: http://www.oecd.org

Oxfam
274 Banbury Road
Oxford OX1 7DZ
Tel: 44 1865 312 389
Fax: 44 1865 312 417

Ozone Secretariat, UNEP
PO Box 30552
Nairobi, Kenya
Tel: 254 2 521 928
Fax: 254 2 521 930
Email: madhava.sarma@unep.no
Web site: //www.unep.org/unep/sec-
  retar/ozon

Peace Child International
The White House
Buntingford

Herts SG9 9AH
Tel: 44 1763 274459
Fax: 44 1763 274460
Email:
  100640.3551@Compuserve.com
Peoples Forum 2001
Maruko Bldg. 5F
1-20-6 Higashieueno Taito-ku
Tokyo 110
Japan
Tel: +81 3-33834-2436
Fax: +81 3-3834-2406
Email: pf2001jp@igc.apc.org

Round Table Secretariat (UK)
John Adams
Room P1/021, 2 Marsham Street
London SW1P 3EB

Third World Network
228 Macalister Road
10400 Penang
Malaysia
Tel: 60 4 226 159
Fax: 60 4 226 4505
Email: twn@igc.apc.org

Un Department for Policy
Co-ordination and Sustainable
  Development (DPCSD)
New York NY 10017 USA
Major Groups Focal Point
Zehra Aydin
Tel: 1 212 963 8811
Fax: 1 212 963 1267
Email: aydin@un.org
Web site: http://www.un.org/dpcsd

CSD Update Coordinator Tarcisio
Alvarez-Rivero Room DC2-2252
Tel: 1 212 963 5708
Fax: 1 212 963 1267

United Nations Development
  Programme
1 United Nations Plaza, New York
NY 10017 USA
Tel: 1 212 906 5000
Web site: http://www.undp.org

United Nations Environment and
  Development UK Committee
c/o UNA, 3 Whitehall Court,
London SW1A 2EL
Tel: 44 171 839 1784
Fax: 44 171 930 5893
Email: una@mcrl.poptel.org.uk
Web site http://www.oneworld.org/
  uned-uk/

UN ECOSOC NGO Unit
Farida Ayoub, Room DC-2 2340
  United Nations New York
NY 10017 USA
Tel: 1 212 963 4842/3
Fax: 1 212 963 4968

United Nations Environment
  Programme
Information and Public Affairs
PO Box 30552, Nairobi, Kenya
Tel: 254 2 623292
Fax: 254 2 623927/3692
Email: ipaunep@gn.apc.org
Web site: http://www.unep.no

UNEP
Environmental Citizenship
  Programme
PO Box 107931
Mexico City Mexico
Tel: 525 202 4841
Fax: 525 202 0950
Email: abarcena@rolac.uneo.mx

UN NGO Committee on the
  International Decade for the
  World's Indigenous Peoples
109 West 28th Street
New York, NY 10001
Tel: 1 212 564-3329

UNEP Publications Distribution
SMI Ltd, PO Box 119,
Stevenage, Herts SG1 4TP
Tel: 44 1438 748111
Fax: 44 1438 748844

UNEP Industry Office
Tour Mirabeau
39–43 quai Andr Citron
75739 Paris Dedex 15 France
Fax: 33 1 44 37 1474

UN Non-Governmental
  Liaison Service (NGLS)
Room 6015, 866 UN Plaza
New York, NY 10017 USA
Tel: 1 212 963 3125
Fax: 1 212 963 3062

UN NGLS, Palais de Nations
1211 Geneva 10, Switzerland
Tel: 41 22 798 5850
Fax: 41 22 907 0057

Youth Campaign on Sustainable
  Sweden, q2000
Docent 315
977 52 Luea
Sweden
Tel: 46 920 989 09
Fax: 46 920 690 30

World Bank
1818 H Street NW

Washington DC 20433, USA
Tel: 1 202 477 1234
Web site: http://www.worldbank.org

World Business Council for
    Sustainable Development
160, route de Florisant, 1231
    Conches, Geneva
Tel: 41 22 839 3100
Fax: 41 22 839 3131
Email: wbcsd@iprolink.ch

Women's Environment and
    Development Organization
    (WEDO)
355 Lexington Avenue, 3rd floor
New York, New York 10017-6603
USA
Tel: 1 212 973-0325
Fax: 1 212 973-0335
Email: wedo@igc.apc.org
Web site: http://www.wedo.org

World Health Organization
1211 Geneva 27 Switzerland

Tel: 41 22 791 2111
Fax: 41 22 791 0746

World Trade Organization
Centre William Rappard
154 rue de Lausanne
1211 Geneva 21 Switzerland
Tel: 41 22 739 5111
Fax: 41 22 731 4206
Web site: http://www.unic.org.wto/
    Welcome.html

World Federalist Movement
777 UN Plaza (12th Floor)
New York
NY 10017
Tel: 1 212 599 1320
Fax: 1 212 599 1332

Worldwide Fund for Nature
Avenue du Mont Blanc, CH-1196
    Gland Switzerland
Tel: 41 22 364 9111
Fax: 41 22 364 4238

List of Acronyms and Abbreviations

ACC	Administrative Committee on Co-ordination
AOSIS	Alliance of Small Island States
BCSD	Business Council on Sustainable Development
CBD	Convention on Biological Diversity
CCD	Convention to Combat Desertification
COP	Conference of the Parties
CSD	Commission on Sustainable Development
CTE	Committee on Trade and Environment
DAC	Development Assistance Conference
DoE	Department of the Environment
DPCSD	Department of Policy Coordination and Sustainable Development
Earth Summit II *see* UNGASS	
ECOSOC	United Nations Economic and Social Council
EMAS	EU Eco-Management and Audit Scheme
EU	European Union
EPA US	Environmental Protection Agency
FAO	UN Food and Agriculture Organization
FSC	Forestry Stewardship Council
G7	Group of 7 Industrialized Nations
G77	Group of 77 Developing Nations
GATT	Global Agreement on Tariffs and Trade
GEF	Global Environment Facility

GNP	gross national product
GPA	Global Plan of Action
Habitat	*see* UNCHS
Habitat II	The Second UN Conference on Human Settlements
IACSD	Inter-Agency Committee on Sustainable Development
IAEA	International Atomic Energy Agency
ICC	International Chamber of Commerce
ICFTU	International Confederation of Free Trade Unions
ICLEI	International Council for Local Environmental Initiatives
ICSU	International Council of Scientific Unions
IGC	Intergovernmental Committee
IIED	International Institute for Environment and Development
ILO	International Labour Organization
IMF	International Monetary Fund
IMO	International Maritime Organization
INCD	International Negotiating Committee on Desertification
IPCC	Intergovernmental Panel on Climate Change
IPF	Intergovernmental Panel on Forests
Istanbul	*see* Habitat II
ITTO	International Tropical Timber Organization
IUCN	International Union for the Conservation of Nature and Natural Resources (previously The World Conservation Union)
LA21	Local Agenda 21
LGMB	Local Government Management Board
MDB	multilateral development banks
MEA	multilateral environmental agreements
NGO	non-governmental organization
NIEO	New International Economic Order
NPI	National Provident Institute
ODA	Overseas Development Assistance
OECD	Organization for Economic Cooperation and Development
OPEC	Organization for Oil-Exporting Countries
Rio	*see* UNCED

SBSTTA	Subsidiary Body on Scientific, Technical and Technological Advice
SME	small- to medium-sized enterprise
TFAP	Tropical Forestry Action Plan
TNC	transnational corporation
UNCED	United Nations Conference on Environment and Development ('Earth Summit', Rio de Janeiro, 1992)
UNCHS	United Nations Centre for Human Settlements ('Habitat')
UNCOD	United Nations Conference on Desertification
UNCSD	United Nations Conference on Sustainable Development
UNCTAD	United Nations Conference on Trade and Development
UNDP	United Nations Development Programme
UNED-UK	United Nations Environment and Development, UK Committee
UNEP	United Nations Environment Programme
UNESCO	United Nations Educational, Scientific and Cultural Organization
UNGASS	United Nations General Assembly Special Session ('Earth Summit II')
UNICEF	United Nations Children's Fund
VOCs	volatile organic compounds
WBCSD	World Business Council on Sustainable Development
WHO	World Health Organization
WICEM II	World International Conference on Environmental Management
WMO	World Meteorological Organization
WTO	World Trade Organization
WWF	World Wide Fund For Nature

UNED-UK

UNED-UK AIMS AND OBJECTIVES

UNED-UK has as its primary objective 'the promotion of global environmental protection and sustainable development, particularly through support of the UN Environment Programme, the UN Development Programme, the UN Commission on Sustainable Development, and all other relevant UN and inter-governmental institutions'. Such commitments have been most fully expressed in Agenda 21 and the Rio Declaration, both agreed at the UN Conference on Environment and Development in Rio de Janeiro in 1992.

Since that Summit, the UN has made the necessary arrangements for a high level Commission on Sustainable Development (CSD), which has taken Agenda 21 as its rubric. The CSD is thus the UN body which coordinates and promotes internationally the work which UNED-UK has set itself, whilst Agenda 21 constitutes the most comprehensive expression to date of sustainable development and environmental protection as urgent issues for the world to address before the millennium.

UNED-UK continues to have close relationships with both UNDP and UNEP.

We aim to carry out the support of UN institutions and processes, as detailed above, through the following means:

278

- dissemination of information;
- UN events in the UK;
- arranging for visits from UNDP, UNEP, and UNCSD representatives;

Other objectives include:

- helping to mobilize the UK political process, particularly through national and local government, the voluntary sector and the commercial and industrial sector, in order to promote sustainable development in the work of the UN institutions both nationally and internationally;
- facilitating input from the membership of UNED-UK to the policy-making processes of UNEP, UNDP, UNCSD, and other intergovernmental institutions;
- contributing to the preparation and implementation of a national strategy for Agenda 21 and to support the work of UNCSD including its reviews of national strategies;
- encouraging other activities that result in multi-sectoral approach to the promotion of environmental protection and sustainable development.

If you would like more information on joining UNED-UK as an organization or individual please do contact us.

Index

Abzug, Bella 152
Administrative Committee on Co-ordination (ACC) 21–3
Agenda 21: CSD programme of work 262; economic issues 248–9; environmental issues 247–8; European perspective 255–61; four areas of weakness 12; institutional issues 250; loss of momentum xviii–xxi; major groups of stakeholders 11; role of children and youth 159–62; social issues 249–50; strategy 246–7
agriculture 11 *see also* trade; banana cultivation 176–7; CSD programme of work 263, 264; desertification 55–7; European issues and action 258–9; water use 120
Australia: forests 77; trade unions 134

Basel Convention 89
Belgium: forests 82; non-hazardous waste 89
biodiversity 248, 263
Birdlife International 195
Boutros-Ghali, Boutros: on NGOs 94, 100; on UN role 15–16, 21
Brazil 252; Local Agenda 21 103, 110; murder over land disputes 130
Brundtland Commission 208; inspires Rio Summit 3; *Our Common Future* 47, 48; poverty causes low standards 171

Bush, George 4–5, 39, 51
business and industry 11 *see also* trade unions; World Business Council for Sustainable Development; before and after Rio 120–3; Cleaner Production Programme 210–11; CSD programme of work 263; and NGOs 235–6; partnership with employees 132–5; production 130–1; progress in Europe 257; responsibility 122

Canada: forests 77, 79
children and young people 11; China 161; continuing difficulties 162–3; CSD programme of work 263; disappointment with Earth Summit 158–9; lack of resources and political will to include 160–1; recommendations for action 163–4; UNCED 158–9
China: Local Agenda 21 campaign 102; water pollution law 86; women's conference in Beijing 154–5; young people 161
climate change: international diplomacy 37–45
Climate Convention: Kyoto conference and the future 42–5
Clinton, Bill: BTU tax undermined by Congress 40; stakeholder approach 13